THE NATIONAL UNIFIED SCHOOL IN ALLENDE'S CHILE

UBC Press—CERLAC
Latin American and Caribbean Studies

1. *The National Unified School in Allende's Chile:
   The Role of Education in the Destruction
   of a Revolution,* Joseph P. Farrell

THE NATIONAL UNIFIED SCHOOL IN ALLENDE'S CHILE

The Role of Education in the Destruction of a Revolution

JOSEPH P. FARRELL

UNIVERSITY OF BRITISH COLUMBIA PRESS
in association with
the Centre for Research on Latin America and
the Caribbean, York University

Vancouver, 1986

THE NATIONAL UNIFIED SCHOOL IN ALLENDE'S CHILE
The Role of Education in the Destruction of a Revolution

© The University of British Columbia Press 1986
This book has been published with the help of a grant
from the Social Science Federation of Canada, using
funds provided by the Social Sciences and Humanities
Research Council of Canada.

Farrell, Joseph P., 1939-
  The National Unified School in Allende's Chile

(UBC Press—CERLAC Latin American and Caribbean studies ; 1)
Includes index.
Bibliography: p.
ISBN 0-7748-0242-1

1. Education and state—Chile. 2. Chile—Politics and
Government—1970- 3. Politics and education—Chile. I. York
University (Toronto, Ont.). Centre for Research on Latin America
and the Caribbean. II. Title. III. Series.
LC92.C5F37 1986   379.83   C85-091568-6

International Standard Book Number 0-7748-0242-1

Printed in Canada

Contents

Figures

Tables

Acknowledgements

The idea for this book originated on a delightful summer Sunday afternoon in Santiago in January 1972, at the height of the popularity and power of the Popular Unity government. During a discussion with a few friends, mostly "gringos" who were working in the Chilean Ministry of Education at that time, we concluded that there was a story which needed to be told. At that point (little did we know what the next eighteen months would bring!), we wanted to explain why educational policy seemed to have such a low priority in a new socialist state, since this seemed to be an historical anomaly. Thus, we resolved to collect all the documents we could and to start noting systematically our thoughts about what we were witnessing. I am writing these words more than ten years later, and history has dramatically changed the aim and contents of this book. A very large number of Chileans have contributed to the production of this manuscript through their willingness to participate in extended, often multiple, interviews, to share their ideas and perceptions with me in informal discussions, and to provide access to their private collections of documents. Many of these individuals are mentioned in the text of the book. Others, by their own choice, are not, but they will know who they are. They all have my deepest appreciation for their assistance and encouragement throughout an enterprise which has been long, often difficult, and sometimes tedious and frustrating.

Throughout 1981 and 1982, Jorge Gilbert worked as my research assistant for this project. He located much useful material and assisted greatly in developing and maintaining an organizational scheme for keeping track of and imposing some coherence upon a huge, initially rather inchoate, mass of detailed information. He also prepared a number of very useful summary papers and background analyses and contributed in many other ways to the success of the venture. During this same period, Cecilia Gomez served as secretary for the project. In addition to her normal duties, she also helped prepare translations of many key documents. I thank Jorge and Cecilia for their valuable contributions.

The physical production of this manuscript, in draft and final forms, has involved the mobilization of the entire secretarial staff of the Department of Adult Education at the Ontario Institute for Studies in Education.

They have cheerfully accepted this interruption in their normal working routines and the occasional postponement of other work for which they were responsible. I am especially grateful to Jeanie Stewart and Lorraine Deason, who were responsible at different stages for keeping the entire effort organized.

The Social Sciences and Humanities Research Council of Canada provided generous financial support during the last two years which made it possible to convert a long-held aspiration into a concrete reality.

I am of course ultimately responsible for the contents of the book.

Finally, this book is dedicated to Chile and Chileans. Chileans have been, and remain today, an open and outspoken people. While many individuals have helped me directly, much of what I know of this society comes from hundreds of casual encounters with Chileans from all walks of life—over fancy meals in clubs and restaurants in Santiago or over wine or beer in soda fountains in remote villages—who have been willing to try to share their understandings of their lives with a wandering North American. Chileans are well aware that while they live geographically in the "farthest corner of the world," as they are fond of saying, they have lived in recent years in the center of world attention, as they have struggled to find their own road to a good life under extremely difficult conditions. Whatever else this book may accomplish, I hope that it will show at least a bit of the terrible, but ultimately hopeful, complexity of life in a society whose reality is often oversimplified.

1

Introduction

Perhaps in their cabins they talk of the fighting, and younger men listen, as though to tales of heroic battle. Certainly the rebellion has not been forgotten in the houses of the gentry. They will over the years construct their twin mythologies, compounded of facts and fables and pride.

Thomas Flanagan, *The Year of the French*, p. 618.

The election in 1970 of the Popular Unity government of Salvador Allende in Chile and its overthrow by the military in 1973 were dramatically significant political episodes in the modern history of the developing world. The publicity surrounding this epoch in Chilean history has been exceeded only by the confusion in subsequent interpretation of its meaning. Chile had a long experience of democratic government and peaceful regime changes and an ability to accommodate within a stable political system the conflicts which have bedeviled much of Latin American history. It also had a well-publicized reputation for having achieved social advances for the poor which were very unusual within Latin America and the developing world generally.

Thus the advent in this nation of the first freely elected "Marxist"[1] government in the world was a major focus of world attention. The elimination of that government by military coup three years later profoundly challenged existing conceptions about the ability of democratically elected governments to preside over massive social transformations and (to put the question in a different form) about the possibility of achieving needed social changes in developing nations by non-violent and non-totalitarian means. Consequently, attempts to increase understanding of this period in Chilean history have significance well beyond the boundaries of that geographically isolated society.

Shortly before the military coup which ended the Allende regime, the defeated Christian Democratic candidate in the presidential election of 1970, Radomiro Tomic, cried out in despair in a speech:[2]

> We are living in a Greek tragedy. Everyone knows what is going to happen. No one wants it to happen. And everyone is doing precisely what is necessary to make it inevitable that it will happen.

This book is an attempt to increase understanding of that tragedy. The particular focus is the proposal for an "Escuela Nacional Unificada" (ENU — the National Unified School), which was the principal educational reform proposition of the Allende government.

I believe that the ENU proposal was one of the major factors leading to the downfall of the Allende regime. It served as a catalyst to unite divergent opposition groups and alienate a significant number of marginal middle-class supporters of the regime (including officers in the military whose support was critical to the eventual success of the coup). Also, in its development, it exemplified and exacerbated the factional conflicts within the coalition government headed by Allende, which were themselves major contributors to its downfall. A number of observers, writing from quite different theoretical and ideological perspectives, have noted the impact of the ENU proposal. Sigmund (1977, p. 204) refers to it as a "very serious political error." Valenzuela (1978, p. 90) speaks of it as "extraordinarily damaging to the government. It not only provided the opposition with an issue capable of mobilizing further sectors against the government, but it also sapped the government of the momentum it needed to continue ruling the country until the 1976 presidential contest." In his analysis of the ideological struggle during the Allende years, Bandeira has noted (1975, pp. 42-43):

> The attack against the ENU united all of the opposition for the first time, from the extreme right to the Christian Democratic sectors closest to the left. The campaign against the ENU above all served to isolate the government and to radicalize the legalist sectors of the opposition. . . . I am convinced that the most effective propaganda — besides the scare-crow of "scarcity" — that mobilized the Chilean women and brought them to collective hysteria was the "threat" to their children represented by the ENU. The specter of the ENU frightened very large sectors of the middle classes. Many military men who were sympathetic to the opposition but who had stayed within the limits of legality lost their "patience" and were radicalized. The ENU was "proof" for a terrorized middle class that "Communism" had already begun to endanger the family.

In the words of a high official in the Ministry of Education at the time the ENU proposal was forwarded:

> ENU was our greatest mistake. It was the wrong policy, in the wrong language, at the wrong time politically. It sealed our fate. Many of us knew it would be a disaster, but we were only one faction in a Ministry that was riddled by factional conflict, and we couldn't stop it.

In spite of the political importance of the ENU proposal there has not yet been published a thorough historical analysis of its development and consequences.[3]

Two questions have been central to the development of this book: 1) How did the Allende government come to advance this proposition for educational change in the form and at the time that it was presented, especially when many of its own education officials were predicting the negative consequences for the regime? 2) How can one account for the devastating effect the ENU proposal had on the political destiny of the regime? Answering the first question will involve a detailed analysis of the internal decision-making structure and process within the Ministry of Education as a reflection of the more general pattern of conflict among factions within the government. Dealing with the second question will require relating the educational system to the more general sociopolitical position in which the government found itself when the proposal was presented and debated.

This book is also meant as a contribution to a more general understanding of educational reform. The literature regarding the causes and consequences of educational reform efforts, particularly but not exclusively in developing nations, is vast but generally inconclusive. What has been clear for some time, however, is that one cannot begin seriously to understand an educational reform proposal and its outcomes without attempting to comprehend the social and political context from which it has arisen. This is especially true of social class conflicts and the sociopolitical position of groups most likely (at least in their own perceptions) to benefit from or be disadvantaged by such a proposal. I know of no other case in which the debate over an educational reform proposal has so perfectly reflected, and so seriously worsened, the sociopolitical divisions within a society. Debates over education do not ordinarily bring down governments.

It is also hoped that this book will contribute to an understanding of the political decision-making process itself. Very little is known about the processes by which governments, particularly in developing nations, actually arrive at crucial political decisions. Generally, decision-making has been treated as a sort of "black box": broad political goals, ideological positions, or class interests are fed in at one end, and specific political decisions somehow automatically come out the other end as directly deducible consequences of those inputs. This tendency is as characteristic of the structural functionalist "systems theory" literature on political systems and planning as it is of the Marxist and neo-Marxist literature.[4]

History is viewed here as the outcome of decisions taken by individuals whose actions are shaped and constrained, but not determined, by their circumstances and their positions within the spectrums of power and ideology within a society. As this book demonstrates, the major educational policy pronouncements of the Popular Unity regime were *not* automatic derivations from the ideological position of the government or any of its sectors. They were rather the product of a richly textured human process in which individual personality styles and histories, judgments and misjudgments of the motives and hidden agendas of others, political calculations and miscalculations, and accidents were very important. There are in this story no "good guys" and "bad guys"; no "white hats" and "black hats." There are only individual human beings, all trying to cope as best they could with a highly complicated and crisis-ridden environment which each perceived somewhat differently. The intent is not to apportion blame. Instead, it is to try to understand how and why a group of well-intentioned, honest, well-informed, and capable men and women managed collectively to create a disastrous political blunder.

SOME NOTES ON METHODOLOGY AND BIAS

This work is an exercise in historical analysis, focussing on events sufficiently recent that most of the key actors are still alive and available. This permits a richness of details and interpretation and the ability to use information from various sources which is not possible when one is limited to surviving documentary records from a more distant past. But this situation also poses some special problems and challenges.

In one sense the methodology employed has been quite straightforward: gathering information from all available sources, crosschecking sources to verify information, and developing from the information a coherent account of what happened and a consistent and defensible explanation of why it happened. The actual process, of course, has been much more complex. Below are some comments on major sources of information, followed by observations on how that information has been used.

1. *Periodical literature.* The Chilean periodical press during the time in question was vigorous and free, with every major current of political opinion represented, in newspapers, newsmagazines and journals of political commentary and analysis. Education was extensively reported, and the

focal event, the ENU proposal, was fiercely debated. Because of the highly partisan nature of media reporting at the time (see Duran and Urzoa, 1978, and Duran, 1976), "factual" accounts of events have had to be treated with considerable caution. However, this very partisanship makes the printed media a very useful indicator of the interpretations various political factions placed on events and/or wished to implant in the public mind.

Following the coup in 1973, the archives of a number of important media sources are either unavailable or incomplete. Fortunately, I was able to locate and obtain access to two sources of information which permitted the development of a virtually complete file of media coverage concerning education during the Popular Unity years. For the period from September 1970 to August 1972, individuals working with an international aid program in Chile subscribed to a "clipping service" which provided a daily file of all articles in the media dealing, even obliquely, with education. For the subsequent period, I discovered that the librarian of an international agency located in Santiago had collected and maintained a complete collection of media clippings related to education.[5]

2. *Documents.* Many government documents, both official and semi-official, regarding educational policy (and related social and economic policy) have been consulted. The debate over ENU and the events preceding it also generated a large number of documents from non-governmental sources—political parties and subgroups within them, teacher unions, student organizations, parent organizations, private school organizations, the Church, and so forth. Some of these documents are publicly available. Once again, however, public archives are largely incomplete. Most of the key documents used in this text were obtained from personal files of individuals who were involved in the events recorded here. Many documents which were thought to be irretrievably lost were eventually uncovered. Some of the material provided to me is highly confidential, dealing with matters which are still politically delicate. In every case in which I obtained a copy of a document from a private source, the individual who owns the material has been allowed to specify if, or in what form, the document can be used or cited.

3. *Interviews with key actors and observers.* Interviews have been conducted with almost all of the central actors, especially officials of the Ministry of Education and important non-governmental actors and observers, particularly from opposition parties, the universities, and the Church. Some of the major figures are dead. In very few cases was it impossible to locate someone with whom I wanted to talk, although a bit of detective work was necessary where people had moved often. In no case did an important informant refuse to be interviewed. In most cases, particularly with those most directly involved in the ENU controversy, there were several extended conversations during the course of three or more years.

Since each informant was involved to one degree or another in the events being discussed, their recollections and perceptions were necessarily shaped by their own positions, and I frequently found that each of the several participants in a series of events or meetings had a different understanding of what had occurred. Memory lapses were frequent. We were, after all, speaking of things which happened a decade or more earlier, and the individuals did not in most cases have recourse to personal files, diaries, minutes of meetings, appointment calendars, or other records. No one can escape completely from the tendency to self-justify and rationalize his or her actions, particularly during critical periods. In only one case, however, did it become quite clear that a person had simply lied to me, and then the explanation, in terms of the past and present situation of the person, was evident. Indeed, I was constantly impressed by the degree of candor and honest self-evaluation encountered. It has been an enriching experience to converse with those who have in many cases been in a concentration camp, in long exile, in jail, or in virtual house arrest and who can, in spite of (*perhaps because of*) these experiences, deal with their own behavior during the Popular Unity years with a remarkable degree of objectivity.

For obvious reasons, some of the information obtained in these interviews could only be acquired if a guarantee were provided of the confidentiality of the source. All key informants have been given the opportunity to review a draft of this manuscript to ensure that I was neither quoting them or using information obtained from them in a manner which might place them in a difficult position. In some cases, information has not been used at all, for there was no way to use it which would not risk revealing the source to anyone closely conversant with the Chilean political scene. Throughout the book, where a direct quotation is not attributed, it is at the request of the source.

4. *Personal Observation.* During the final ten months of the Frei government and the first eight months of the Allende regime, I lived in Chile and worked in the Ministry of Education. I returned to Santiago for six weeks in early 1972 to work with Ministry of Education officials and practicing educators, conducted an intensive training course in Toronto for selected Chilean Ministry of Education officials during July and August of 1972, and was again in Chile, working with an educational research institute associated with the Catholic University for three weeks immediately preceding the coup in September, 1973. I returned to Chile for at least a few weeks every year thereafter until 1978, when I spent the entire year there working with another private educational research institute associated with the Catholic Church. Much of the texture and detail of this book is thus the product of three sources: my own personal observations as a North American participant observer in the Chilean Ministry of Education

during the early months of the Popular Unity government; the observations of many Chilean friends and colleagues with whom I have discussed the educational policies and the general situation and conduct of the Allende government over many years; and the understanding of the workings of the Chilean educational system (as well as the political social and economic systems) derived from more than a decade of research and living in the society.

The idea for this book originated during the 1971-73 period, and I began then to assemble information, although I was not able to give much attention to it until 1978. During that year, I began to explore seriously the possibility of acquiring the kind of detailed data which would be required to do a proper job. In 1980 I obtained a generous multiyear grant from the Social Sciences and Humanities Research Council of Canada, which included both release time from academic duties and sufficient financial resources to return to Chile several more times and to locate and interview Chileans in other parts of the world.

It is now more than a decade after the idea first began to grow and several years after I started the investigation in a concentrated fashion. In writing this kind of book one can never completely escape one's own intellectual biases; one can only try to identify as many of them as possible and to deal with them openly. One starts with a series of working hypotheses, some explicit, others implicit. Through constant interchange between the evidence at hand, an often changing interpretation of that evidence, and one's understanding of social theory and broader questions of epistemology, there gradually emerges a coherent account of what happened and why. Intellectual honesty demands that the guiding principle in an endeavor of this sort be a search for evidence which will *refute* the hypotheses (or, more properly, hunches) with which one started. There have been any number of occasions in which I have been surprised by the testimony of informants and by documentary evidence. Several of the working questions which guided early interviews have had to be completely rephrased and in some cases discarded. Some of my original beliefs about what happened turned out to be completely wrong. The discipline of going back to interviewees several times to check out preliminary hypotheses that emerged from the data has been very salutary. The need to deal with the reactions of most of the key actors in the story to a preliminary draft has been particularly useful in identifying implicit biases as well as in correcting errors of fact.

As with any history or social investigation this account is an *interpretation* of the events being discussed. Metaphors from drama are frequently found in the text; I believe that "the historian is inevitably an artist of a kind as he composes his narrative, selecting, shaping, coloring" (Muller, 1957, p. 33). Ultimately, the problem one faces is phenomenological. The actors, as well as the observers, are creatures of their own personalities and histories, ideological stances, and theoretical preconceptions. They interpret their own actions and those of others from those differing frames of reference.

But the process is not wholly subjective. There are objectively obvious facts that must be dealt with as well. As Muller has noted:

> We cannot simply stick to the facts but we cannot disregard them either, and must derive our meanings from them in the knowledge that they are both stubborn and ambiguous. Our distinctive interests and beliefs make it possible for history to be relatively disinterested and impartial. Through Marx, Freud, Sumner, Pareto, Boas, Spengler, and many others, we have become more aware of the inveterate habit of rationalization and the sources of bias — the class interests, the *mores*, the conditioned reflexes of culture, the unconscious assumptions, the "climate of opinion." Although we can never entirely escape or control our climate, never attain a God's-eye view, we can more freely discount and supplement, at least when we read the other fellow's history. (p. 33)

There is no claim here for a uniquely valid interpretation of what happened in Chile between 1970 and 1973, nor do I believe that there is, or can be, one. But the existence of a variety of interpretations is a benefit, except perhaps to those whose understanding of social reality is so rigidly narrow-minded that they regard any deviation from received truth, as they understand it, to be heresy which is only to be extirpated. As Muller again has observed: "When historians offer some fifty different reasons for the fall of the Roman Empire, we may at first be simply confused; yet we have a better understanding of the fall than if we assumed there was only one reason, or no reason except Fate" (p. 32).

A few additional observations may be useful. It has become fashionable in recent years to categorize the many distinct ways of understanding developing nations into two general camps: modernization theory and dependency theory. These are, of course, essentially applications to the special case of developing nations of the more general structural-functionalist and conflict modes of understanding societies. In my view, a complete reliance on either of these modes seriously limits one's ability to understand complex social processes. Rather, I attempt to operate from what Paulston has referred to, and urged, as "a dialectical research perspective that is locked into neither functionalist nor conflict theory yet draws selectively and critically from each orientation" (in his important analysis of the relation between theoretical perspective and the ability to understand educational reform — 1976, p. 44).

It should also be clear that I am strongly committed to the value of open and democratic political systems which permit individuals and collectivities to influence their own destinies and that of their societies, to choose freely among competing visions of their society's future and to remove from power in a non-violent fashion governors to whom they are opposed. In spite of their imperfections, the institutional forms of parliamentary democracy which have grown up historically in the West (in which I include Chile) have served relatively well — at least better than any of the competing governing arrangements which are available. I am utterly opposed to the increasingly common position that authoritarian or totalitarian regimes, whether of the left or the right, are the best or only means of controlling or resolving the inevitable conflicts attendant upon rapid and needed social change; a benevolent dictatorship is still a dictatorship. But as the experience of Chile demonstrates, in times of heightened conflict, democratic institutions are exceedingly fragile, their maintenance is a delicate and subtle art, and the consequences of their destruction can be tragic. For those of us who live in parliamentary democracies, and those who wish they did, Chile's recent history provides some sobering lessons. Within this context I have been strongly influenced in my understanding of the general Chilean situation by the work of Arturo Valenzuela (1978), which is part of a broader effort by Juan J. Linz and his colleagues (1978) to understand what they call "the breakdown of democratic regimes."

THE ORGANIZATION OF THE BOOK

As the development of complex social systems such as nation states unfolds, there is an important sense in which everything is somehow related to everything else. Some readers will approach these pages knowing almost nothing of the history of Chile; some will be quite familiar with the vast literature that has been generated about that nation in the past decade or so; still others will have themselves lived through the events in question. I write these pages fully aware that a single book cannot completely satisfy these diverse audiences. But while I believe that the story to be told here is of potential interest and importance to all three groups, I do not intend to write three separate books.

As noted, writing any history is necessarily an act of (over)simplification. This is especially apparent in the subsequent three chapters. Clearly, one cannot understand what began to occur in 1970 without knowing something of what went on before that time in Chile. But Chile has a long and complicated history, and an extensive literature has developed particularly regarding the post-1960 period. The objective of the next three chapters is to provide sufficient historical background to permit the reader to understand the remaining chapters without writing yet another general history of Chile. Only those events and patterns which, in my judgment, have a relatively direct bearing on the questions to be addressed in later chapters are dealt with.

Chapter 2 is concerned with the general political history of the nation, particularly since the 1930's. It focusses on the major political parties, their development, their general ideological stances, and their educational policy positions. In Chapter 3, the development of the educational system is considered, with special attention to those events of the postwar era which directly affected the educational policy initiatives of the Popular Unity government. Chapter 4 examines the electoral campaign of 1970 and the results of the presidential election itself, concluding with a consideration of the situation the winners faced when their victory became apparent.

The remaining chapters deal with the Popular Unity epoch, recounting in detail the gradual development of the regime's educational policy positions. Throughout these chapters, there are brief discussions of the developing political, social, and economic situation of the nation which formed the backdrop against which the educational policy development process was played out. These are not meant to be comprehensive treatments. They are designed primarily for the reader who is not already familiar with the history of the Popular Unity years and focus only on those elements of the overall situation which I judge to be most salient to what was occurring within education.

Chapters 5, 6 and 7 deal with the educational policy development process from the day after President Allende's election until late 1972. It was during this period that the various trends and conflicts which converged upon and determined the final development of the ENU proposal gradually evolved. Chapter 8 focusses upon the political fight within the Popular Unity during November and December 1972, and January 1973, which gave ENU its ultimate shape. The next two chapters provide an account of the extraordinary, and extraordinarily damaging, political dispute that arose when the ENU project was presented publicly in early March 1973 and which led to an almost complete retreat from the policy by the end of April. Chapter 11 recounts the continuing educational debate during the last months of the regime, ending with discussion of a final compromise on education reached between the government and the opposition just before the coup, too late to have an important impact or to counteract the damage that had already been done. The last chapter returns to the two central questions noted above and includes a discussion of the relative importance of the ENU proposal within the myriad factors which culminated in the tragedy of 11 September 1973.[6]

2

The Political Parties and Their Positions

Chile is often thought of as an almost archetypical model of political stability and peaceful transitions between democratically elected regimes—at least until 11 September 1973. While Chile certainly has been unusual in this respect, the popular image masks a more complex reality. Throughout the previous century, after independence from Spain was consolidated, contests for political office were basically disputes among different factions within a narrow oligarchy. What was unusual about the Chilean case in that epoch was the extent to which political philosophies distinct from mediterranean corporatism, inherited from Spain and Portugal by all Latin American states, came to penetrate Chilean politics. These non-traditional political ideas had been used symbolically by the leaders of the independence movements throughout Latin America. The French and American revolutions were rhetorical touchstones for the creole aristocracy who were trying to free themselves from the power of the Spanish Empire so that they would have unfettered control over their own societies. But these new ideas did not generally have a deep impact upon the post-independence political structures. In Chile, however, particularly from the 1840's onward, the "liberal" social philosophies of the protestant West (that is, utilitarianism, libertarianism, positivism, and social Darwinism) gained powerful adherents. A few decades thereafter, with the rise of a strong middle class, European radical socialism and masonic anti-clericalism began to penetrate the Chilean political system. The peculiar genius of that system was its ability to accommodate these non-traditional ideas, to translate them into a body of social legislation, and to implement such legislation to a degree which was very advanced for that time and region.

It was not until the early years of the present century that the great mass of laboring poor began to have a significant political voice and impact, particularly during the reign of Arturo Alessandri, who served as president from 1922-25. The traditional political system became increasingly unstable and polarized until in 1927 Colonel Carlos Ibañez installed a military dictatorship. By 1931 the dictatorship itself had collapsed, followed by a brief period of great political turmoil. Within fifteen months there were two general strikes, a naval revolt, and nine different governments, including a somewhat improbable "socialist republic" installed through a coup led by Colonel Marmaduke Grove. In 1932 presidential elections were again held, although the old political parties were still badly disorganized as a consequence of Ibañez' dictatorship. This election, won by Arturo Alessandri, who had been out of power for seven years, marked the start of the final four decades of the stable democracy for which Chile was so well-known.

It is the developments within those years, from the Depression of the 1930's until the election of 1970, which are the focus of attention here. The discussion is organized around the development and positions of the major political parties of this era. This is appropriate since the role of the political parties was one of the most distinctive features of the Chilean political system. The party system in Chile was quite similar to those found in much of Europe, especially in France of the Third and Fourth Republics. The parties served to align and demarcate the political forces in the society, but in a highly fractionalized fashion (in the 1930's there were more than thirty distinct parties operating). As Valenzuela notes:

> Chile's party system was everywhere, not only determining the political recruitment process for important national posts but also structuring contests in such diverse institutions as government agencies, professional and industrial unions, neighbourhood organizations, and even local high schools. Parties were so much a feature of national life that in a survey conducted in Santiago, only 22.2 percent of Santiago residents felt that parties could be dispensed with in governing the country. (1978, p. 3)

If, as was often said, "politics is Chile's national sport," the parties were the players.

Since this discussion will not be completely chronological, Figure 1 is provided to help keep track of the players and their changing fates. For each presidential election from 1938 onwards, when Arturo Alessandri's term of office ended, the candidates, the vote percentage obtained, and the parties that supported them are listed.

To a considerable degree, the remarkable stability and durability of the Chilean system during the post-Depression era, in spite of increasing socioeconomic polarization and a fractionalized party system, was owing to the presence of a numerically strong middle sector which distanced itself from the extreme left and the extreme right. Also important was the presence within this sector of powerful individuals who were able to play the role of political negotiators, who could, in Luis Maira's words, "find 'the just middle ground' between apparently irreconcilable positions, thus amassing sufficient support to gain approval for new policies" (1979, p. 247). (This, of course, was a role which could be played only so long as the basic legitimacy of the system was widely accepted.) It is appropriate, then, to start this account with the parties of the middle.

THE PARTIES OF THE MIDDLE: THE RADICAL PARTY

Until late in the 1950's this political middle ground was occupied by the Radical party. Long an important force in Chilean politics and with their roots in French and Italian radical socialism of the previous century, the Radicals maintained this centrist position by having a vague and undefined ideology (many radicals refer to their party as ideologically "eclectic"; members of other parties frequently use harsher language) and being prepared to enter into governing coalitions with parties on either side of the ideological spectrum as one or the other wing of the party gained dominance. Throughout the 1930's the Radicals worked with leftist parties forming with them the Popular Front, which captured the presidency in 1938 and retained power for more than a decade. By the late 1940's the party was moving to the right, and by 1962 it was in coalition with the Conservative and Liberal parties in support of President Jorge Alessandri.

By 1964, however, the coalition supporting Alessandri had dissolved in the face of by-election defeats, and the forces of the right united with the Christian Democratic party in support of Eduardo Frei, while the Socialist and Communist parties supported Salvador Allende. The Radicals ran their own presidential candidate, Julio Duran, and were crushed electorally, receiving only 5 per cent of the popular vote. This election campaign signalled a major split within the party because many of its leaders openly urged their supporters to vote for Frei rather than Duran. Following this defeat, the party moved rapidly back to the left. By 1969 the more conservative sectors had been driven out of the party, and control was taken by a group who believed that the party could play a key role in the formation of a coalition of the left which, because of the Radical presence, would not be identified as totally Marxist in orientation.

If there was a central core to Radical thinking within all of the vacillations, it is captured by Gil:

FIGURE 1
PRESIDENTIAL ELECTION RESULTS, 1938-1970

Year	Candidate	% of Vote	Supporting Parties[1]
1938	Pedro Aguirre Cerda	51.6	Radicals, Socialists, Communists (Popular Front)
	Gustavo Ross	48.4	Conservatives, Liberals
1942	Juan Antonio Rios	56.0	Radicals, Socialists, Communists, Falange (Democratic Alliance)
	Carlos Ibañez	44.0	Conservatives, Liberals, Nazis
1946	Gabriel Gonzales Videla	40.2	Radicals, Communists
	Eduardo Cruz Coke	29.8	Falange, Socialists, Christian Socialists
	Fernando Alessandri	27.4	Conservatives, Liberals
	Bernardo Ibañez	2.5	Socialists
1952	Carlo Ibanez	46.8	"non-political"
	Arturo Matte	27.8	Conservatives, Liberals
	Pedro Alfonso	19.9	Radicals, Christian Democrats
	Salvador Allende	5.5	Socialists
1958	Jorge Allesandri	31.6	Conservatives, Liberals
	Salvador Allende	28.9	Socialists, Communists (Popular Action Front)
	Eduardo Frei	20.7	Christian Democrats
	Luis Bossay	15.6	Radicals
	Antonio Zamorano	3.3	left breakaway from Popular Action Front
1964	Eduardo Frei	56.1	Christian Democrats, Conservatives, Liberals
	Salvador Allende	38.9	Socialists, Communists (Popular Action Front)
	Julio Duran	5.0	Radicals
1970	Salvador Allende	36.3	Socialists, Communists, Radicals MAPU (Popular Unity)
	Jorge Allesandri	34.9	National Party
	Radomiro Tomic	27.8	Christian Democrats

1. Very small parties or political fragments are not mentioned.

A consistent feature of Radical philosophy, however, has been its reliance on improving the lot of the lower classes by evolutionary methods rather than by revolutionary. It is a firm Radical philosophy that vital economic issues can be solved by peaceful means through evolutionary development. Official party documents define its ideology as based on "socialist democratic doctrine" and proclaim the party's faith in the secular state and the system of political parties, its endorsement of free obligatory education, and its opposition to all forms of dictatorship or totalitarianism. (1966, p. 259)

Two aspects of the Radicals' situation are particularly important for the analysis here. First, even though it had lost a great deal of electoral support, the Radical party had long been, and still was, an extremely powerful element within the ever-expanding public service of the nation. Within the teaching force of the society and among Ministry of Education bureaucrats, it was the strongest party. For this reason, the one ministry controlled consistently by the Radicals throughout the Popular Unity period was education. However marginal the party was in most areas of government activity, it was a key player in the education sector. Indeed, it could be said that the Chilean educational system in the mid-1960's, which in spite of many problems was remarkably advanced for a poor nation, was fundamentally a product of Radical thought and action. Nonetheless, partly because of its internal rupture and swing leftward after 1964, the party entered the Popular Unity epoch without a clearly defined educational policy position beyond general affirmation of the need for democratization of education, careful technical planning, and strong support for free public, as opposed to private, Church-controlled, schooling. These were all longstanding general Radical principles, particularly the last, which was reflected in the concept of estado docente (the teaching state). This notion, central to Radical thinking, embodied the anti-clerical idea that the state rather than the Church should control education. But in Radical thinking it also carried with it much of the traditional principle of the tutelary state; that the state must teach the people (as opposed to government learning from the people). It was not until late in 1972 that the party formally adopted a detailed educational policy document.

Second, because of its ideological vacillations, the Radical party was not trusted as a member of the coalition by many of the other members, especially the more extreme left members of the Socialist party. Although Allende continually insisted on the importance of the Radical presence in Popular Unity, at its 1967 Congress the Socialist party had formally rejected the idea of Radical participation in the coalition, claiming: "These attempts to incorporate radicalism into the heart of the left mean assuring, artificially, the survival of a senile party, which expresses no socially or ideologically progressive force, and which aspires to subsist as a political force through opportunistic movements within the national political landscape, permitting them to put a price on their declining parliamentary and electoral power'' (Jobet, 1971, p. 129). Since the extreme left Socialists became the other truly powerful force within the Ministry of Education, the potential for deep suspicion and intense ideological combat was built into the educational sector from the first day of the Popular Unity regime.

THE PARTIES OF THE MIDDLE:
THE CHRISTIAN DEMOCRATIC PARTY

Founded in 1938 as the National Falange, the Christian Democratic party started by the late 1950's to be a serious contender with the Radicals for the support of the middle sectors. Labelled by one observer in 1957 as a ''kind of Radical party which is not anticlerical'' (Silvert, 1957, p. 15), the Christian Democrats gained about 20 per cent of the popular vote in the 1958 presidential election, and by the 1963 municipal elections had become the strongest single party, with about 23 per cent of the popular vote, slightly more than the declining Radicals. In the following year the party's candidate, Eduardo Frei, with the support of the rightist parties which did not enter their own candidate, achieved the presidency with an absolute majority (56.1 per cent) of the vote.

Although considerably less ''eclectic'' than the Radicals, there were right- and left-wing elements within the Christian Democratic party. However, the core ideology at the time of the 1964 victory is well expressed by Gil writing shortly thereafter.

> The essence of Chilean Christian Democratic doctrine is the belief in social pluralism and political democracy. The party [has a] neo-socialistic economic platform, derived from the acceptance of the need for a limited class struggle as a means of achieving social justice. . . . Most Christian Democrats see themselves as leftists and Catholics. As Catholics they see themselves as anti-Marxists, but as leftists they cannot allow themselves to be undemocratic in their anti-Marxism. They criticize capitalism on the United States model as being opposed to Christian morality. Old-style liberalism is considered thoroughly un-Christian and pernicious by many Christian Democrats. Some important leaders of the Christian Democratic party are in actuality not distant from Marxism in their political philosophy. In advocating what they term the ''communitarian society,'' they agree with Marx that private capital is the root of nearly every evil and therefore they support the abolition of private ownership of all property save con-

sumer goods. In general, Christian Democrats have no particular commitment to the free enterprise system and would abandon it if they thought it wise to do so. Eduardo Frei, who stands in the philosophical center of the party, constantly hammers away at the need for replacing the obsession for profit that inevitably vitiates capitalism with the spirit of Christian brotherhood. (1966, pp. 268-69)

Under pressure of actually governing in an increasingly polarized society, the internal division within the party became more marked, with President Frei becoming identified with the rightists. By the end of the decade the left wing had won predominance, nominating Radomiro Tomic as presidential candidate and developing a platform which was not far removed from that of Popular Unity. However, during the process of thrust and counterthrust between what had come to be the Frei and Tomic sectors of the party, the minority farthest to the left split off in mid-1969 to form the Movement of Unitary Popular Action (MAPU), which eventually formed part of the Popular Unity coalition.

Implementation of the most massive and thoroughgoing educational reform in Chilean history was a primary goal and accomplishment of the Frei regime. The details of this reform, its effects upon the educational system, and what it failed to accomplish will be considered in the following chapter. Here it will be most appropriate to note the general ideological orientation of the party toward education, which colored both the nature of its particular educational reform and its view of educational change attempts under the Allende regime.

Fundamental to the Christian Democratic view was the belief that education was essential to, indeed a promoter of, socioeconomic growth. They held that the major social structural changes required by their society could only be fully accomplished with a well-educated citizenry. It was also felt that individuals could participate fully in the "communitarian" society they envisaged and could have full and effective access to political power only if they were educated. These beliefs led to a very strong emphasis on quantitative expansion of the schooling system. The Catholic doctrine of free will—the notion that every individual is the agent of his/her own destiny, constrained but not determined by broader social forces—led to an emphasis on the right of individuals or, in the case of children, their families to choose the type of education suited to their needs. A corollary to this was a concern for the preservation of private (in Chile, basically Catholic) schooling as the best effective guarantee of freedom of choice. In the area of curriculum and teaching methodology, this basic orientation also produced a desire to encourage participatory learning—"learning by doing." An awareness of the constraints upon the ability of poor children to survive and learn within the school systems produced such ancillary programs as the provision of free breakfasts and lunches at school and even to such things as providing free boots and raincoats to poor children in the rural areas of the cold rainy south of Chile.

The general position of Christian Democracy on education was well captured in a declaration of the Third World Conference of Christian Democrats, held in Santiago in 1961:

> Christian Democracy declares that real possibilities for profound change in the socioeconomic structure are not possible without a change and expansion of education at all levels. . . . This change must be realized within [the parameters of] a real guarantee of and regard for the family's right [to choose] education, a right that supersedes that of the State, which must [at the same time] meet the need of the community in educational matters. . . . Christian Democracy considers urgent an Education Reform. . .that develops efficient programs to eradicate illiteracy, that increases the period of basic schooling and diversifies education in such a way as to produce. . .skilled laborers, technicians of various levels, scientists and professionals. . . . This Reform must give priority. . .to an effective democratization of education, which will ensure a real opportunity for every person to freely pursue studies to the highest level, in accordance with his intellectual and moral capacity. (cited by Fisher, 1977, p. 52)

However, it should also be noted that the Chilean Christian Democratic party came to power with the support and cooperation of a large cadre of young to middle-aged professionals and technicians who, while not necessarily completely in agreement with the ideology of the party, saw it as the only alternative to the non-expert bureaucratism of the traditional governing parties and the disorganized fragmentation of the left. In Gil's words, this group "cherished the thought of a sort of political truce under the PDC that would endure for a period during which a 'government of technicians' directed by a neutral governmental mechanism and operating within a democratic framework could achieve needed aims" (1966, p. 273). This influence gave to much of the party's governance, including its implementation of the educational reform, a notably technocratic, top-down, and somewhat manipulative style. While this approach allowed them to accomplish a great deal in a very short period, it also greatly irritated many teachers, particularly the leaders in the teacher union bureaucracies. One product of this was an insistence, when Popular Unity came to power, that any educational reform carried out by the Allende government had to be subject to extensive consultation with "the bases." Thus educational change proposals in the 1970-73 period were constrained not only by the ideology and objective accomplishments and failures of the Frei educational reform, but also by the style in which it was carried out.

THE PARTIES OF THE RIGHT

Not surprisingly, what we would now call right-wing or conservative parties or political groupings governed Chile for most of its independent history until the 1930's. Although a number of smaller parties sprang up from time to time on this side of the ideological spectrum, the constants from shortly after independence from Spain until the right-wing collapse just before Frei's election were the Conservative and Liberal parties. Both represented the interests of the traditional oligarchy, with the Conservatives strongest among the large landowners and the Liberals predominantly the party of the mercantile and industrial new rich. They shared a commitment to the established order and the Mediterranean corporatist worldview with its emphasis on a rigidly stratified hierarchical society and strong tutelary government. Moving into the twentieth century, they both became champions of free enterprise, private property, and the essentially North American competitive capitalist development model, albeit with a strong commitment to protection of domestic (their own) enterprise. The only issue which historically separated the two parties in a fundamental sense related to the role of the Church in society; the Conservatives being a clerical party and the Liberals anti-clerical. Once this issue was settled, starting late in the 1900's and finishing with the formal separation of Church and state in 1925, the differences between segments of the political right were those of nuance and style rather than substance. After about two decades out of power, the Conservative and Liberal parties joined forces for the 1958 election, forming the Democratic Front whose candidate, Jorge Alessandri, gained the presidency. By-election results late in Alessandri's term of office convinced the parties of the right that they could not win the next presidential election and, indeed, that if they ran their own candidate, they might well ensure the victory of Salvador Allende, the perennial leftist candidate (Allende had been a candidate in both of the two previous presidential elections). Thus, the Liberals and Conservatives threw their support to Frei, the Christian Democrat, as a lesser evil. However, by 1970 the coalition between these two traditional parties had reemerged, now called the National Party, with Alessandri once again their candidate.[1]

Although Chile had built up one of the most advanced educational systems in Latin America during the long years of Liberal and Conservative rule, by the 1950's education was not a high priority item on the rightist political agenda. There was support for expansion of schooling in a general sense, and maintenance of private schooling as a guarantor of "freedom of teaching" was taken for granted—although the Conservative party in its 1961 platform suggested that the Church should have the right to provide religious instruction in all schools, both public and private (Gil, 1966, p. 246). This linkage of schooling and religion by the Conservative party is important to an understanding of some of the debates over education during the Allende years, and Gil's observation about the strength of feeling on the issue during the mid-1960's is worth noting.

> Fundamental to an understanding of the ideological position of Chilean Conservatives is the recognition that religious issues still play a very important role in party thought. There are many party members who believe that although the historical "theological question" may have been solved, some aspects related to family, marriage and schools, particularly, are still valid policy issues. These Conservatives have the image of their party not chiefly as the defender of vested economic interests but as the sustainer and defender of Catholic ideals in politics. (1966, p. 247)

It should also be noted, however, that during the Alessandri regime the need for a major reform and expansion of the educational system was recognized, and a national Commission for Integral Educational Planning was established. This commission published its report in the last year of Alessandri's presidency (Ministerio de Educación Pública, 1964); however, the background research undertaken and the data which were gathered and analyzed by this commission were very important in permitting the educational reformers of the Frei government to move rapidly once they were in power.

THE PARTIES OF THE LEFT:
POPULAR UNITY AND ITS FOREBEARS

Although it was not until the 1950's that the leftist parties formed a powerful electoral bloc, there had been organized political party activity at this end of the spectrum since early in the century. The Chilean political left has been constantly plagued by fragmentation, dissension, and internecine warfare; however, the two dominant forces which emerged were the Communist party and the Socialist party, the first founded in 1912 as the Workers' Socialist party and the other in 1933. Throughout the 1930's and 1940's these two parties (or more properly, the Communist party on one side and various combinations of splinters and fractions on the Socialist side) were in bitter conflict over: 1) ideological hegemony over the workers' movement; 2) the workers' votes; and 3) control of workers' organizations. This conflict was brought under at least minimal control (it was never really resolved, even during the Popular Unity reign) in the early 1950's so that the Popular Action Front (FRAP), combining the Socialists, Communists, and splinter groups, could be formed in 1956. This coalition ran Salvador Allende as its presidential candidate in the 1958 election, and he very nearly won, receiving 28.8 per cent of the vote versus the 29.1 per cent obtained by the winning Alessandri (a considerable improvement over the 5.4 per cent Allende had gained as a Socialist candidate in 1952).

In the following presidential election, Allende and FRAP were overwhelmed by Frei, even though Allende's share of the popular vote had risen to 38.9 per cent. And, of course, in 1970 Allende finally achieved presidential victory, although in this case with a smaller percentage of the popular vote than in 1964 (36 per cent).

As a result of the electoral failure in 1964, the Communist and Socialist parties began to diverge ideologically to a greater extent than had been true over the previous decade or so. The official ideology of the Communist party was Marxism-Leninism, as interpreted at any particular time by the Communist party of the USSR. Although this rather slavish adherence to the Moscow line led to some remarkable turnabouts on foreign policy issues, the Communists maintained a relatively consistent general position with reference to internal national politics. The party was well organized, with a strong base in the labor movement (enabling it to survive a decade of official proscription, 1948-58, with its structure and support-base virtually intact), and followed a relatively conservative and cautious line on national issues. Its basic political program is summarized as follows by Gil:

> (a) Anti-capitalism and anti-imperialism; (b) broad reforms toward democratization of the educational system; (c) full state participation in all economic activities (and the concomitant principles of agrarian reform, nationalization of banks and insurance companies, strict control of foreign trade, etc.); (d) electoral reforms to extend suffrage to illiterates, all eighteen-year old citizens, and members of the armed forces and the police; and (e) reforms of the political system to achieve a true democratic order of national liberation, under which all power resides in the hands of the people. (1966, p. 278)

In pursuit of its goals, the Communist party was long an advocate of unity among the leftist parties and of the need for collaboration with the "middle classes" in order to achieve political power through electoral and parliamentary means rather than through armed revolution. This stance, however, did not signify total or ultimate rejection of the need for armed insurrection. As Arriagada has observed with reference to all of the Moscow-line Communist parties in Latin America in the mid-1960's, "this rejection of the 'armed path' did not mean that the Communist parties ceased to see socialism as the work of an active minority which, based on a combination of political and military elements, where the latter would be predominant, could seize total power, independently of the opinions of the majority. For them, the relationship with guerrillas or insurrection continued to be a question of tactics" (1978, p. 161).

The Socialist party was far less ideologically homogeneous, including everything from advocates of armed revolution to non-Marxist "humanistic socialists." However, a Trotskyite position tended to predominate, at least in the party's rhetoric. In general terms, the party defined itself as anti-capitalist, anti-imperialist, revolutionary, accepting a Marxist historical materialist understanding of the world and assuming the inevitability of class warfare which would lead to the establishment of a socialist "workers' state" and dictatorship of the proletariat. Eventually, the various currents of thought and splinter groups in the party coalesced into two general tendencies or lines which came to be identified as the reformists versus the revolutionaries or the soft-liners versus the hard-liners. The former took a strategic position similar to that of the Communists. They held that Chile was fundamentally a salaried middle-class society (this group being very different from the "petit-bourgeois" in classical Marxist thinking because of its historical development in the Chilean context), with a large urban proletariat who had middle-class aspirations, and a small and diminishing peasant class. Under such conditions, the only viable route to power was to form a wide front ("frente amplio") of proletarian parties and those many elements of the middle classes already sympathetic to the working-class cause. With such a coalition, one could achieve political power through electoral means and begin a process of gradual transformation from the capitalist system to a socialist state. The revolutionaries rejected this analysis, maintaining that it would be impossible to use the institutions of the bourgeois such as elections, Congress, and the courts to change that very state radically. Rather, in their view, the only way to power was through open class warfare, in which the working class, unsullied by alliances with the middle sectors, would use force of arms to overthrow the existing institutions and install a dictatorship of the proletariat.

A tendency which is observable throughout the history of the Socialist party was for its official rhetoric to reflect more the hard line (in official party declarations, for example, or resolutions passed at party congresses), while its actions followed the soft line. (It formed part of the Popular Front government of Pedro Aguirre Cerda from 1938 until 1940, when it withdrew from the coalition and promptly disintegrated. Shortly after it had regained a measure of cohesiveness in the mid-1950's, it joined the FRAP.) The conflict was never fully resolved, and the tendency to talk "hard" while acting "soft" had serious consequences for the conduct and fate of the Allende government as a whole and for the education sector in particular. Therefore, it is worthwhile devoting some attention to the final stages in the development of that conflict in the years just preceding the 1970 electoral victory.

After the 1964 election, the Communist party interpreted the defeat of FRAP as indicating that Chile was not prepared to support a government composed only of Socialists and Communists. A movement with a wider socioeconomic base was needed. Hence the party began to enter into serious conversations with potential allies among "progressive" elements from the center, particularly with the Radical party, which was moving to the left as a result of its own electoral defeat.

Within the Socialist party, however, the 1964 election results strengthened the revolutionary wing; in its 1967 Congress in the city of Chillan, the party officially rejected any possible alliances with "bourgeois center" elements and affirmed the inevitability and legitimacy of revolutionary violence in order to take power. However, as was typically the case with this party, the situation internally was more complex.[2]

The key resolution debated and approved at the Chillan Congress had been developed and presented by party locals from the south and east sectors of Santiago. The most important sections read:

1. The Socialist party, as a Marxist-Leninist organization, establishes the seizure of power as the strategic objective to be achieved by this generation, in order to install a Revolutionary State which will free Chile from dependency and economic and cultural backwardness, and will initiate the construction of Socialism.
2. Revolutionary violence is inevitable and legitimate. It is a necessary result of the repressive and armed character of the class state. It is the only road which will lead to the seizure of political and economic power, and its later defence and reinforcement. Only by destroying the bureaucratic and military apparatus of the bourgeois state can the socialist revolution be consolidated.
3. Peaceful or legal forms of warfare will not, in and of themselves, lead to power. The Socialist party considers these as limited instruments of action, incorporated into the political process which will bring us to armed warfare. Consequently the alliances established by the party can only be justified to the extent that they contribute to the realization of the strategic objectives just noted. (Jobet, 1971, p. 130)

The resolution then went on to a rather didactic and academic discussion of the Workers' Front Policy which had originally been formulated by the party ten years earlier. This policy "proposes the unity of action of the proletariat, the peasants, and the poor middle class, under the leadership of the first group. The Workers' Front will be reinforced by the incorporation into the political fight for socialism of revolutionary students and intellectuals" (Jobet, 1971, p. 131). However flamboyant some of the language, the authors and promoters of the resolution did not see it as militaristic or extreme, but rather as a somewhat moderate position which, while recognizing that eventually class conflict would have to come down to an armed fight, held that it was necessary and appropriate to work carefully and within traditional and legal insitutions in the long preparation for that event. Moreover, it affirmed that large sectors of the salaried middle class were not bourgeois in the traditional Marxist sense but were potential allies of the proletarian forces.

However, "as so often happened in the Socialist party" (interview with Ivan Nuñez, 27 September 1982), the same congress which approved this rather moderate—in Chilean Socialist terms—resolution also elected a central committee, the majority of whose members were either unconvinced of the validity of, or misinterpreted, the resolution.

This committee produced for general distribution an "edited" text of the resolution which glossed over the "moderate" qualifications, emphasizing the need for revolutionary violence and speaking only of "the people" or "the workers" rather than the wider Workers' Front concept. This fixed the public image of the party as highly revolutionary. Meanwhile, the text actually approved by the congress was used as a reference point by many of those who had drafted and promoted it. Two of these individuals came to occupy key posts in the Ministry of Education after Allende's 1970 triumph: Ivan Nuñez and Lautaro Videla. The ideological position they advocated, which had more nuances than the officially promulgated hard-line posture, influenced the style of educational reform they eventually encouraged.

Neither the Socialist nor the Communist parties placed much emphasis on education in their official party documents and platforms. Following orthodox Marxist thinking, they held that true educational reform could only come as part and as a consequence of profound change in the socio-economic structure, in the forms and relations of production. Contrary to the Christian Democratic (and Radical) understanding that educational change was a necessary condition for economic growth and social change, these two parties held that education could only be "an accelerator; the motor is the economy" (Retamal, 1971, p. 93). In terms of specific policies, there are calls for elimination of illiteracy, increasing democratization of the educational system not only with reference to expanding enrolments but to more popular participation in decision-making, emphasis on polytechnic education, the integration of academic and manual work (as Fischer points out, this is one of the few concrete educational objectives which can be derived directly from the writings of Marx and Lenin—1977, p. 120), and calls for the abolition of private schooling. There was, however, a "lack of an educational policy for the workers' movement; our parties respond pragmatically, on the defensive; our offensive actions are limited and occasional, fruits not of a general strategy but of pressure from the masses (local fights for expanded enrolments or better buildings, etc.). We have been unable to *politically* appraise the educational process" (Conferencia Nacional de Trabajadores de la Educación del Partido Socialista, 1968, pp. 43-44). The only area of education in which the leftist parties were consistently active was in struggles for influence or control in the various teachers' unions.

However, late in the pre-Allende period (January 1968) the Socialist party teachers (the National Conference of Socialist Party Educational Workers) produced a lengthy educational policy statement (Conferencia Nacional. . . 1968). This document was used on a number of occasions thereafter, particularly after the Popular Unity government came into power. For example, it formed part of the curricular material for a seminar on "Perspective on the Structure and Functioning of Chilean Education" held at the State Technical University in the summer of 1971. It was also used, in whole or in part, in a number of courses and seminars at the Center for In-Service Teacher Training. Thus, it was perceived by many to represent the official Socialist party position regarding education and was understood by a number of people to represent the "real" objectives of the Allende government with respect to educational policy. It is therefore worth some examination.

In its analysis of the socioeconomic juncture in which Chile found itself, the document paralleled the resolution that was actually approved at the Chillan Congress the year before. It mentioned, for example, that the revolutionary mission of the Socialist party would be carried out by the proletariat, "aided by the peasants and the salaried middle class" (p. 45). However, much of its rhetoric was even more flamboyantly revolutionary than the language in either version of the Chillan resolution. For example:

The transition to socialism has not been and will not be peaceful. (p. 44)

There is neither time nor the possibility for a "peaceful revolution" nor for a revolution in liberty, except as tactical and propagandistic maneuvers of imperialism, which they will soon be seen to be. (p. 45)

Accomplishing the revolutionary task will require the destruction of the bureaucratic-military apparatus of the bourgeoisie, which can only occur through armed warfare. (p. 45)

In order to "defend the new order" a variety of Popular Councils and Popular Committees was proposed, supported by the general arming of the people. "The Revolutionary State will be, from the viewpoint of the masses, a more democratic political system than the wider bourgeois parliamentary democracy. But, the Revolutionary State will also be a most implacable dictatorship with respect to counterrevolutionary tendencies which might try to turn the situation around." (pp. 46-47)

The new society will have to defend itself with the rifle as well as ideology. (p. 47)

Turning to education itself, the document argued that the conditions necessary for a true educational revolution were the following: 1) ownership of the means of production by the workers as the only way to ensure the necessary finance and support for schooling; 2) direct participation in educational decision-making by the masses, in order to give dynamism to the system; 3) a system of integral national social and economic planning, in which educational planning would be inserted, in order to ensure the most efficient use of resources; 4) a Marxist-Leninist orientation to all aspects of schooling, which would permit science to truly penetrate the educational system; 5) a revolutionary dictatorship of workers, peasants, and the poor middle class as the only means of ensuring an effective democratization of schooling; 6) abolition of distinctions between intellectual and manual work in the wider society as the only condition under which a polytechnical approach could erase the distinctions within education.

The socialist teachers were also quite clear in stating that there would be no ideological pluralism in the new school:

> The content of education will change radically. When the educational system is in the hands of the workers, who have nothing to fear from and much to take advantage of in science, we will realize the ideal of a scientifically structured education. Education will be organized and planned scientifically, its methods will have a scientific basis, and will produce much greater achievement than presently, and it will transmit a scientific doctrine, dialectical materialism, as a set of principles and as a method to interpret reality. If pedagogical work in a capitalist regime is inspired by determined doctrines—such as christianity, fascism or liberalism, the proletariat will take their right to use their own philosophical instrument—Marxism, to orient and provide content for the educational tasks of the new society. . . . Neither superstition, nor religious dogmas, nor patriotism will have a place in the New School. These will be replaced by the scientific materialist conception of nature and history. Patriotism will be replaced by a just and proper valuation of internationalism. Individualism and competition will be replaced by socialist forms of living together. (pp. 49-50)

Reading that statement in conjunction with the call for an "implacable dictatorship" to stamp out "counterrevolutionary tendencies" led many

Chileans several years later to have great difficulty believing the claims that the Allende government intended to maintain ideological pluralism within the schools.

RELATIVE PLACEMENT AND STRENGTH OF THE POLITICAL FORCES IN 1970

To summarize this brief history of the main political groups, we may consider their relative position in 1970 on three dimensions: 1) their degree of commitment to the existing socioeconomic order or conversely their commitment to the need for a reordering of the distribution of economic and political power within the society; 2) their degree of commitment to the maintenance of the existing constitutional order and the parliamentary democratic institutional structure; and 3) their support among the electorate. Figure 2 locates each of the major parties, as well as smaller groups which have not been discussed above, on these three dimensions. Placement on the first two dimensions is taken from Arturo Valenzuela's work (1978, pp. 45-48), adapted somewhat. The estimates of electoral strength are based upon the results of the 1969 congressional elections adjusted to account for the probable effect of subsequent events.

It is particularly important to take into account the joint and interacting importance of the first two dimensions. The political struggle in Chile was not simply a "left" versus "right" fight between those who desired a major redistribution of social, economic and political rewards and power in favor of the "dispossessed" and those who wanted to maintain the status quo from which they themselves had benefited (the horizontal dimension). It was also a conflict between those who had a strong commitment to the existing parliamentary institutional structure and those whose support for those institutions was either qualified or non-existent. Significant portions of both the right and left had only qualified commitment on this vertical dimension. That is, their commitment was ultimately dependent upon the degree to which those institutions served their interests or the interests they understood themselves to be representing. Thus, to the extent that the strong supporters of the socioeconomic status quo (in 1970 predominantly the adherents of the National party and the Radical Democracy) perceived the success of Popular Unity to be eroding their own status, they were likely to join the small fraction who supported Fatherland and Liberty and supported and stimulated a military intervention to destroy the existing political institutions. Conversely, to the extent that Popular Unity supporters saw the actions of the traditional "right" as blocking their efforts to achieve radical socioeconomic change within the parliamentary framework, they were likely to move to the position of MIR and the revolutionary-line Socialists, who were already convinced that their

FIGURE 2

PLACEMENT AND STRENGTH
OF KEY POLITICAL PARTIES AND GROUPS, 1970*

Commitment to Existing Socioeconomic Order

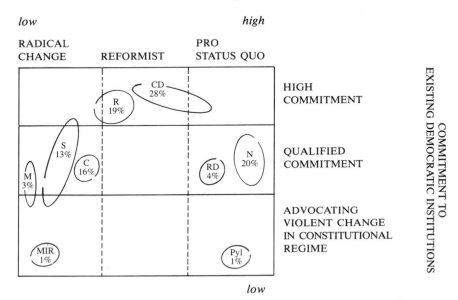

Legend:

M = MAPU; MIR = Movement of the Revolutionary Left; S = Socialist Party;
C = Communist Party; R = Radical Party; C.D. = Christian Democratic Party;
RD = Radical Democracy; N = National Party; Pyl = Fatherland and Liberty.

*Adapted from Valenzuela, 1978, p. 46. The estimates of electoral strength sum to
95 per cent. The remaining 5 per cent cannot be easily attributed to any particular
group or party.

goals could be achieved only through the destruction of the parliamentary
system.

Only the Christian Democrats and the Radicals were firmly committed
to the existing political "rules of the game." The Allendista Socialists generally considered their commitment to these institutions to be temporary
and tactical. Allende observed on several occasions that eventually the
traditional procedures and institutions would have to be replaced. His
conviction was that this could be accomplished *within* that institutional
framework without having to first destroy it. (See particularly his famous

interview with Regis Debray, *Punto Final*, 16 March 1971, pp. 25-63.) Thus, calling the Christian Democrats and Radicals "centrist" refers to their reformist position regarding socioeconomic change. In 1970 they were not "centrist" regarding the existing political institutions. On the other hand, the "centrist" elements with Popular Unity are those committed to the existing democratic institutions; all within the coalition were committed to the need for radical change in the socioeconomic structure.

If Popular Unity was to be successful, it had to achieve a stable governing coalition which would be able to resist the tendency of both the extreme left and extreme right to move toward advocacy of violent overthrow of the constitutional order. This tendency was particularly strong at the end of a decade in which the ability of the Radicals and then the Christian Democrats to hold together, from the center, the compromise state which had maintained Chilean democracy for so many decades was being seriously eroded by growing social polarization. The Radical party had already split under this strain, and the Christian Democrats were increasingly divided between those who favored radical change and those inclined toward a reformist or pro status quo stance. It is instructive to note that the joint "center" on both scales in Figure 2 is empty and that electoral strength was fairly evenly divided between the traditional parties of the left, the right, and the center.

At a very minimum, the Allende regime had to ensure that the Christian Democrats did not move toward the lower right-hand corner of the figure. This task was complicated by the inability of Popular Unity forces, even those most "centrist" in their own terms, to recognize the importance for the middle-class sectors represented primarily by Christian Democracy of a dimension not included in Figure 2—*culture*. Contrary to traditional Marxist thinking, this was to some extent independent of socioeconomic and political status. It was when the government's educational policy was seen by a coalition of forces which cut across traditional class and party lines as threatening fundamental cultural values related to the family and religion that many of those who were strongly committed to the constitutional regime were persuaded that they might have to sacrifice that system in order to preserve what was most dear to them: the welfare and destiny of their children and their religion.

3

Development of the Educational System

Chile has long been considered to have one of the most advanced educational systems in Latin America. While many Chileans have concerned themselves with trying to explain why they have not done better educationally, foreign observers more typically have tried to understand how they have managed to do so well.

When it achieved independence from Spain early in the nineteenth century, the nation then had the rudimentary educational system typical of Spanish colonies of that time: very few schools offering a simple and inflexible curriculum to a small and almost exclusively male proportion of the population. Two small universities in Santiago provided limited opportunity to study the few academic fields then recognized in the Spanish-speaking world. The importance of education to the consolidation and development of the new nation was quickly recognized by the post-independence governments, and this recognition was converted into public policy and action much more rapidly than was typical in Latin America.

Chile was the first Latin American nation to formally establish a system of public instruction, in 1842. Before 1850 the University of Chile had been established (it became a major focal point for bringing the "liberal" political philosophies of non-Mediterranean Europe into the nation), experimental science had penetrated the classical curriculum of the university-preparatory *liceo*, and the first normal school had been founded, just a few years after the first such school had been established in the United States.

In 1860 an Organic Law declared primary education to be free, and additional secondary and normal schools were established. Later in the century, secondary education was opened to females, and Chile became the first Latin American nation to admit women to the university and to allow them to practice the liberal professions. By the turn of the century approximately one-third of school-age children were enrolled in schools—a remarkable achievement for the time and place.

During the early part of the present century the slowly growing political power of the working class produced a spreading perception of social imbalances and inequalities as social problems rather than inevitable conditions. This led, among other things, to the enactment of the first social security law in Latin America and, in education, to the establishment in 1920 of compulsory education for all children under fifteen years of age. Expansion continued steadily, particularly at the primary level, in response to ever-growing social demand for schooling. This in turn created greater demand for secondary and higher education, which put increasing strains on the physical and administrative capacity of the system. Nonetheless, the growth in the educational system was impressive, as shown in Table 1, which notes the change between 1865 and 1952 in the percentage of school-age children enrolled in school. The increase in access to formal schooling was also reflected in the adult literacy rate, which grew from 17 per cent in 1865 to 50 per cent in 1920 and 80 per cent in 1952.

TABLE 1

PERCENTAGE OF SCHOOL-AGE CHILDREN IN SCHOOL, 1865-1952

Year	Percentage	Year	Percentage
1865	10.9	1907	35.5
1875	17.1	1920	46.2
1885	20.4	1930	60.6
1895	27.7	1940	57.5
		1952	61.6

Source: E. Hamuy, "La evolución de la educación elemental y el problema educacional," in E. Schiefelbein and N. McGinn, eds., *El sistema escolar y el problema del ingreso de la universidad* (Santiago: CPU, 1975), p. 103.

However, the quantitative expansion of schooling was not only creating more and more difficult administrative and financial problems within the educational sector itself as more and more students wished to attend the more expensive upper levels, but it was also not solving the underlying problems of socioeconomic inequality in educational opportunity. A number of major reform plans were developed, starting in the 1920's. While none was fully implemented, they served as models of what might be done within Chilean schools for reform-minded educators at a later time.

TWENTIETH CENTURY REFORM EFFORTS

The first attempt at global reform occurred in 1928. In that year massive change in the educational system was decreed. Administration of the system was radically altered, both by unifying disparate "directorships" within the bureaucracy and by decentralizing some decision-making. Teachers were given freedom to experiment with new styles of teaching and learning in their classrooms, and local school communities involving teachers, parents and students were to be formed. Curriculum and teaching methods were to be developed to take into account both the psychobiological needs of the growing child and the requirements of national or regional development. Technical subjects were to be introduced as options in the traditional humanistic curriculum of the *liceo*. But the reform was shortlived; within less than a year it had been cancelled. As Nuñez notes, "it went beyond what the existing social system would permit" (1979, p. 18). However, the force behind the reform was sufficiently strong that even in eliminating it the educational traditionalists had to permit some of its elements into the system. "The principles of the new pedagogy were incorporated into the official doctrine for the Chilean primary school. Some elements of a modern and realistic secondary education came to be recognized by Decree. In-Service Teacher Training, and the possibility of experimentation within the classroom and in the internal organization of the school were accepted" (Nuñez, 1979, p. 19). With these modifications, the Chilean school system took on the form and character that it would maintain with little change until the reforms of the 1960's.

Just after the Second World War two other important reform attempts were started. One was the Gradual Secondary Education Renovation Plan. This plan, which had rather wide political support as well as North American technical and financial aid, was designed to gradually introduce major changes in the traditional *liceo*, starting with a few experimental demonstration schools. In these schools more flexible programs of study were introduced, with more active and participatory teaching-learning methods, which attempted to prepare youngsters from a wider range of social backgrounds not only for university entrance, but also for the necessities of their family, social, and economic lives as adults. Although bureaucratic and traditionalist opposition did not permit these reforms to spread beyond the first demonstration schools, these experimental *liceos* achieved and maintained great prestige, being generally recognized as among the best schools, private or public, in the nation. For many they served as a model of what could be done within the walls of the classical Chilean secondary school.

In 1945 another experiment was started, with ministerial support, by a group of educators in San Carlos, a rural district in the south of Chile.

The San Carlos Plan attempted to develop a local educational system which integrated all levels of schooling under a single administration (within the Ministry of Education primary, secondary, normal, technical-professional, and other forms of schooling were each under a separate directorate each with its own lines of authority to local schools under its jurisdiction) and attempted to establish much closer links between the schools and the local community—in essence using the school as a center for community mobilization. For a variety of national and local political reasons, this experiment was abruptly terminated in 1948. However, it served as a model for a number of "consolidated schools" which were established over the next two decades, primarily in peasant or mining communities, or in the marginal areas of the large cities. By 1962, thirteen such schools were in existence; by 1974 there were thirty-one (Nuñez, 1979, p. 22). Although always few in number and marginal to the standard operation of the vast traditional schooling system, these schools had an important influence upon the educational policy of the Popular Unity government. They provided an example of what "unified" schooling could be in a local community, and they served as training grounds for some of the most influential figures within the Allende Ministry of Education.

Particularly important was the consolidated school located in San Miguel, a working-class district of Santiago. The director of the school was Luzmira Leyton, a powerful personality and an important veteran of the long struggle for some form of "consolidated" schooling. One of the leaders within the school was Lautaro Videla, who became a key Socialist figure in the Ministry of Education between 1970 and 1973. Starting in the early 1950's Leyton, Videla, and their team of teachers (and later Videla's wife, who worked as a community organizer) slowly built the school into an institution which served some three thousand students and was a center for mobilization of the local community (one example: using the school as a base, the community organized itself to turn a deep block-square hole from an abandoned construction site, which was a danger to the children, into a large planted plaza), as well as a meeting site for a wide array of community organizations. In addition, this school served as a training ground for a group of young teachers who were emerging as important socialist teacher union leaders. Most important among these was Ivan Nuñez, who became superintendent of education and was the prime motivating force behind the educational policy propositions of the Allende government. Both Videla and Nuñez claim (Nuñez, 1979, p. 23; Videla, interview, 18 May 1981) that, for them at least, this experience in San Miguel was the start of the idea for the National Unified School proposal.

Finally, in 1961 the Educational Integration Plan for Arica was established in the northernmost province of the nation. This experiment, which continued on into the Allende years, attempted once again to develop a unified local administrative system which would overcome the traditional barriers within the Ministry of Education and produce an educational structure and curriculum adapted to the local needs of this distant region. The plan drew heavily upon the experience of the experimental *liceos* and the consolidated schools and was relatively successful, particularly in reducing dropout rates.

THE FREI REFORM: 1965-70

All of these reform efforts were either partial, temporary, or circumscribed within a particular area. It was not until the Christian Democratic regime of Eduardo Frei came into power in 1964 that it was possible to implement a major national reform program. The Frei regime placed high priority upon educational reform and backed it up with the necessary financial resources (including substantial aid from the United States). Starting with the technical work that had been done by the planning commission in the last years of Alessandri's government, the Frei reformers were able to move quickly.

The first move was to increase the system's capacity. Theoretically, the existing stock of schools could have met, or even exceeded, the forecast total demand for places. However, because of chronically high repetition rates, much of the already existing enrolment was "bunched up" in the lower grades. For example, the first grade enrolment was 70 per cent greater than the total population of seven-year-old children in the nation. Thus, it was concluded that in order to accommodate both the repeaters and new cohorts who would hopefully pass more smoothly from grade to grade, it was necessary to increase classroom capacity. Resources were provided to build new buildings and to increase the production of trained teachers.

At the same time the decision was made to begin restructuring the system to break the traditional pattern of six years of primary schooling and six years of secondary education. The primary level was increased to eight years, designed as a common and compulsory cycle for all children from six to fifteen years of age. By 1970 new curricula had been designed and implemented for all eight grades. The new curriculum aimed: 1) to stimulate the overall personality development of children, rather than concentrating solely on academic achievement as preparation for higher levels of education, 2) to prepare students for more active participation in a democratic society as adults through active participation in their learning in school, and 3) to provide a foundation for a wise choice between entering the labor market and continuing in school once past the limit of compulsory education.

With the expansion of the primary level, the secondary cycle was reduced to four years, the first two years providing a common base and the last two years allowing diversified specialized preparation for university or the world of work.

To permit adaptation of the curriculum to regional or local requirements and to the needs of individual students, detailed central specification of curriculum was avoided; rather, general guidelines were issued with the expectation that teachers and school directors would be able to adapt them to local needs. Although this flexibility was not always attained, it was at least encouraged. Mechanisms were also introduced to provide for easier lateral movement between the technical-professional schools and the university preparatory *liceos*. Under the traditional system essentially irrevocable vocational decisions had to be made by or for children by the end of the sixth grade; under the new system youngsters had, theoretically at least, four more years before the die was cast.

To attack the class-linked problems of dropout and repetition more directly, several ancillary strategies were adopted. School breakfasts and lunches, school uniforms, learning materials, shoes, and even raincoats and boots where the climate demanded were provided free of charge to children from poor families. A system of automatic promotion through the early years of primary schooling was instituted. An emphasis on formative rather than summative evaluation was encouraged.

To provide support for all of these changes a Center for In-Service Training and Educational Experimentation was established. This organization mounted a massive program of in-service teacher training and preparation, testing, and distribution of new curricula, teachers' guides, textbooks, workbooks, and other didactic material. Examples of the scale of this effort can be seen in its accomplishments by 1970: three-quarters of all teachers had received at least one in-service training experience averaging three weeks in duration; 3.65 million primary school texts had been designed, printed and distributed (just over two books per enrolled student); 1.3 million children were receiving free breakfasts at school every day; and 0.6 million were receiving free lunches (the meal program reached practically all children in school with potential or real nutrition problems).

RESULTS OF THE REFORM

The literature regarding major attempts to reform educational systems is littered with examples of spectacular failure; it tends to confirm the old adage that "it is easier to move a graveyard than an educational system." Within this context the Chilean reform under the Christian Democrats was remarkably successful. As with any massive social change effort, many of the proposals were never fully implemented; some of the successes created problems for the next administration; and many of the consequences, positive or negative, have never been adequately identified. Nonetheless, the results were quite substantial. Schiefelbein and Farrell have noted the following quantitative changes:

> Between 1965 and 1970, primary enrollment doubled and enrollment at the secondary and university levels tripled. While in 1964, 87% of the population aged 7 to 12 were in school, by 1970 the figure was raised to 95% and by 1972 had come close to 100%. By 1970, 85% of those entering grade 1 were doing so on time (at 7 years of age) and primary repetition rates were drastically reduced. Roughly 0.2 million children who had previously been denied access to a meaningful basic education were accommodated in the schools, to the point that by March, 1970 all children who requested entrance to primary schools were enrolled. Whereas before the reform only about a third of those who started grade 1 completed the then 6-year primary cycle, by 1970 half of the entrants completed the full 8 years of basic education. Whereas before the reform about a third of those who completed primary school did not continue on into grade 7, by 1970 almost all students who completed grade 8 enrolled in secondary school, and about 40% of secondary starters completed the cycle. (1982, p. 31)

This growth also marked a notable improvement in the probability that poor children would not only enter primary school but also complete the now longer primary cycle. Table 2 compares the proportions of children from various occupational strata who completed primary schooling in the 1943-53 period and in 1970.

TABLE 2

COMPARISON OF SURVIVAL POTENTIALS BY SOCIAL STRATUM
AT THE PRIMARY LEVEL OVER A 20-YEAR PERIOD

	1943-1953		1970
Group	*Percentage surviving to grade 6*	*Percentage surviving to grade 7*	*Percentage surviving to grade 8*
Rural poor (primary resource exploitation)	15.3	5.6	18
Urban poor (urban industrial)	27.8	13.9	48
Middle class (white-collar middle-class)	48.4	32.1	71
High class (professionals and managers)	79.8	73.3	100

Source: Schiefelbein and Farrell, 1982, p. 65.

Clearly in 1970 the probability of completing primary education was still strongly associated with the socioeconomic status of the family. Moreover, children of all social strata benefited somewhat from the quantitative growth; in each case the completion percentage in 1970 is higher than in the earlier period. The group that appears to have benefited most is the children of the urban poor, which was itself a rapidly expanding economic group during this time period. The proportion of this group completing an eight-year primary education in 1970 was almost twice the percentage completing a six-year primary education two decades earlier and more than three times the percentage completing grade seven. Obviously, the group that benefited least was the children of agricultural laborers—the peasantry, an occupational group which was, however, rapidly diminishing in size during the 1950's and 1960's. (In 1970 only about one-quarter of economically active males were engaged in agricultural labor.)

One also notes the very strong screening effect in the earlier period of the transition from primary to secondary schooling—from grade six to grade seven. Among the relatively few children of poor families who completed primary education, less than half entered grade seven; the screening was especially marked among the rural poor. Even for middle-class children this was an important sorting point; about one-third of the children from this group who completed primary school did not go on. Only for the small professional and managerial class was this transition not an obstacle. By 1970 this had ceased to be a problem; practically all children who completed primary schooling, of whatever family background, enrolled in secondary education. The critical decision was the type of secondary school in which the student would enroll (a university preparatory *liceo* or one of the several types of technical-professional schools), and at this point family socioeconomic status was a prime determinant (Schiefelbein and Farrell, 1982, p. 73). It appears that the main social impact of the Frei reform was to improve dramatically the educational opportunities available to the children of the urban working class: the "proletariat" in the language of the left. This was not an inconsiderable accomplishment, but it still left much to be done.

The reaction of the leftist parties, particularly as expressed through the teachers' unions they controlled, was somewhat ambiguous. On the one hand, they supported many of the objectives of the Christian Democratic reform, and many of the accomplishments could neither be ignored nor criticized, except to note that they were limited with respect to the total set of education problems faced by the society. The main objections were the following: 1) the educational changes were not accompanied by the broad socioeconomic structural changes which by the left's analysis were necessary for a truly significant educational reform; 2) the changes were too strongly influenced by North American thinking; 3) given the style of

implementation, the changes did not appear to be part of an integral reform, but rather a set of separate policy measures, implemented in a top-
down, manipulative, and sectarian fashion;[1] 4) the previous problem was
aggravated by the lack of a clearly enunciated statement of the philosophical foundations of the reform and a precise statement of aims and objectives (Nuñez, 1982b, pp. 78-79).

EFFECTS ON THE TEACHERS' UNION MOVEMENT

The educational policy initiatives of the Frei regime had a direct effect
upon structural developments and policy propositions advanced within the
teachers' union movement. These in turn significantly constrained the
educational policy initiatives of the Allende government. The teachers'
union movement in Chile had a long history of fragmentation reflecting
the administrative divisions within the Ministry of Education. The three
principle organizations were the Union de Profesores de Chile (UPCH),
which was the primary teachers' union; the Sociedad Nacional de Profesores
(SONAP), the union of *liceo* teachers; and ASTECO, the union of technical and commercial school teachers. In 1944 these three unions, plus several smaller associations, joined together in a loose federation called the
Federación de Educadores de Chile (FEDECH). This mechanism allowed
support across the organizational lines, but each constituent union maintained its own separate identity, its own resources, budget, and so forth.
Propositions to form a single union had been advanced from time to time,
but they had never been seriously pursued.

Several aspects of the Frei government's activity in the area of education created a more propitious climate for formation of a single union.
First, the very success of the Frei initiatives on a wide array of fronts, its
attempts at global educational planning, and the inability of opposition
teachers' groups to resist most change propositions convinced a number
of powerful actors in the various unions that resistance to further reform
initiatives would be possible only through a single organization. Second,
in early 1968 there was a long and bitter nationwide teachers' strike over
salary issues. This strike, which Nuñez describes as resulting in a "prolonged
and painful tie" between the government and the teachers (1982b, p. 121)
also suggested to many the need for a framework for more effectively
coordinated action among teachers from different sections of the educational system. At the same time, several moves tended to reduce the traditional prestige gap between *liceo* teachers, who were generally university
graduates, and primary teachers, who were predominantly graduates of
secondary level normal schools and were very poorly paid: 1) normal schools
were raised to post-secondary status in 1967; 2) much greater emphasis

was placed on using the education faculties of the universities as training sites for primary teachers; 3) although the effect was limited, the reforms were bringing a socially more broadly based student body into the traditional *liceos* (Nuñez, 1982b, p. 14).

These developments produced increasing support for the idea of forming a single union. They also led many of the union leaders to conclude that organized teachers needed an agreed alternative policy so that they could move from a reactive to a proactive stance against the Christian Democrats and that such a policy alternative had to be developed through extensive consultation with teachers, parents, students and other members of local school communities to counter the top-down planning style of the Christian Democrats. At the same time, and partly as another reaction to the Christian Democratic policies, there was a discernible shift farther to the political left within the teachers' unions. The Communist and Socialist parties were gaining power within the movement at the expense of the long-dominant Radicals, who were themselves moving to the left, although they were still very far removed from the extreme public positions of the Socialist teachers. This in turn led to increasingly sharp competition for power and membership, which greatly complicated and constrained the development of a single union and an agreed alternative policy.

Within FEDECH a three-part program was devised to be proposed to and hopefully accepted by each of the constituent unions. The first proposition was that FEDECH be replaced by a Single Union of Educational Workers (SUTE—Sindicato Unico de Trabajadores de Educación). Second, a policy for educational transformation was proposed—or more accurately a *name* for such a policy was proposed: The School for Development. The points of view among the different political factions were so disparate that only a name could be agreed upon; and, even that name was interpreted differently by different groups, representing itself a compromise between the Socialists and the Radicals. The Socialists preferred the title "Consolidated School." However, given the history of the consolidated school movement, the Radicals perceived that name as giving too much of a Socialist imprint to the new policy. Hence a name was found which both parties could accept. Third, it was suggested that a National Congress of Education be held, bringing together representatives from all levels and sectors of the educational system to debate policy.

The three propositions were seen as closely interrelated. The School for Development was to be the basic policy direction. The National Congress was necessary in order to achieve consensus on the detailed content of that policy, and a unified teaching force in SUTE was essential to fight for the reform idea. The fundamental notion was to use an attractive educational reform proposal and well-organized teachers to mobilize masses to fight against and act as a constraint upon the Christian Democrats. This was conceived as a long-term strategy of *opposition* on the assumption that the left would lose the 1970 election and organized teachers would be facing another six years of battle against the same group of educational policy-makers. It was not conceived as a strategy for policy formulation within a new leftist government, which is what it turned out to be.[2]

During 1968 and 1969 the three propositions were approved by all of the separate unions, and SUTE was formally constituted in 1970. However, the National Congress of Education, which was originally to be held in 1968, did not occur because of the teachers' strike. It was also not held in 1969, apparently owing to the proximity of the presidential elections (Nuñez, 1982b, p. 80). Consequently, the "School for Development" remained a name without content. Moreover, the decision to form SUTE neither signalled nor created a reduction in interparty rivalries and jealousies within the teachers' union movement. It was simply seen as a politically expedient device to oppose the Christian Democrats more effectively. Indeed, the decision to create SUTE provided a new issue for political maneuvering among the parties: who would control the new organization? The presidency of SONAP, the *liceo* teachers' union, was in the hands of the Communists. The Socialists controlled ASTECO, the union of technical and commercial teachers. The Radicals controlled the union of primary teachers, UPCH, the largest of the groups, and also had the presidency of FEDECH. The question was whether the Socialists and Communists could use the competitions for directive posts in the new organization as a means of further eroding the power of the once dominant Radicals. The leadership elections for the new union, which would finally resolve this issue, were not held until after the Allende government came into power.

These teachers' unions never represented all of the teachers in Chile. Useful statistics comparing union membership to total teaching force in the relevant sector of the educational system cannot be found (as Nuñez, 1982b, p. 15, notes in the most exhaustive study of the Chilean teacher union movement available). However, from the evidence that is available, the following observations can be made. First, private school teachers were excluded from these unions. These individuals, who constituted about one-quarter of the teaching force, had their own organizations. Second, many public school teachers who did not share the political orientation of the Radical, Socialist, or Communist parties either did not join the union movement or would participate actively only when the unions were involved in a conflict with government over salary, other economic benefits, or working conditions. It appears that primary teachers were the most unionized and that large proportions of technical and commercial teachers at the secondary level also participated actively in the union movement. *Liceo* teachers were least likely to be union members. Among this group, the sense that union activity was not compatible with the professional dignity of their calling was particularly strong. Indeed, in the 1950's a rival organization to SONAP was formed, the Association of State Teachers (one had to have a university degree to be certified as a state teacher), which aspired to achieve the same status as the College of Engineers, the doctors' and lawyers' associations, and other organizations representing members of the traditional professions. While this organization never became as large as SONAP, it was an important counterforce.

The importance of the teachers' union movement for the analysis here does not, however, reside in its general representation of the teaching force or lack thereof. Rather, when Popular Unity assumed power, virtually all major administrative and policy posts in education were filled by leading figures from the teachers' unions. They carried the history of the union movement in education into the ministry with them. For example, the first minister of education was Mario Astorga, the Radical president of the primary teachers' union. The subsecretary of Education (the chief administrative officer within the ministry), Waldo Suarez, was an important Socialist teacher union leader. The main policy-formulation post in the ministry, that of superintendent of education, was filled by Ivan Nuñez, another of the powerful Socialists from the union movement (although Nuñez was chosen for this particular post because of his academic credentials). Still another of the Socialist union leaders, Lautaro Videla, became "visitor general"—a rather unusual but powerful position in the Chilean educational bureaucracy, which involved travelling throughout the nation to act on behalf of the minister in solving local problems and collecting information (both technical and political) of importance to the ministry.[3]

In addition, Carlos Moreno, a Socialist and president of the union of technical and commercial teachers, was named director of technical education. Jorge Espinoza, a Communist and president of the *liceo* teachers' union, became director of secondary education (he was responsible for *liceos* only—Moreno's directorate had charge of all other secondary institutions). Since Mario Astorga was named minister, another important Radical from the same union, Fresia Urrutia, became director of primary education. The position of technical secretary in the superintendency of education, another key policy formulation post, was filled by Hugo Araya, yet another of the important Radical union leaders.

What these individuals and many other key actors in the union movement brought with them to government, then, upon the unexpected electoral victory of Allende, were the following constraints:
1) a long history of interpersonal and interparty antagonisms, except for a few individuals who had developed the ability to gain the respect of and work with people of very different ideological persuasions;
2) awareness that the educational system had just absorbed the most abrupt and massive set of changes ever experienced by teachers, bureau-

crats, students and parents. This led many to the conclusion that it would be several years before most individuals working in education would be ready to entertain seriously, let alone implement, yet another wave of major change;

3) a new single union which was just being formed and which was serving not to unite the teaching force, as had been planned, but rather, through the on-going fight over control, to exacerbate old interparty conflicts. Moreover, this was a union which was to be decapitated at birth through the transfer of almost all of its powerful leadership figures into government positions;

4) a commitment to organize and hold a National Congress of Education, with participation from all levels and sectors, before developing the details of an educational policy;

5) no educational change propositions of important substance which had been discussed among, let alone agreed by, the various parties to the Popular Unity coalition. This lack of program content can be seen clearly in the Basic Program of Government of Popular Unity, the agreed campaign platform document of the coalition. This document can best be discussed, however, in the context of the electoral campaign and results in 1970, which is the subject of the following chapter.

4

The Campaign for 1970:
The Constraints Imposed by Victory

Chilean presidential campaigns generally began long before the election. Throughout 1969 there was much maneuvering for position within parties and searching for coalitions between or among them. The right was reunited as the National party. Just as by-election results in 1964 had convinced this sector not to nominate its own candidate for the presidency, but to support Frei, so a strong showing in the 1969 congressional elections convinced the National party that this time it should nominate its own candidate: Jorge Alessandri, who was still a popular political figure and was again eligible to run for the presidency. The Christian Democrats, who appeared to be losing electoral support steadily, were badly divided. Another alliance with the right, formal or informal, was seen as neither possible nor desirable. The division was between those who sought an alliance with the left and the nomination of a single "popular unity" candidate who would, it was hoped, be a Christian Democrat, and those who proposed that the party nominate its own candidate (with the possibility of negotiating for wider support from the left thereafter). At a key meeting of the party's assembly in early May 1969, the "own candidate" supporters won a narrow victory. This event triggered the resignations which led to the formation of MAPU. A few months later, in August, Radomiro Tomic was selected as the party's candidate, in spite of the fact that Tomic had declared firmly some months previously that "without popular unity coalition there will be no Tomic candidacy" (Sigmund, 1977, p. 78).

Given the historical divisions among the parties and fragments of the left, and particularly the Socialists' firm official rejection in 1967 of any possible alliance with the Radicals while the Communists and Allendista Socialists supported such an alliance, it took a great deal of negotiating to reach the point where, in early October, representatives of the Socialists, Communists, Radicals, MAPU, and two splinter groups (the Social Democratic Party and API—Accion Popular Independiente) met and agreed to draft a Basic Program for a Popular Unity coalition and to select a single candidate. Work on the program document began first, and within two months (by mid-December), an agreed text had been drafted. Shortly thereafter, on 26 December, a Popular Unity Pact was signed by the six groups. This document set out the rules for campaign coordination, but more importantly it affirmed that, if elected, the popular government would be multiparty in character. Among mechanisms specified to ensure this were the following: 1) the establishment of a "coordinating committee" representing all of the parties, which the president would have to consult regularly on all major matters of government policy (this committee was established and replaced the cabinet of ministers as the main decision-making body—or, as Tapia says, "non-decision making body" [interview, 9 December 1981] of the government); 2) an agreement on exactly how many ministries of government would be apportioned to each party; and 3) an agreement that in each ministry the "sub-secretario" or deputy minister would be of a different party from the minister. These latter provisions were the first signs of the "quota" system for dividing administrative posts among party adherents which plagued the government almost from the day of its election. Less than a month later, on 20 January 1970, after several weeks of very intense negotiations among the parties, Salvador Allende was selected as the coalition's presidential candidate. It is important to note, as Tapia indicates, that "Salvador Allende was not necessarily the most popular figure. This was particularly the case in his own party, where he achieved a narrow victory" (1979a, p. 28). One consequence was that even as president, Allende's authority and influence over his own party and the rest of the coalition was much less than might have been expected given his previous stature within Chilean politics.

THE BASIC PROGRAM OF POPULAR UNITY

General Characteristics

In both its text and its tone, the Basic Program of Popular Unity appeared to reflect the reformist or soft line within the coalition. The general theme, as expressed not only in the campaign platform but also in speeches during the campaign, was that the Popular Unity regime would not immediately bring into existence a socialist state, but rather that it would, using existing legal and constitutional mechanisms, initiate a "peaceful transition to socialism." The program itself, however, was very vague about both the nature of the eventual goal (in other words the kind of end-state society envisioned) and the detailed means for getting there. This was necessarily the case since there were many different understandings of "socialism" within the coalition, ranging from the position of the extreme revolutionary wing of the Socialist party, who were more in favor of armed revolt than electoral disputes and wished for the "implacable dictatorship" of the proletariat of which the socialist teachers had written (see Chapter 2), to Christian socialists (who felt abandoned by the Christian Democratic party) and those members of the Radical party who envisioned a kind of social democratic state on the European, especially Scandinavian, model. So divergent were the understandings within the coalition that one of the most prominent Radical ministers during the Allende years could say afterward that: "It is important to keep in mind that the socialist goal of the program was never defined as Marxist-Leninist. This was historically and politically impossible. To be more exact, the goal was never a Marxist-Leninist regime, because if it had been, the Chilean road to socialism would never have existed" (Tapia, 1979b, pp. 298-99). Yet, it was very clear that for large sectors of the coalition, such a Marxist-Leninist regime was precisely the intended eventual outcome. Zemelman (1979, p. 283) suggests that this lack of agreement was tolerable because the parties to the coalition did not really expect to win the election. They were thus able to lay aside their ideological differences and "interpret the program in a certain utopian light." Tapia (1979a, p. 28) outlines a broader analysis of the situation:

It is worth emphasizing the nature of consensus on the program. Unlike what had happened in 1964 and on other occasions, there was no concerted effort to define the key points of the program in terms of intermediate goals and strategies to facilitate coherent government action. In some cases this seemed to reflect skepticism about the likelihood of victory, in others, the conviction that the important thing was electoral triumph—afterwards there would be time for details. Lastly —and no less important—it reflected the conviction among some sectors that any attempt to spell out the key concepts of the program would lead inevitably to internecine clashes. In the long run these apprehensions proved critical. Apart from the program's real commitment to effect profound changes in Chilean society, there was no apparent agreement on goals or strategies—so basic to a program advocating revolutionary transformations.

Of greatest long-term importance, this lack of definition left unresolved — indeed, built into the very heart of the Popular Unity program — the conflict between the two lines: those who held that elective power, once achieved, should be used to exacerbate class conflict on every possible front so as to lead as rapidly as possible to the armed conflict and a true workers' state; and those who believed that the objective of acquiring elective power was to begin gradually transforming the society through peaceful means, using the power of government to mobilize increasingly broad sectors for support of increasingly profound changes.

One can best interpret the systems established by the Popular Unity Pact (for example, the coordinating committee and the careful apportioning of ministerial and sub-ministerial posts among the parties) as a set of within-coalition checks and balances designed to ensure that neither of these two "lines," nor any of the parties or movements within Popular Unity, would achieve ideological hegemony or too much organizational power within the government. The effect was to build in from the very inception of the coalition a systematic inability to arrive at a single clearly defined and strongly supported policy specification regarding any of the important propositions in the Basic Program.

Although the overall program represented a series of compromises, the various sections were most influenced by the party or group which took most interest in a particular theme. Thus, for example, the sections on agricultural reform were most heavily influenced by MAPU, whose leader, Jacques Chonchol, became Popular Unity's first minister of agriculture. The education section, while taking into account the Radical party interest in the area, was drafted in its final version by Ivan Nuñez from the Socialist party teacher union contingent. However, one aspect of the drafting process which was very damaging to the image of the Popular Unity coalition both during the campaign and once it had gained power was, as Sigmund points out (1977, p. 89), that "the program was most influenced in content and phraseology by the platform adopted by the Communist Party at its fourteenth National Congress held in the last week of November. As Alessandri supporters were to demonstrate during the campaign, whole sentences of the Popular Unity program were taken word for word from the statements of the Communist Party Congress."

Non-Educational Policy

Politically, the program proposed a Popular State, whose centerpiece was to be a unicameral legislature, a People's Assembly elected by vote among all citizens above eighteen years of age, literate or illiterate, and with a mechanism for popular recall of a legislator between regular elections. There was also to be integral national planning of the economy, a reorganization of the judiciary system making it more dependent upon the People's Assembly, and mechanisms for greatly increased participation in policy-making by workers and peasants through their unions and community organizations.

The *economic system* was to be divided into three areas: the area of social property, the area of private property, and the mixed area. The most striking feature of the economic proposals was the suggested dramatic expansion, through expropriation, of the social property area, which would include the following ("with full protection of the interests of the small shareholder" but no mention of compensation for the major owners):

1) the large copper, nitrate, iodine, iron and coal mines;
2) the national financial system, particularly the private banks and insurance companies;
3) foreign commerce;
4) large enterprises and monopolies of distribution;
5) strategic industrial monopolies; and,
6) in general, all activities which have a decisive influence on the economic and social development of the nation, such as the production and distribution of electrical energy, rail, air and sea transport, communications, refining, production and distribution of petroleum and its derivatives, including liquid gas, and the steel, cement, petrochemical and heavy chemical, cellulose and paper industries. (Programa Basico de Gobierno de la Unidad Popular, 1970, p. 20)

The private area was to include the remaining small non-monopolistic and non-strategic enterprises to which financial and technical assistance was pledged. The mixed area was left undefined except to note that it would include combinations of state and private capital. This proposed expansion of the social property sector must be seen in the context of an already massive extension of the Chilean state into the national economy. As Valenzuela observes (1978, p. 13):

> Even before the election of Salvador Allende to the presidency, the state played a greater role in the nation's economy than it did in the economy of any other Latin American country with the exception of Cuba. By the end of the 1960's direct public investment represented well over 50 per cent of all the gross investment, and the state controlled over 50 per cent of the GNP and 13 per cent of the economically active population. A state agency, the Corporación de Fomento de la Producción (CORFO), owned shares in eighty of the country's most important enterprises and institutions, and majority shares in thirty-nine of the same. Most private groups and institutions were closely regulated by the state and relied on its favorable dispensations. Not only did it chart the course for economic growth and control prices, it also ran the major social security programs and had a dominant role in collective bargaining.

The other key element in the economic program was a massive expansion of the agricultural reform program started during the Frei regime.

All agricultural holdings larger than the equivalent of eighty hectares of irrigated land were to be nationalized along with abandoned land and that judged to be poorly utilized. Preferably, these lands were to be organized cooperatively with the peasants receiving title to their homes and small garden plots. Allowance was made, however, "when circumstances warranted" for division of expropriated lands into privately owned parcels, as well as for the formation of state-owned large farms.

Under the heading of *social tasks,* the program provided a brief list of general promises, such as: limitations of high public salaries, extension and improvement of the social security system, provision of preventative and curative medicine to all, expansion of the government housing program, granting full civil rights to married women, and the like. The *foreign policy* section was similarly brief and general, stressing national autonomy and anti-imperialism. Support for the Cuban revolution and extension of diplomatic relations to all countries, whatever their political or ideological system, were also included. The Organization of American States was denounced as an agent of North American imperialism and all treaties were renounced which limited Chile's national sovereignty, especially bilateral treaties with the United States.

Educational Policy

The educational policy propositions of the Basic Program were embedded in a wider concept of "popular culture":

> The profound transformations which are to begin will require a socially conscious and solidary people, educated to exercise and defend their political power, scientifically and technologically capable of developing the economy of transition to socialism, and massively open to the creation and enjoyment of the most varied manifestations of art and intellect. . . . The new State will undertake the incorporation of the masses into intellectual and artistic activity, both through a radically transformed educational system and through the establishment of a national system of popular culture. . .[which will] stimulate artistic and literary creation and multiply the channels of communication between artists and writers and an infinitely vaster public. (Programa Basico, 1970, pp. 28-29)

With reference to the educational system itself, the first promise in the program was the establishment of a national scholarship plan:

> sufficiently extensive to assure the entrance and survival in the school system of all children of Chile, especially the children of workers and peasants. (p. 29)

In addition, an extraordinary plan for school construction was proposed, including expropriation of "sumptuous buildings" for use as schools and dormitories, with the aim of creating:

> at least one unified school (primary and secondary) in each rural area and in each neighbourhood or marginal settlement in the cities of Chile. (p. 29)

In addition, a rapid expansion of the system of day-care centers and nursery-school/kindergartens was proposed, concentrating on the poorest sectors so that:

> the children of workers and peasants will be better equipped to enter, remain in, and take advantage of the regular school system. . .and to make possible the incorporation of women into productive labor. (p. 29)

The use of teaching methods which required the active participation of students was also called for.

A campaign to eliminate the remaining pockets of adult illiteracy was proposed, along with a program to raise the general educational level of the adult populace, primarily through programs organized at their work sites where general, technological, and social education could be combined.

With reference to system planning and administration, two promises were made:

> 1) The transformation of the educational system will not be the work only of technicians, but will be discussed, studied, decided and executed by the organizations of teachers, workers, students and parents, within the general line of national planning.
> 2) In the executive direction of the educational apparatus there will be effective representation of the social organizations already mentioned, integrated in Local, Regional, and National Councils of Education. (p. 30)

None of these promises were especially controversial. Just as it had been difficult for the opposition to criticize the Frei educational reforms vehemently, so it was awkward for those outside of the Popular Unity coalition to criticize calls for further quantitative expansion, additional assistance to the children of the poor, or provisions for wider participation in the governance of the system. Indeed, many of the Christian Democrats with a strong interest in education and commitment to their reform efforts appear to have seen these propositions by the Popular Unity as natural next steps—the sorts of things they would be doing if they continued in power. Nor was there great controversy surrounding the three educational items in a companion campaign document outlining the First Forty Measures of the Popular Government:

1) free enrolment, plus free textbooks and school supplies for all children in primary school;
2) free breakfasts in school for all primary children, and free lunches for children in need;
3) a scholarship system at the primary, secondary and university levels based upon academic achievement and family need. (pp. 35-40)

However, the final educational proposal was the subject of great controversy during the campaign, since it struck at the heart of Christian Democratic and conservative thinking regarding education: the elimination of private schooling. "In order that educational planning, and the unified national democratic school, will be a reality, the new state will take under its responsibility private establishments, beginning with those which select their student body on the grounds of social class, national origin or religious belief. This will be carried out by integrating the personnel and other appurtenances of private education into the educational system" (p. 30).[1]

THE UNEXPECTED VICTORY

As Sigmund notes, "In retrospect, it is difficult to understand why more students of Chilean politics had not predicted a victory for the left in 1970" (1977, p. 106). Nonetheless, the Allende victory did come as a surprise, not only to observers outside of Chile but also to many of the victors themselves. Certainly the educational strategy of the Popular Unity-controlled teachers' unions was based on the assumption that they would continue past 1970 in opposition. In my research I never encountered an informant from Popular Unity who claimed to have expected to win the election. As one member put it: "*Hope*, yes, of course. We hoped to win, like the cancer patient hopes that a cure will be found before he dies. But *expect* to win? Never!"

And it was a very narrow victory. Allende received 36.3 per cent of the popular vote, a smaller percentage than he obtained when he lost to Frei in 1974. Alessandri obtained 34.9 per cent, which was slightly greater than his winning percentage in the 1958 election (31.6 per cent). The margin of victory was less than forty thousand out of about three million votes. Tomic's third-place percentage, 27.8 per cent of the vote, was very close to Allende's percentage when he narrowly lost to Alessandri in 1958. This victory clearly *did not* reflect a sharp turn to the left among the Chilean electorate. Careful analysis of the voting patterns in the election indicate that 1) new voters during the late 1960's (resulting from both population increase and higher voter registration) were not significantly channeled to the left; and 2) in a two-way race between Allende and Alessandri, most Tomic voters would have preferred Alessandri (Valenzuela, 1978, pp. 39-42, and Sigmund, 1977, p. 109). As Valenzuela has suggested, "heightened radicalism was not a principal characteristic of Chilean electoral politics in 1970. Instead, Salvador Allende's election was the result of the inability of Chile's polarized political system to structure a winning majority coalition before the election and was further evidence of erosion of traditional mechanisms of political accommodation" (1978, p. 39). Moreover, those same analyses indicate that the support for candidates was far from perfectly correlated with the social class positions of the voters. Although Allende acquired substantial majorities in many working-class areas, his support also included many middle-class and even some upper-class voters, and significant proportions of lower-class voters did not support his candidacy. A survey conducted just before the election found that 45.9 per cent of lower-class voters would refuse to vote for Allende (Valenzuela, 1978, p. 43). In summary, the results of the election on 4 September 1970 produced a regime which 1) was a minority government that did not even represent, electorally, all of the working class for whom it claimed to speak; 2) was a "coalition of convenience" among political parties with long histories of animosities and with internal divisions, which shared few perceptions of appropriate strategy and tactics or even of basic social and economic policy goals; and 3) had not expected to win the election, and hence achieved power with neither an agreed program nor an effective means of reaching one.

This was a particularly unfortunate set of circumstances because whatever the differences among the parties to the Popular Unity coalition, the one thing they did agree upon was that they wished to begin a process of profound transformation in Chilean society. This immediately raised the fundamental question of the legitimacy of the government. Was it legitimate for a government elected by a minority of the populace to propose to use the very rules under which they had been elected to alter the rules themselves to produce a different kind of society, a type of social order not clearly supported by the majority of the electorate? Landsberger and Linz (1979, p. 434) put the problem very well.

There was in itself nothing at all new and unsettling about the fact that the representative of a coalition who had obtained only 36 per cent of the vote assumed the presidency. After all, Jorge Alessandri had received only 31 per cent of the vote in 1958. What was perceived to be challengeable by the opposition was the attempt to completely reorient Chilean society on this very narrow basis of support. Previous major shifts in policy, none of which in any case even approximated what the *Unidad Popular* promised to do, had occurred only under Presidents who had been elected with substantial majorities. Both Pedro Aguirre Cerda, head of the Popular Front in 1938, and Eduardo Frei, head of the Christian Democrats in 1964, were seen as representing a considerable break with the past. But both candidates had obtained over 50 percent of the votes, i.e. a clear majority, The opposition never forgot that the *Unidad Popular,* offering a much more drastic program, had obtained far less support.

Under such circumstances, the loyalties of the middle groups, those who were neither firm supporters of the newly elected regime nor adherents of the extreme right position that the regime was by definition a non-legitimate government, were critical. For the right, the task from the moment of the election was to recruit the members of the middle by establishing a polarized definition of the situation, a contest between Marxism on the one hand and traditional Chilean democracy on the other. (See Maira, 1979, p. 251 for a useful discussion of the National party position.) For the Popular Unity itself the problem was more complex, since there was a sharp division between those who believed that mobilization of support among the middle sectors was both possible and essential and those who held that such support was impossible to obtain and undesirable.

The position of the middle groups at the moment of the election is difficult to specify with precision. Many of the existing analyses, especially those written from a left perspective, reflect the authors' ideological views of how one ought to understand the middle groups—a subject of fierce internal debate within Popular Unity. (See, for example, Bandeira, 1975, and Smirnow, 1981, especially chapter 2, "The Debate over the Middle Classes.") My own impression, based not only upon the literature but also upon extensive conversations before and after the election with middle-class and comfortable working-class Chileans, is that the prevailing attitude was a mixture of affirmation of existing institutional arrangements— one might not like the results but Allende had been fairly elected—and hope that the new government could accomplish long-needed changes without destroying the society itself, turning Chile into "another Cuba." It appeared to be a compound of pragmatic support among those who had voted for Allende and a willingness to "give him a chance" among those who had not voted for him—so long as the understood constitutional rules were not violated. The mood of this strategic group was well captured by a comment heard toward the end of a large family party in a middle-class district of Santiago shortly after the election. After a long and heated argument about the election results, one individual, himself a middle-ranking military official, declaimed loudly with the approval of all there: "Look, this country needs some changes. In '58 we tried Alessandri and nothing happened. In '64 we gave Frei a chance and some things improved, but not enough. Now we'll give these guys a turn and see if they can do it. If they can't we'll throw them out in '76 and try something else."

In summary, large segments of this middle group appear to have been available for mobilization by the Popular Unity government, but with important qualifications. Those who had voted for Allende did so on pragmatic grounds; their continued support was contingent upon government performance. Those who had opposed him electorally but were prepared to grant legitimacy to his assumption of the presidency did so on two conditions: 1) adequate government performance; and 2) no serious violations of the constitution or other understood norms of political behavior.

All of these factors created serious constraints upon the Allende government's ability to act in education as in all other policy fields. To them must be added a final complication. Although Popular Unity had won the presidency, it did not control the other important agencies of government in the Chilean system: the Congress, with its Senate and Chamber of Deputies, the Judiciary, and the *Contraloría*.

In the Chilean system there were two mechanisms for making law. The first was congressional legislation. The president could *propose* legislation and have it introduced in the Congress by his supporters, but without a majority in one if not both houses, there was little probability of following this route successfully. The president could also veto legislation, either in whole or in part, that was passed by an opposition majority in the Congress. The second mechanism was executive decree. In this case, the *Contraloría General de la Republica* was required to rule on the constitutionality of the decree. If a decree was judged to be unconstitutional, it was returned to the president either to be withdrawn or modified. Under both systems the constitution provided complex mechanisms for resolving impasses between the presidency and the Congress or the *Contraloría*. These mechanisms had often been used, since this was not the first time Chile found itself with a president whose party or coalition controlled only the executive arm. However, they depended ultimately upon skillful negotiators, "honest brokers" who were respected by and could deal with both sides and who could function only so long as the basic legitimacy of the system was not in question—a condition which was denied as of 4 September 1970 by both the extreme left and the extreme right.

AFTERMATH OF VICTORY: THE STATUTE OF DEMOCRATIC GUARANTEES

Allende's victory signalled the final change from a political system based on conciliation to one based on confrontation. This was seen most immediately in the open doubts expressed as to whether Allende would be allowed to assume office in November. Under the Chilean constitution, if no candidate gained an absolute majority of the vote for president, then the full Congress would decide between the two leading candidates. Although it was not constitutionally required, the Congress always in the past had selected the candidate who had received the largest popular vote. However, on this occasion the outcome was not so clear. Of the two hundred votes in Congress, parties supporting Allende accounted for eighty, and Alessandri supporters, forty-five. The seventy-five Christian Democratic members, who could not vote for their own candidate since he had finished third, were clearly the swing vote. The Alessandri forces, determined to prevent Allende's accession if at all possible, immediately began to maneuver for Christian Democratic support. Five days after the election, thanking those who had supported him, Alessandri declared that if he were elected by Congress, he would resign the post, producing a new election in which he pledged not to participate. (*El Mercurio,* 10 September 1970). The invitation was clear. If the Christian Democrats voted for Alessandri, there would be a new election in which Frei would be eligible to run (since there would formally have been an intervening president) and which he almost certainly would win. Four days later, on 13 September, Allende responded at a mass rally by threatening that if "the people" were robbed of their victory by those machinations, they would bring the country to a standstill.

Under enormous pressure from both directions, as well as from the United States government, which was doing everything in its power to block Allende's victory through the CIA as well as official diplomatic channels,[2] the National Council of the Christian Democratic party met the next day. It was decided that the party would support Allende in the Congress, but only if Popular Unity agreed to incorporate into the constitution, through amendment, a Statute of Democratic Guarantees which would ensure the freedom from political control of such things as party organizations, education, trade unions and other private associations, the mass media, and the armed forces.

The simple fact that the Christian Democrats, the centrist party, whose candidate and platform had been in many ways very similar to that of Popular Unity, considered it necessary to extract such a statute of guarantees as a condition for their support, is itself an indicator of the crisis of legitimacy created by the Allende victory. There was widespread and real fear that, even if Allende himself could be trusted, he would be pushed by the more extreme sectors of his own coalition into the elimination of traditional Chilean institutions and the establishment of a one-party Marxist state on the Cuban model. As Valenzuela observes, the demand for the statute:

was a vivid illustration of the serious polarization of Chilean politics and the severe erosion of the traditional rules of the game. Those rules in the final analysis are based on a degree of trust, and the need to extract a formal declaration from Allende that he would preserve the constitution showed the deterioration of confidence between political leaders who had been close for decades and for whom a respect for the rules of the game had been implicit. (1978, p. 49)

On 23 September, representatives of the party formally presented their demands to Allende. Allende promised that he would consider the demands carefully, consult with Popular Unity, and provide his response as soon as possible. The version of their demands provided for the public indicated that the Christian Democrats were "concerned" in five areas, which reflect the party's high degree of commitment to the existing constitutional order and suspicion of Popular Unity's commitment to those democratic institutions. The demands were the following:

1) maintenance of political pluralism and constitutional guarantees;
2) continued reign of the state of law;
3) that the armed forces and police continue being a guarantee of democratic co-existence;
4) that education remain independent of all official ideological orientation and that university autonomy be respected; and,
5) the free existence of labor and social organizations. (*La Segunda*, 24 September 1970)

Within Popular Unity, Allende's own party, the Socialists objected most strongly to entering into such an arrangement, as did the more conservative elements within Christian Democracy. However, by early in October the less extreme elements on both sides had prevailed, a joint committee was appointed, and a text for the statute was drafted, approved by both groups and submitted to Congress. There it was passed by both houses, with the final vote taking place just two days before the full Congress met and formally elected Allende as president of the Republic.

Education was clearly one of the prime areas of concern in the negotiations which produced the Statute of Democratic Guarantees. The strength of feeling in many sectors over the issue of freedom of education was very high. The most extreme fears are illustrated in an editorial in the newspaper, *El Diario Illustrado*, which appeared on 6 October. It noted that the intention of Christian Democracy was to forestall "any possibility that Chilean education would be transformed into an element for 'brainwashing' infants and transforming Chilean children into mental slaves of communism." It observed that the concern of Christian Democracy was understandable, "since contemporary history demonstrates without the least doubt that one of the fundamental concerns of communism, once it arrives in power, is to capture all of the educational apparatus so that it may serve as a colonizing and transforming element, in its desire to create a new man with communist roots and a communist mentality." Moreover, in order to accomplish its objectives, Popular Unity would have to "take absolute control of education, so that while using adults in their work of transformation, they can be preparing the seedbed of new Chileans who will arrive to national activity with a communist mentality infiltrated into their brains and spirits because they will have been thus educated since their most tender infancy." The editorial finished with the claim that preservation of the right of parents to educate their children in the religion which they professed was fundamental to the maintenance of individual freedom and hence of democracy. This style of rhetoric, the easy identification of Popular Unity with communism (aided by the fact that large portions of the Popular Unity program were taken word for word from the Communist party's platform), and concerns regarding "mind control" and the explicit use of education as an instrument of official ideology, remained characteristic of much of opposition commentary regarding education whenever an issue arose during the Popular Unity reign.

However, even among moderate sectors of the opposition, the proposed abolition of private education was troubling. It must be repeated that "freedom of choice" in education, as guaranteed by the existence of non-state schools, had long been a central element in Christian Democratic educational thought and policy. At the same time, the Chilean Church, itself in the vanguard of the theological revolution that swept through Latin American Catholicism in the 1960's, was finding more and more the few elite schools run by religious orders for the sons and daughters of the wealthy to be an embarrassment. Attempts were already underway in some quarters to alter the class composition of such schools, to turn them over to non-Church agencies, or even to incorporate them into the public school system. The best available estimates for the late 1960's indicate that about 25 per cent of all Chilean primary and secondary students were in private schools and that of these only about one-fourth were attending schools which charged fees, the remainder being in private schools which charged no fees and received government subventions to supplement the support received from the Church or other agencies (Cariola and Garcia Huidobro, 1970, p. 456). In a brief but penetrating analysis, two of the leaders in the private education reform movement noted that there were substantial similarities between the basic principles and goals of the popular Unity educational program and the policy statements adopted at meetings of the Federation of Private Secondary Schools. They particularly emphasized, given the Popular Unity's concern for local participation in forming educational policy, that these meetings "were held with equal participation of parents, teachers, and students; there are already a number of [private] schools which are attempting systems of self-government with the participation of all [in Arica, Antofagasta, Valparaiso, various schools in Santiago, Chillan]" (Cariola and Garcia Huidobro, 1970, p. 461). Under such circumstances, it would be inconsistent, they argued, for Popular Unity to take over and submit to a central control private schools which had already begun developing their own distinctive locally based programs (p. 462). This article thus raised, in the first month after the election, another issue which was to bedevil educational debate for the next three years: the strain between central planning and local control; the more there is of one, the less there can be of the other.

Out of this ferment of argument came a lengthy constitutional amendment regarding education; it was in fact the longest single section of the Statute of Democratic Guarantees. Since these provisions were a constant source of reference in the debates that followed, they must be considered in some detail. (All the following quotations are from the text published in *El Mercurio*, 16 October 1970).

> Education is a primordial function of the State, which is carried out through a national system formed by official teaching institutions and private institutions which collaborate in its execution, following the plans and programs established by the educational authorities.
>
> The administrative organization and the designation of personnel in private establishments will be determined by the private organizations themselves, subject to legal norms.
>
> Only free private education, and not that which is profit-making, will receive economic contributions from the State guaranteeing its financing in accord with the norms established by law.

These three articles were intended to enshrine constitutionally the legitimate existence of private education, while recognizing that it must, as it always had, follow official plans and programs of study. They also recognized that it was not legitimate for the government to subsidize fee-charging private schools; but, on the other hand, they made clear the government could not squeeze the others out of existence economically by refusing to continue the subventions upon which they depended.

> The education provided through the national system will be democratic and pluralistic, with no official party orientation. It will also be modified only democratically, after free discussion in competent agencies which represent all lines of thought.
>
> There will be a Superintendency of Public Education under the au-

thority of the government, whose Council will be composed of representatives of all sectors linked with the national educational system. Representatives from these sectors will be democratically selected. The Superintendency will be responsible for inspection of national education.

The superintendency and its council (called the National Council of Education) already existed. They were the principal technical policy formulation and planning agencies within the ministry, with staff rather than line authority which cut across all of the other administrative subdivisions within the organization. These provisions gave them constitutional legitimacy and were designed to ensure that the widely representative and democratic nature of the National Council would serve as a block on any attempt to impose an "official party orientation." The remaining provisions were also designed to protect against the infiltration of a single official ideology. The plethora of such provisions in the constitutional amendments is a good indicator of the degree of suspicion regarding the ultimate educational aims of Popular Unity.

Competent technical organizations will select textbooks on the basis of public competitions which will be accessible to all qualified educators whatever their ideology. Facilities will be available for the printing and distribution of all such texts, and educational establishments will be free to choose those they wish.

Public universities, and the private universities recognized by the State, are juridical personalities provided with academic, administrative and financial autonomy. The role of the State is to provide financing adequate to permit them to fully carry out their roles, in accord with the educational, scientific and cultural requirements of the nation.

Admission to the universities will depend solely upon the academic ability of the applicants, who have completed secondary education or its equivalent, which will permit them to fulfill the objective academic demands of their studies. Access to and promotion within academic careers for professors and researchers will depend solely upon their capacity and aptitude.

Academic personnel are free to develop their subject matter in conformity with their own ideas, always subject to the obligation to provide necessary information to students regarding other doctrines and principles.

University students have the right to express their own ideas, and, to the extent possible, to search out the professors and tutors they prefer.

Government negotiators saw these provisions as restricting the actions only of the most extreme elements within their own coalition (Interview with Jorge Tapia, 24 May 1983). However, combined with all the other constraints discussed earlier, it is clear that the educational policy-makers of the new regime had very limited room for action. That this was known by most of the new officials will be evident in the next chapter.

5

First Attempts at Policy Definition and Early Problems

THE FIRST POLICY DEVELOPMENT

In mid-September 1970 a number of policy development commissions were appointed by the Popular Unity government to develop specific proposals for action with reference to the general propositions contained in the Basic Program. One of these commissions, headquartered in the central building of the primary teachers' union (UPCH), was charged with educational policy. Hugo Araya, a powerful Radical party teachers' union figure and a member of that party's central committee, was appointed chairman. Araya had already been giving the question considerable thought, since Allende had called him the day after the election and asked him to start working on an educational policy document.

The first meetings of the educational commission were well attended by more than eighty people, but none of those present seemed to know what it was that they were supposed to accomplish. Araya understood clearly, however, that the mandate was limited to producing recommendations for concrete measures which could be implemented immediately upon taking office or at least before the opening of the next school year in March 1971 (the Chilean school year runs from March to December with the summer vacation from Christmas through mid-March). Fundamental long-term policy development had to wait upon the promised consultations with parents, teachers, other community organizations and the holding of a National Congress of Education. Only when that process was completed, and only if it produced a consensus among the ideological positions within the coalition, would it be possible to move beyond short-range structural and procedural changes.

Over time, fewer and fewer people came to the meetings. Finally, in late

October, Araya wrote the report himself. This report, entitled "Educational Policy of the UP Government: Immediate Measures" (1970), was available for the new officials who assumed their posts early in November, and clearly they used it in the following months. (Information regarding the production of this document is taken from interviews with Hugo Araya, 23 November 1980 and 8 May 1981.)

In response to its limited mandate, this first policy document included only a brief theoretical or ideological introduction and consisted almost entirely of precise recommendations, costed where possible and appropriate, with a detailed timetable for implementation covering the months from November to March. The document begins by noting that education is only part of the global process of societal transformation and cannot be expected to resolve all of the problems and contradictions of a capitalist society. "The objectives of education are therefore integrated into the general objective of the popular government, which is the transformation of a capitalist society into a socialist society" (p. 1). Within this framework, the general objectives for the educational system were to be: 1) guaranteeing access to school for all children of school age and opening the schools to adults to form a system of permanent education; 2) assuring that students would not drop out of the system; 3) achieving real participation by educational workers, students, parents, workers' organizations, and the people in general, in the transformation of the educational system within the framework of national planning; 4) orienting the educational system toward a commitment to the interests of the working class rather than the interests of the bourgeoisie and imperialism; 5) redefining the role of the educator in terms of the requirements of the proposed socioeconomic transformation; and 6) producing graduates who would be critical and creative, who would feel solidarity with their fellow citizens, and who would "have the disposition and the capacity to contribute to the construction of a socialist society" (p. 2).

This two-page introduction was followed by twenty-nine pages of specific recommendations for immediate measures. The most important of these were the following:

1. To increase the capacity of the system in order to be able to enrol all students who would apply, and to adopt a series of measures to simplify the administrative process for enrolment, since the very complexity of the enrolment process had often discouraged students or their parents from trying to find a school place.
2. To increase the funds available to the National Commission for School Assistance by 100 per cent (this was the organization which administered scholarships and other forms of aid to poor but able students), and to rationalize its administrative processes

to ensure that the aid was delivered to the students who required it.

3. To improve the control and supervision of existing private schools, and to ensure the democratic participation of the private school community in the academic and administrative affairs of such schools.

4. To eliminate state subventions to fee-charging private schools, and to ensure that all private school teachers would be licensed to teach in Chile.

5. To ensure where necessary that private school teachers received the same salaries as equivalent public school teachers.

6. To ensure that foreign texts would be used in private schools only if approved by the Ministry of Education.

7. To ensure that new private schools would be established only with the approval of the Ministry of Education, and that all private schools would be registered with the Ministry of Education before 21 February 1971.

8. To train university students as literacy instructors for a literacy campaign during January and February 1971.

9. To organize a series of courses for teachers in the Center for In-Service Teacher Training to train them to carry out the tasks specified in the report, using a decentralized training system.

10. To increase by 100 per cent the available spaces for pre-school education.

11. To begin work on a National Education Census to improve the quality and credibility of the data available for central planning and programming, and to detect problems that had escaped the attention of central authorities.

12. To bring teachers actively and immediately into the policy reformulation process not only by ensuring their participation in local councils, but also by incorporating them, along with secondary and university students, into a National Plan for Summer Work to cover such areas as literacy training, housing, and health.

13. To adopt a set of 17 different administrative and legal changes to provide better salaries and improved career stability for teachers.[1]

The Radical party teacher union orientation of this first policy document is evident in several of its features: the concentration upon quantitative expansion of the formal system; the concern with administrative improvements; the focus upon controlling private education (as the document was being written, it was already evident that the campaign promise to take over private education could not be fulfilled); the concentration upon teacher welfare measures. Nonetheless, the document was clearly a product of the restricted mandate given to its author, particularly in its introduction.

FIRST POLICY ANNOUNCEMENTS

Early policy pronouncements by officials of the Popular Unity government were similarly cautious and concrete. However, the first education-
related news items carried in the press following the 3 November inauguration pertained not to the educational policy of the new government, but
to the continuing struggle for power within the teachers' organizations. At
issue were ten positions on the directive council of the National Teachers'
Welfare Service. Seventeen candidates were presented by the new opposition forces and an equal number by Popular Unity, carefully apportioned
between the Radical, Communist, and Socialist parties. However, since
there were more candidates on the government list than there were positions, each of the three parties devoted considerable newspaper space to
identifying and promoting its own set of candidates. A Communist tab-
loid went so far as to identify the three Communist party candidates as
the only members of the Popular Unity list (*Puro Chile*, 17 November 1970).
Thus, the first image of the new government available to the public in the
area of education involved not policy pronouncements but internecine political struggles.

It was not until after this election campaign was completed that policy
statements first began to appear. On 16 November, the new minister of
education, Mario Astorga, formally received a delegation of leaders from
the new single teachers' union (SUTE) headed by the organization's president, Humberto Elgueta, another Radical. SUTE gave its "combatative
greeting and total support" to the new minister, indicated that teachers
expected to be directly involved in the planning of future changes, and
responded positively to a request that teachers assist in the national literacy campaign being planned for the summer (*Puro Chile*, 17 November
1970; *La Nacion*, 17 November 1970). On 23 November, Astorga announced
that "not a single kid will be left out of school,"[2] indicating that the government was making provision to ensure that all new primary and secondary students and all continuing or repeating students would find places in
the system. He also announced a series of administrative measures to simplify the enrolment process and to speed the delivery of scholarships and
other financial aid to recipients. In both the statistics cited and the administrative measures announced, Astorga's declaration closely paralleled Araya's policy document (cf. *Clarin*, 24 November 1970).

The following week Carlos Moreno, the new director of professional
education, announced a series of measures to simplify and rationalize administration of the schools under his jurisdiction. This again closely followed Araya's recommendations and emphasized that "In this first stage
we are not yet going to define an overall policy. The idea of the govern-

ment is to dedicate all of next year to designing an overall educational line
. . . . In this first stage we are only going to deal with some conflict-laden
problems that need a more or less rapid solution" (*El Mercurio*, 3 December 1970).

The next day, Sergio Arenas, head of a newly established Commission
to Rationalize Enrolment for 1971, followed Astorga's main theme, noting
that the government's slogan was "Free enrolment for all" and providing
more detail regarding the steps involved in and calendar for the new enrolment procedure (*Clarin*, 4 December 1970). At the same time, the director of secondary education, Jorge Espinoza, declared that his immediate
goals were "expansion, modernization and democratization" (*El Mercurio*, 1 December 1970) and provided more details regarding the enrolment
process for secondary level, where the most complicated problems had tended
to occur in the past (*La Segunda*, 9 December 1970; see also *El Mercurio*,
15 December 1970).

IMPROVEMENTS IN THE ENROLMENT PROCESS

The administrative measures adopted by the new government did make
the enrolment process less complex, and, particularly at the secondary level, significantly higher proportions of age-eligible youngsters were enrolled.
Following a general emphasis on increasing technical/professional education rather than university-preparatory, humanistic-scientific courses, enrolments in 1971 in industrial schools were 52 per cent greater than in 1970.
In agricultural schools the enrolment increase was 55 per cent (Comisión
Racionalizadora de Matricula, 1971. This report, published in May 1971,
provides a detailed summary of the administrative measures undertaken
and their quantitative results.) In the two most populous provinces, Santiago and Valparaiso, the enrolment process was computerized, providing
a more effective means of matching students to available school spaces.[3]

In achieving these immediate improvements, the government was able
to rely not only on newly appointed officials but also on cadres of highly
trained technicians in the educational planning and budgeting offices who
had been trained by and inherited from the Frei government.[4] At least for
these first few weeks, there was little observable friction at the working-
team level between the new appointees and the civil servants already in office. Rather, throughout November, December, and January (February is
vacation month in Chile), the offices of the superintendency were filled
with teams of people working long hours to accomplish the immediate objectives.

However, the weight of traditional bureaucratic procedures and chaotic
communication and command links between Santiago and the rest of the

nation within a highly centralized governance system quickly began to create problems. These were exacerbated by the fact that few of the new officials had effective command of anything more than the most elementary technical planning techniques. Even most of the Radical officials, who were often pejoratively labelled "the technicians" by Socialist party members, were more nearly traditional Chilean bureaucrats than skilled technical operatives.[5] Consequently, small errors accumulated to produce major difficulties. By March, when the new school year was about to start, serious problems began to surface, and they quickly became political issues. Early in March, Astorga announced that a number of "irregularities" were occurring in the enrolment process because school directors were not complying with new ministry directives (*La Prensa*, 10 March 1971). On 17 March, five days before classes were to begin, the Christian Democratic newspaper *La Prensa* headlined a story regarding enrolment problems: "More than 200,000 children unable to enrol in primary school." One father's story was quoted as an example:

> At the end of last year I put my 8 year old daughter on the list for enrolment at School No. 55, Jose Arrieta, in the Borough of La Reina [in Santiago]. When they opened up the enrolments in early March, I went there and they told me that nothing could be done because the first year primary class was full, and everyone else on the waiting list had to go to Brown Ave. where they would assign us a school. So I went to that office where a functionary told me that she didn't have any list, and she asked me for the data about my child. She took down the information and told me to come back March 8. I went back that day and they said the only information they could give me was that I would have to wait until after March 22, when classes begin, to see if there were a "possibility" that she could be enrolled in some school.

It was not that such administrative problems were new or unusual. Rather, it was the fact that such problems had routinely affected large numbers of worried parents which had made the new government's pledge to streamline the process a politically popular move and which made its failure to fulfill that pledge completely politically damaging.

The government's response was to attack the critics. For example, on 21 March, *El Mercurio* reported that a government official explained to concerned students, parents, and teachers in the city of Santa Cruz that the problems they were facing regarding secondary school arrangements were caused by the fact that the opposition-controlled Congress had reduced the 1971 education budget to the level of 1968, an assertion which was denied several days later by the president of the Congressional Budget Committee (*El Mercurio*, 21 and 26 March 1971).

Since it took office in November and the school year began in March, the government was unable to build enough new classrooms to accommodate the increased enrolments immediately; it could not assign teachers to all of the new classes by the time the school year began; and it encountered great difficulty in delivering the promised increased quantities of various forms of school aid to poor children, which was particularly embarrassing for a self-proclaimed "people's government."[6]

All of these difficulties resulted in a wave of "takeovers" of schools by students and/or parents (this was a common form of protest in Chile at this time) during March and April, which was an added embarrassment to a government whose constituent parties had frequently used the same tactic to oppose previous regimes. Finally the minister responded, claiming that the problems were caused by lower level officials who were "boycotting" or "sabotaging" government plans. (This declaration was reported almost identically in both supporting and opposition media. See *El Clarin* and *La Prensa*, 29 April 1971.)

What was particularly unfortunate about this series of events was that the well-publicized failures of the government to accomplish goals which were beyond its technical capacities tended to obscure the fact that it had made a considerable improvement in the annual enrolment process and that some quantitative gains in enrolment and school aid had been achieved. This was the first example in education of one of the problems which plagued the Allende government throughout its reign: underestimating technical and political problems while overestimating its own capacity to overcome them, promising more than it could deliver, and creating expectations it could not fulfill, and thus an image of incompetence even in policy areas where more modest pledges could easily have been achieved. Throughout the Allende years, the fact that the government achieved substantial increases in quantitative aspects of educational development often went unnoticed because of this pattern. Expansion was not the main focus of the regime's efforts in education (indeed, the worrisome long-term fiscal implications of continuing expansion were an important factor in determining the direction of later proposals for qualitative change), and Popular Unity's accomplishments built on the results of the massive expansion that had occurred during the Frei years. Nonetheless, the results were important. Between 1970 and 1972 the proportion of all public expenditures devoted to education increased from 11.1 per cent to 12.3 per cent. Primary level enrolments, which were already high, increased slightly, and enrolments at the secondary and university levels increased substantially, with most emphasis being placed on the technical fields of study. In 1970, 33.5 per cent of the age-eligible children were enrolled in secondary schools. By 1973, the figure was 42.9 per cent. Corresponding figures for the university level are 9.0 per cent and 16.1 per cent. In addition, the volume of assistance to poor children approximately doubled, and there were great increases in the distribution of free textbooks and other school supplies (see LaTorre, 1981; Nuñez, 1982a; and Bermudez, 1975 for more detailed considerations of the quantitative results during the Popular Unity period).

EARLY DEVELOPMENT OF INTERNAL PROBLEMS

Although certain of the new teams within the ministry worked effectively in these early months, throughout the ministry several very serious operational problems began to appear from November onward. The first was what became known as the "cuoteo": the establishment of quotas for each party of the available positions in the government or under the government's control. Much time and energy were devoted to debates over each party's fair share. Moreover, as another part of the checks and balances between the parties, care was taken to ensure that heads or directors within the public service had subordinates who were members of the other parties (a lower level reflection of the decision that each minister would have a sub-secretary of a different party) and/or had "coordinating committees" of some sort with representatives of all parties to supervise their actions (lower level reflections of the overall Popular Unity Coordinating Committee). It was not uncommon in these early days and thereafter to hear officials jokingly refer to the "spies" in their offices from other parties in the coalition. The "cuoteo" was applied not only to high-level government posts; arguments over distribution of positions also affected quite low-level administrative posts. This problem was recognized in Popular Unity's review of its own first year in power (see Chapter 7).

Soon after the election, a multiparty committee was given the responsibility of nominating individuals for all of the available primary school directorships in the nation—approximately eighteen hundred posts in all. For almost nine months, the committee was unable to agree on the proportion of these directorships which should be given to each party, an issue they felt had to be resolved before the parties could start naming people to them. The lack of directors, the presence of interim directors, and the continuing presence of directors from the "wrong" political party for a neighborhood, were more of the many causes for the mounting wave of school takeovers. Finally, Allende authorized Lautaro Videla to resolve the dispute. Videla called a meeting of the committee, indicated that he had authority directly from the president, and gave each party twelve hours to come in with a list of nominees—specific individuals for specific directorships. The Radicals brought in about six hundred names, the Socialists about thirty, the Communists none. Videla accepted all of each party's nominees and filled all of the rest of the positions on the basis of qualifications and seniority without regard to political affiliation. Videla observed that the ironic, indeed "stupid" thing about the entire affair was that months were wasted in arguments when only the Radicals had a large number of qualified nominees[7] and between them the three parties could fill only about one-third of the available positions. "The same thing happened at all levels" (interview with Lautaro Videla, 18 May 1981). Given the traditional Radical predominance in education, it was not surprising that they would have many qualified nominees on hand. The problem was caused by representatives of the other two parties fighting stubbornly for positions.

This process also illustrates the Popular Unity government's chronic difficulty in finding qualified party members to fill all of the available posts. The problem was partly caused by the operation of the quota system, but it was aggravated by the fact that, in contradistinction to the Christian Democratic regime, very few Popular Unity people came into government from the universities. Videla suggests that part of the explanation was that even high-level Ministry of Education posts paid less than university faculty positions (interview 18 May 1981), although this had not been a problem for the Christian Democrats in 1964. Nonetheless, for whatever reason, an important pool of manpower did not make itself available. As a result, 1) able people had to work very long hours, often, in effect, doing several jobs, which lowered their effectiveness in any given area; and 2) many posts were filled by unqualified individuals.

Adding to the factors which made it difficult for the government to formulate or implement policy in education, as in other areas, was the almost immediate appearance of fundamental ideological and strategic disagreements between parties and factions which had been publicly submerged for the electoral campaign. It was within government offices and committee meetings that the differences first appeared; they were sharp, clearly visible from the beginning, and often paralyzing. In many such settings the high degree of distrust, at times bordering on hatred, was palpable. Epithets such as "traitor," "stupid technocrat," or "incompetent ideologue" were frequently heard, often in face-to-face confrontations between officials holding different ideological perspectives. (It was particularly common for hard-line Socialists to refer to all who did not share their views as traitors.) This interparty mistrust not only made many government offices impossible working environments, it also created a situation wherein offices controlled by one party would withhold important information from offices controlled by other parties in order to gain a power advantage or would pursue independent policy initiatives along their own ideological line without coordinating with other offices. By May, these interpersonal conflicts within the Ministry of Education were becoming public. At the National Conference of Socialist Educational Workers held late in that month, Suarez, Nuñez, and Videla were the principal speakers. Astorga was strongly attacked, along with Radical-led SUTE, for being too bureaucratic, obstructionist, and slow to act in the new situation. A motion was passed demanding the removal of the Radical director of primary and normal education, Fresia Urrutia (*La Prensa*, 31 May 1971).

PUBLIC POLICY DIFFERENCES WITHIN THE GOVERNMENT

At the level of public discourse over policy, the differences also became obvious but in a somewhat slower, more subtle and indirect fashion. Partly this was because all parties within Popular Unity were committed to the use of a common rhetoric (for example, education must form the "new man" needed to "build the new socialist society"), however different were the meanings they attached to the words. Moreover, although the main split that could be identified in public documents and speeches was between Radicals and Socialists, the fundamental difference within the ministry was between: 1) the hard-line socialists (the three most visible Socialists within the ministry, Suarez, Nuñez and Videla, were all inclined more toward the revolutionary than the reformist position within their party, even though Nuñez and Videla both perceived themselves as being moderating forces within the overall party context) and 2) everybody else. That is, on most issues the differences between the Radicals, the Communists, the soft-line Socialists, and the other smaller groups were less than their collective differences from highly vocal revolutionary Socialists.[8]

The differences between the "two lines" can be most clearly seen in two small books published early in 1971 by the Radical and Socialist parties. The Radical document, *Formulation of a New Education in the Popular Unity Government*, contained chapters written by Astorga and Araya and a position paper from the Radical party teachers' group. The Socialist publication contained papers written by Suarez, Nuñez, and Videla and was entitled *Contributions to the Formulation of an Educational Policy*. These two books, supplemented by several speeches, form the main basis for the following comparison of positions.

The fundamental ideas that the Popular Unity government had as its goal the transformation of Chile into a socialist society and that education had to contribute somehow to that transformation were found in both documents. But the differences in their conceptions of "socialism" were quite apparent and reflected the distinctions discussed in Chapter 2. Although the Socialist party papers were less militant than the declaration of the Socialist teachers in 1968, the language and concepts used were evidently Marxist-Leninist. Thus, for example, Nuñez could state:

The presidential mandate of comrade Allende is not an isolated or casual occurrence. It is the clear result of the contemporary historical trend, defined since 1917 as the *transition from capitalism to socialism*. This transition, which is happening violently and irreversibly throughout the world, has been manifested in our continent since 1959 in the Cuban Revolution and in Chile, with the installation of the Government of Popular Unity. Chile could not remain on the margins of history. (Suarez, Nuñez and Videla, 1971, p. 4)

The Radicals, on the other hand, took great care to define their socialism as *not* Revolutionary Marxist-Leninist:

> We aspire to a socialist society in which there is an equilibrium between the value of the individual and society as a whole, in order to avoid falling into the opposite errors of anarchic individualism or sectarian authoritarianism.
> There can only be freedom among equals, and there can only be equality among free people.
> There cannot be democracy without socialism and there cannot be socialism without democracy.

Democracy was defined in terms of the rule of law as established by an authority which was legitimated through secret and universal suffrage (Astorga and Araya, 1971, pp. 60-63). In contrast, Suarez could speak of local groups of teachers "imposing authority, overstepping legality and not waiting for orders from the authorities. One must make decisions, take the initiative, neither seeking permission nor allowing one's actions to be sanctioned by legal formulas." And Videla could speak of "revolutionary action to extirpate the last residues of reformism from the educational system" — both propositions which would be unacceptable to the Radicals. (*La Prensa*, 31 May 1971). When the Radicals used the word "socialism," they tended to refer to income redistribution, meeting basic needs of people, taking over basic resources by the state, and other social democratic propositions. (See Astorga's first major speech, in late January, as reported in *La Nacion*, 24 January 1971 and *El Mercurio*, 23 January 1971).

The diagnosis by both parties of the educational system they had inherited in 1970 was similar. It was anti-democratic both in its coverage and decision-making structures, classist and elitist, and overly influenced by foreign models. Their view of the Christian Democratic efforts differed, however. Astorga claimed in his first speech that there had not yet been an educational reform in Chile (a proposition to which the Christian Democrats strongly objected; see *La Prensa*, 23 January 1971), but he did allow that there had been partial changes in the previous six years, many of which were "admittedly positive" (*La Nacion*, 23 January 1971). The Socialists, on the other hand, were reluctant to admit that there could have been any positive change in education without the total restructuring of society, which they believed to be a necessary precondition for meaningful educational reform.

In their books and speeches, both parties devoted much space to explanations of the importance of the educational system to society in general and the importance that it would have within the Popular Unity regime. This was hardly surprising from professional educators, whatever their political affiliation. However, the Socialists carefully adhered to the standard Marxist-Leninist position that education could reinforce but could not lead a process of fundamental social change. The Radicals, particularly Astorga, assigned a more active role to schooling. For example, the title of the minister's paper in the Radical party book was "Education: Motor of Social Changes" (in contrast to Retamal's claim that education could only be the accelerator, not the motor). In his first speech, Astorga also referred to education as the "great promoter of change" (*La Nacion*, 23 January 1971).

The most important differences between the positions of the two parties, however, related to two issues: 1) the relative emphasis on technical as compared to theoretical issues, particularly in their understanding of the educational planning and policy-making process; and 2) the relative degree of local decision-making autonomy to be permitted. With reference to the first issue, the Socialists placed great emphasis on political and ideological discourse and paid almost no attention to operational or technical details. Radical documents typically provided a general theoretical introduction followed by pages of operational, administrative and technical detail. The Socialists' position was clearly stated on the second page of their policy book. While talking of the road that would have to be traversed in order to arrive at an educational system which would contribute to the "process of revolutionary change initiated in Chile with the ascent of the Popular Government," Nuñez observed that "it will have to be a *political road rather than a technical* one" (emphasis added). In contrast, Astorga asserted that "Educational planning is a *technical and political* process" (p. 4, emphasis added).

The Socialists' book consists of page after page of ideological and political rhetoric, followed by general statements of what the new school for the new society ought to be like. One of the high-ranking Communist officials in the Ministry of Education has referred to these Socialist documents as "one long introduction, which never got down to concrete policy measures. They never told us how they would get from here to there."

The Radical book, in contrast, complemented its general theoretical arguments regarding the inherited deficiencies in the school system with a number of statistical tables and graphs and followed most educational goal statements with specific operational or administrative proposals for achieving the goal. Astorga's first speech was also a good reflection of the Radical emphasis on technical concerns, with much attention devoted to the administrative measures already undertaken, or still needed, to have an effective system of educational planning and implementation. The minister claimed that the major problem the nation's teachers would face when they participated in the policy planning effort was not ideological confrontation but *economic constraints*—the lack of resources such as schools, teaching aids, and teachers—in a poor country facing an explosive enrolment increase as a result of population growth patterns. (*La Nacion*, 24 January 1971). The Socialists gave little indication that lack of resources might in any way limit the government's ability to accomplish its educational objectives.

In the view of a number of hard-line Socialists within the ministry, a difficulty with this Radical concentration on the technical and administrative side was that it led to policy proposals which were not uniquely "socialist," which could have been proposed and implemented by governments of widely varying ideology. They considered it to be fundamental that any specific policy proposition must not only be consistent with but deducible from the general ideological position of the Popular Unity government as they understood it, or wished it to be.

This insistence that policy must be directly connected to ideology led to the other major difference between the Socialists and the Radicals. The basic issue was the role to be assigned to local units (for example, the teachers, students, and parents in a school, or a community council, or even regional and provincial groupings) in the overall national planning process. To what extent were they to have autonomy to reach conclusions which differed from those already established by the central authorities? The issue first surfaced with respect to the planned program of national consultation regarding educational policy, which was scheduled to start in March with discussions among the teaching staff in individual schools and then work progressively upward to the promised National Congress of Education to be held at the end of the school year.

The Socialist position was most clearly expressed by Nuñez in a speech delivered to mark the opening of in-service training courses for secondary teachers at the Center for In-Service Training on 25 February 1971. His theme was "This is the Year of Educational Democratization." His interpretation of democratization was as follows:

[Chile,] finding itself at a decisive crossroad, democratically deliberated and chose a path. This path is oriented toward the liquidation of unjust socio-economic structures; toward the conquest of true national independence, toward an accelerated development effort and an authentic democratization. It is a path which has a target: SOCIALISM. (Nuñez, 1971)

Since the nation had already chosen this new goal, education had to reorganize itself to contribute to its realization. "We will have to redefine the aims and objectives of our educational system; we will contribute to forming the NEW MAN, the citizen who will live socialism." He then observed that "we [the central level officials] have a theoretical conception of the New Education" and that it was the role of experienced teachers to show how to "transform it into concrete practice." In short, the goals had already been established; the job of the teachers and all other contributors to the national consultation was to collaborate in accomplishing them, not to criticize them or suggest others.

The Radicals, having a much less structured ideological position, expected the agenda of the consultation process to be wider. Speaking of SUTE's role in the proposed National Congress of Education and in all preliminary meetings, Elgueta claimed that the objective was "to determine the aims and objectives" of education, as well as proposing specific structures, plans and programs for their realization (*El Mercurio*, 14 March 1971). In his first speech, Astorga spoke of the teacher's role in the consultative process as "active, creative, and at the same time critical. We don't want passive elements, but individuals who can criticize, think and act" (*La Nacion*, 24 January 1971). In an interview, Astorga noted that "we want to provide a great national debate in which we will redefine the objectives of Chilean education" (*Ercilla*, 3 March 1971).

The start of the new school year tended to focus national attention on the confusion and debates surrounding Popular Unity's educational policy. Allende delivered a major address on educational policy on March 25 in the National Stadium (Allende, 1971). The speech, based in part on background papers the president had requested from Nuñez and Suarez, was mostly an extended but still very general elaboration upon the education-related themes contained in the Basic Program (except for the section on private education). Consequently, it did little to clarify which policy line the government would eventually follow.

He started by noting that all society must be a school and that the individual must be an integral part of the greater school which is society. (The fact that this observation echoed a slogan frequently used by Fidel Castro did not escape the attention of opposition commentators.) He emphasized that the whole nation was about to begin a great debate regarding educational policy, which was to be part of a broader process of public participation in all aspects of policy formation. Such active and continuous participation was what was meant by a "people's government." But in order for this conception of democracy to be possible, all children would have to have equal possibilities to learn to participate. The objective was to ensure that they all had an equal chance to develop their capacities. This, however, could not occur if children arrived at school hungry, from illiterate homes, or with mental deficiencies caused by infant malnutrition. To eliminate such problems would require not only educational solutions but elimination of the unjust social structure which created them. It also demanded a common basic education.

Allende noted that many adult Chileans could not participate fully in the economic or cultural life of the society because they lacked basic training. He proposed that a parallel system of education be formed under the supervision of, if not the authority of, the Ministry of Education. This system would include all educative agencies in the community outside of the regular formal school system such as child care centers, adult education programs, educational programs of other ministries such as Agriculture, Labor, Health and Justice, INACAP (the National Training Institute), university extension centers, and so on. This would permit a closer linkage between the school and its community. He also proposed that each school form, if it had not already done so, a council of educational workers, which would have full technical and administrative authority within the school, and a council of the school community, which would include not only teachers and parents but also representatives of community organizations to plan and supervise the school-community linkage.

He concluded that creation of the New Man would require a profound redefinition of Chilean education. First, this required a critical knowledge of the Chilean educational reality as part of the diagnosis of the problems. Second, it required "the will to incorporate our education into the process of transition toward the new society, which implies a commitment to the goals we have adopted."

The increasingly apparent policy differences between sectors within the Ministry of Education produced several consequences. First, lower level government officials were frequently confused about what their government's policy was on issues. Some would do nothing at all for fear of violating whatever the policy might be or come to be. Others followed whichever line or version was closest to their own political position or simply ignored all the official statements and followed their own inclinations. This led to contradictory policy applications.

Another consequence was a great deal of honest confusion and mistrust among the opposition, who did not know which version of government policy to believe. In October, the newsmagazine *Que Pasa* asked, "Is there an educational plan?" It answered as follows:

> In contrast to the sureness and speed with which the Popular Unity has attacked important sectors of the national reality, such as the econ-

omy, the area of education has remained without basic changes. The discrepancies among the parties of Popular Unity in this area are notorious and could explain the lack of a common objective.

After recounting some of the public positions taken by Socialist educational officials, the report then noted:

> The Radical bases have been moving in defense of a scheme which is defined as socialist but still defends democratic values. Their position is found in a green-covered pamphlet of very limited distribution [the Radical book cited above], which, although it carries the seal of the Ministry of Education, is clearly of Radical inspiration. Even though the wording is sufficiently ambiguous that one can draw various conclusions from it, there is a clear difference between these ideas and those proclaimed by the Marxist educators, and this promises to produce an acidic debate within government. . . . Now we have to wait for the reaction of the Socialists and Communists to this new demonstration that in education we do not lack a plan, but we have too many plans. (14 October 1971)

A view which appeared to be widely held among the middle sectors who were neither firm supporters nor committed opponents of the Popular Unity government was a hope that the soft-line version of educational policy, as expressed by the Radicals, would prevail. This was combined with a fear that the revolutionary socialist position would win out in the internal struggle or that it represented the true intentions of the government, which was simply using the Radicals to mask its goals from the public.

A frequent experience of ministers of education trying to explain the government's educational policy to worried organizations was to receive as a reply, a list of examples of ministry officials speaking or acting in contradiction to the minister's version of policy. That portion of the opposition mass media which was controlled by right-wing opponents of the regime routinely exploited policy divergences, citing statements and documents from the hard-line socialists to stimulate mistrust of government intentions. (*El Mercurio* was particularly effective at this.)[9]

These differences over policy direction, combined with other internal problems, produced a government which tended to reinforce the confusion surrounding its intentions. The first major policy error had to do with private education. It surfaced within three months of the inauguration and originated both in the Ministry of Education and in the Ministry of the Economy, which had responsibility for a pervasive system of wage and price regulations that had developed over many years to cope with chronic high inflation.

PRIVATE EDUCATION: THE FIRST ERROR

Given the centrality of the private education issue to the negotiations which produced the Statute of Democratic Guarantees and the strength of feeling surrounding the issue, as well as the fact that Allende was determined to maintain good relationships with the Church, it would seem that elementary political wisdom would have dictated that the private school sector be treated with caution. This was not to be the case. The government paid various subventions to private schools which charged no fees, or which charged fees only to some students, or only to cover some of their costs. These schools were under the financial jurisdiction of the Ministry of Education. In December, the ministry announced that the fees charged in 1971 would be frozen at 1970 levels (*El Mercurio*, 4 December 1970). Late in January, the Ministry of the Economy, which controlled the fees charged by private schools which did not receive state subventions, announced that the fees for these schools also had to be held at the same level as in 1970. The official reason given was that "The Supreme Government is pledged to detain inflation, which requires effective participation from all sectors of the nation" (*El Mercurio*, 30 January 1971), quoting from the circular directed from the Ministry of the Economy to all the affected schools. The circular closed by saying, "This Directorate thanks you for your valuable support in the anti-inflationary battle.")

The schools in question were already required to provide approximately a 35 per cent increase in salaries to all of their employees as a "readjustment" to cover the official rate of inflation during the previous year. This measure was therefore interpreted by many as an attempt to force these private institutions into bankruptcy so the state could then take them over in an attempt to accomplish by indirection what it had pledged in the Statute of Democratic Guarantees not to do.[10] Ironically, several of the schools which appeared most likely to be affected were Church-related establishments which had just decided to adopt a sliding scale of fees based on family income in order to broaden the social class base of their student body. The assistant director of one such well-known school, San Ignacio de El Bosque, was quoted in the opposition press as claiming that if the government did not reconsider its position by mid-May, "there will be nothing left for us to do but close the school. We're going straight to bankruptcy" (*La Tarde*, 16 February 1971). The report, with the inflammatory headline, "Death Penalty for Private Education," followed the quotation with its "guess" that "the closure of the establishment will be very brief, since the state will take it over."

Astorga denied that this was the government's intent. In an interview published in the middle-class women's magazine, *Paula*, he declared that the government wanted to ensure that the programs of study in private schools followed the policies established for public schools, that the two systems were better coordinated, and that government subventions to such schools were better controlled so that education could not be a profit-making business. "Private schools which stay within the rules of the game have nothing to fear." He also stated that all of the rumors regarding the government's desire to eliminate private education were only "fantasy, without foundation." It is indicative of the mistrust of government intentions in some sectors of the opposition that the report of the minister's statements concluded by noting that these were his positions "for the moment . . . . One will have to wait until March to resolve his doubts" (*Paula*, 4 February 1971).

In early March, another interview was published in another women's magazine. Once again, Astorga asserted that private schools had nothing to fear so long as they followed the plans and programs fixed by the government, but that the government would exercise strict control over the subventions to avoid being swindled by school proprietors who manipulated budget and enrolment figures. In the same article, Isabel Dominguez, president of the Federation of Private School Parents and Guardians (FEDAP), noted that Allende himself had assured her that the government's only desire was that everybody receive education "without discrepancies between one type of schooling and another." The federation's position was that the problems which concerned the government involved only a small minority of schools, which were owned by individuals rather than institutions, which charged very high fees and were subject to no control, and which sprang up and disappeared like mushrooms. She also claimed that private schools were not going to suffer because of the government's fee-control policy, since the schools were already finding ways to survive under the new regime by using their facilities more efficiently—for example, by increasing enrolment by going into a double-shift system (*Eva*, March, 1971).

At the same time, Astorga noted in another interview Allende's affirmation that "his administration would be pluralistic, respecting the rights of religious congregations and other private institutions to have their own schools." He went on to claim that "we haven't heard the last word on this; right now there is a commission examining the costs of private education. If the requested increase is justified, it will be authorized" (*Ercilla*, 3 March 1971). In his first official policy statement regarding education, Allende reaffirmed Astorga's position.

Nevertheless, doubts about the government's intentions continued. They were fueled by reports that lower level government officials contradicted the minister's position. For example in the Christian Democratic newspaper, *La Tarde*, Lautaro Videla was quoted as telling a group of teachers who were taking a summer course at the Center for In-Service Training that "private education in Chile will disappear in two months. If we haven't taken the necessary measures before, it is because of the compromise we entered into with the Christian Democrats regarding freedom of education.'' He was also alleged to have said that the buildings belonging to private schools would be ''dispossessed'' by the government (19 March 1971). On the next day, the Ministry of Education issued an official denial that Videla had made such statements (*Ultima Hora*, 21 March 1971), but the damage had already been done.

It is not clear whether Videla actually made the statement reported or if this was an example of malicious invention by the opposition press. Nonetheless, similar statements were frequently made on semi-public occasions, particularly by those Socialists who had opposed the Statute of Democratic Guarantees in the first place; and they quickly filtered out to the wider society through the active Chilean political gossip system. Thus, even if the quotation was not precisely correct, it was taken as representing a widely understood position within the ministry. For opposition private school supporters, the question was whether the official position, as expressed by Astorga and Allende,[11] or the position of the hard-line Socialists would ultimately prevail.

For the next several months, debate, attacks, and counterattacks regarding the nature of government policy with respect to private education continued. In August the situation became even more confusing when it became known that discussions were underway between the government and several religious congregations, particularly the Jesuits and the Sacred Heart Fathers, regarding the ''delivery to the state'' of a number of schools owned by these orders. These included some of the most nationally prominent institutions, several of which had been identified in February and March as likely to be driven into bankruptcy by the fee-control policy. This led to a heated and complex argument.

The Church took the position that it did not wish to continue supporting ''classist'' education. On 20 August, Cardinal Silva Henriquez told a group of Christian Democratic parliamentarians, who had asked him to clarify the Church's position, that the Conference of Bishops had ''asked all the educational organizations of the Church to study means for terminating the situation of some private schools. This means democratizing our education'' (*El Mercurio*, 20 August 1971). At the same time, some Church statements hinted that it would have been preferable to continue Church control of democratized private schools, but that government financial policy made this impossible. This left the impression that government policy was forcing the Church to turn schools over to the state. For example, the leaders of the Jesuit and Sacred Heart congregations in Chile declared on 24 August, responding to a campaign against their initiatives led by *El Mercurio* in the name of freedom of education, that ''genuine freedom does not exist in some private schools since they cannot offer their services to everyone without economic discrimination [suggesting that they could have done so if the government had not frozen fees] nor can they convert themselves into schools without fees under the existing rules without compromising their very existence" (*El Mercurio*, 24 August 1971). About three months later the bishops of Chile sent a public letter to all those responsible for Catholic private education emphasizing that "all of *our* fee-charging schools should be free" and that "we do not want *our* schools to be or appear to be classist" (*El Mercurio*, 13 November 1971, emphasis added). Thus, the Church's position appeared to be that it would prefer to maintain control of its schools and democratize them in its own way, but that it would support their delivery to state control if that were fiscally necessary. The federations of private school students, private school parents, and private school teachers all declared themselves to be firmly opposed to any takeover of private schools, as did the Christian Democratic party.

This put the government in an awkward position since it appeared that some sectors of the Church, in the name of eliminating classist education, which was also a government policy objective, were forcing the government to do what it had pledged not to do just months before—take over private schools. In mid-August, Astorga repeated that the government would respect private education (*El Mercurio*, 15 August 1971). Shortly thereafter, however, his director of secondary education, Communist Jorge Espinoza, was reported as declaring that within six years the state would have taken over all private schools. Espinoza denied that he had made such a claim, but in the course of his denial, he made a statement which was almost as damaging from the point of view of the opposition:

> I do not consider that freedom of education is desirable. . . . According to Latin American thinkers it is a utopian idea, already cast aside by history. The government is conscious of the need to guarantee pluralism, and will respect the constitution, but the State cannot renounce its right to direct and orient all of education. (*Las Noticias de Ultima Hora*, 23 August 1971).

Astorga insisted that this was not government policy and noted that even if it wished to, the government did not have the financial capacity to take under its control the approximately 25 per cent of all Chilean children attending private schools (*El Mercurio*, 20 and 22 August 1971). Finally, the minister appeared on a national television and radio network to insist that it was *not* government policy to take over private education (*El Mercurio*, 26 and 27 August 1971).

Negotiations between private school owners and the state continued, however. By the end of the year, the director of primary and normal education announced that 220 private schools had become public schools, "not through pressures, but on the initiative of their owners or administrators" (*La Tercera*, 30 December 1971). The government's handling of these negotiations served to demonstrate that the operative policy regarding private education was as Astorga had described it. The debate gradually diminished, and the issue effectively disappeared during 1972. (Indeed, many private school sources refer to relationships with the government during 1972 as being more cordial than during previous regimes.) Nonetheless, a residue of suspicion about the government's long-term intentions was left, and the issue surfaced once again in 1973 as part of the wide debate regarding the National Unified School proposal.

EDUCATION OR INDOCTRINATION? THE POLITICAL USE OF SCHOOLING

Lying beneath the confusion and disagreement about private education was the most fundamental educational policy dispute between the government and the opposition. This was the extent to which ideological pluralism, in the society as a whole and in its schools, would be permitted to exist. A continuing fear among the opposition, both centrist and extreme right, was that the Allende government would turn Chile into a totalitarian one-party state on the Russian or Cuban model. Within this concern, the possible use of schooling to indoctrinate children into an official ideology was a constant, very sensitive, and absolutely basic preoccupation. Many supporters of private education saw it as a bulwark against complete state control of their children's minds, a necessary guarantor of their freedom to choose for their children the kind of education they thought best.

The regular emphasis in government statements, from whatever source, on the need to use schooling to create the New Man for the socialism toward which Chile was moving created widespread worry that schooling would be used to communicate a single ideological line. There was much within the rhetoric of the hard-line Socialists to reinforce that worry, but even the Radicals did not seem to recognize the symbolic importance of the rhetoric they had adopted because they felt obliged to use a revolutionary vocabulary as a token of their legitimacy as members of a left-wing coalition.

Early in January, in the midst of an editorial concerning the new government's plans for a campaign to eradicate the remaining illiteracy, *El Mercurio*, which adopted a generally positive stance (describing the plan as "a new and perhaps decisive step in the war to substitute knowledge for ignorance"), warned that "it would be desirable if the plan is carried out without any political partisanship" since illiterates, because of their very lack of education, were likely to accept "the first slogan shouted at them" (2 January 1971). Later in January, a Christian Democratic union official was quoted in that party's press as warning that "one can already see the beginning of a stage of massive indoctrination. . . . There is a grave danger that in a short time Chile will lose its freedom of thought" (*La Tarde*, 16 January 1971).

A month later, *El Mercurio* referred editorially to Chile's position in the just completed meetings of the ministers of education from Peru, Bolivia, Ecuador, Columbia, Venezuela, and Chile (representing the "Andres Bello Agreement" for educational and cultural cooperation among the Andean Pact nations). Noting the general agreement at the meetings that education should contribute to socioeconomic transformations in the member societies, help to free them from cultural dependency, and contribute to the formation of the "New Man," the editorial observed that such a position was hardly surprising since the ministers from Chile, Peru, and Bolivia represented Marxist governments or dictatorships which were committed to changing the existing social order through legal or revolutionary means. Claiming that no one would object to the proposition that education in the Latin American nations ought to open students to the widest array of perspectives with which to confront their future, the editorial then suggested that "nonetheless, subordinating education to political indoctrination is something which belongs only in those totalitarian societies which believe that the way to change the existing state of affairs is by spreading proposals which are extreme, if not violent" (*El Mercurio*, 15 February 1971).

Early in March, a newsmagazine reported that:

> The Marxist currents of officialism are fighting to incorporate into compulsory education their own economic, social and historical analysis. The principal changes will be seen in social science and history, where they have incorporated themes such as the Russian Revolution, the Vietnam War, the Cuban Revolution, and Imperialism, and the bibliographies which included the *Diary* of Che Guevara, and the speeches of Fidel Castro and of Salvador Allende himself.

Asked about these changes Astorga replied that he was not familiar with the details of curricular changes, since these were the responsibility of the Superintendency of Education, but that in any case such changes would be provisional until the planned national consultation had taken place (*Ercilla*, 3 March 1971).

Shortly thereafter, *El Mercurio* printed an article titled, "Threats to Educational Pluralism." It observed that the objective of the Statute of Democratic Guarantees was to prevent the further spread of ideological dogmatism from those in the government who wished to place education at the service of the construction of a future socialist society. After noting some examples of intolerance of opposition opinion by Popular Unity supporters in university councils, the article concluded that "the eagerness with which education is made a vehicle of Marxist indoctrination is a serious threat to the Constitutional Guarantees" (15 March 1971). At about the same time, *La Prensa* warned of the dangers in a plan announced for implementation in 1971 which would stimulate collaboration between the USSR and Chile in the production of school texts and allow exchanges of teachers between the two nations. This would mean opening the doors to Soviet influence from which would follow "ideological penetration" (19 March 1971). Also in mid-March, *El Mercurio* referred to the "ideological blockade" created by the fact that all of the key positions of power in the Ministry of Education were held by Marxists whose desire to "dogmatize" the educational system was confirmed by their actions, their private statements and their public speeches (18 March, 1971).

The search by the opposition press for examples of "ideological infiltration" often took on hysterical tones. An innocent plan to expand the number of extracurricular clubs, such as folklore groups, so that all children would have a chance to participate was strongly criticized in an article whose headline read, "Communists Won't Leave Students in Peace Even during Recess" (*La Tribuna*, 30 August 1971). Although Marxist-oriented educators had for years possessed and exercised the freedom to teach their beliefs and test students on what they had been taught, there were also regular alarmed references to Marxist doctrines and slogans being taught in school and to tests which covered Marxist material.[12]

In the midst of this constant barrage, the central issues were joined early in March in an editorial in *El Mercurio* and in a guest column by a Christian Democratic educational official and university professor featured on its editorial page. The editorial began by noting that:

> The country is living through an experience which, according to official declarations, ought to lead Chile to a socialist model. The heart of the problem is not in questioning the model itself, but in defining its characteristics. In this respect, the educational question assumes an especially important role.

It then reviewed the major educational changes introduced by the Christian Democrats during their reign and underlined the fact that even though that government was elected by an absolute majority of the electorate, it had consistently regarded ideological pluralism as an "untouchable" feature of "our national community. . . . This respect for the moral autonomy of parents and guardians, students and teachers was possible because the Reform was designed from an essentially technical and professional angle.'' Since definitions of this "socialist model" found in official statements were vague, the editorialist argued, one had to resort to the fact that "the most enthusiastic spokesmen are none other than educational authorities who belong to the Socialist party." Consequently, the model could only be Marxist-Leninist since these individuals were known for their doctrinal single-mindedness. But the imposition of Marxist postulates in the schools could not be supported because "the immense majority of the country subscribes to a position absolutely opposed to Marxist principles" (11 March 1971). In sum, a minority government could not legitimately use the schools to impose its own ideological position on the children of the majority who did not share that view of the world.

This theme was picked up by Hugo Montes in a long opinion column about two weeks later. Montes' argument clearly reflected the Christian Democratic view that society was *not* composed of classes which were inherently in conflict and in which the only basic question was which class had power; rather, it was a "community," which tolerated and was enriched by differences in position and opinion (although not necessarily differences in economic status); and in which the value of the free individual was paramount. Nothing, he claimed, could be a greater enemy of authentic education and culture than sectarianism, taken in its dictionary sense of fanatical or intransigent adherence to a party or an idea. After developing this theme, he concluded:

> Education is the patrimony of all. It has grown up through many generations and diverse creeds and ideologies. Parents and guardians, teachers, students, unions, authors of texts, politicians, sociologists, men of letters and scientists, artists, and manual labourers have all created this thing which must continue to serve everyone. . . . *Education is not at the service of those who won today and lost yesterday. The wheel of fortune spins and spins; it will keep turning in the world, and in Chile as well.* (*El Mercurio*, 23 March 1971, emphasis added)

Here Montes touched upon the heart of opposition objections to the educational policy they feared would be developed: the assumption embedded in much of the rhetoric that the transition to socialism was historically inevitable and therefore that the main task of education was to prepare children for the kind of society in which they were to live. If one believed that the "wheel of fortune" would keep turning and that other political ideologies might win in future elections, then the New Man rhetoric was utterly unacceptable. Nuñez himself has noted that while he did not believe that the transition to socialism would occur automatically, he felt that his job was to do whatever he could to make it inevitable (interview with Ivan Nuñez, September 1982). It is worth noting that Allende did not share this view. He frequently observed that he might well lose the 1976 election, in which case he would peacefully turn over power to his successor (Tapia, 1979b, p. 297). Once again, for the middle sectors, the problem was who to believe.

The depth of feeling on this issue, even very early in the regime, was dramatic. One frequently heard, in casual conversations, the sentiment which was echoed in a letter from a father reported in *La Segunda* (21 June 1971). Observing that secondary education was in the charge of a powerful Communist, Jorge Espinoza, he concluded that there could be no confidence in an educational system in which children's consciousness would be assaulted, their human spirits attacked, and "dogmatic and pseudo-religious lies of Marxism" imposed on their minds. "Let it be known once and for all," he said, "that we shall not send our children to schools where the education is Marxist oriented, even if the price to be paid is life and persecution for us, and self-education for our children. At least they will be free." The constant references in the opposition press to the "political indoctrination" issue doubtless reinforced such fears, but they were touching an already very sensitive nerve.

The government did not develop an effective response to this issue. The Radicals and Allende kept insisting that ideological pluralism would be maintained, and the revolutionary Socialists continued with their own style of rhetoric and action. A typical response was in an editorial published in *La Nacion* (18 May 1971). "To speak of educational policy and social conscience does not mean, in the pejorative sense, politicizing students nor turning them into card-carrying socialists, as the reactionary opposition would cunningly have us believe." The editorial then went on to repeat the "inevitable transition" argument, noting that education was necessarily a reflection of the predominant social orientation. Education in Chile would thus necessarily have to orient itself toward socialism, which was the "democratic, massive, popular and general" orientation of the society —precisely the proposition which the opposition denied.

To a considerable extent, conflict was inevitable, since it touched upon fundamental differences between the belief systems of the government and opposition forces and was part of the broader dispute regarding the basic legitimacy of a government such as Popular Unity. However, because of their internal problems, government forces frequently undertook unnecessary actions which excited the worst suspicions among both its firm opponents and still-neutral sectors. One notorious example during the first year involved a magazine which was sent to all teachers in the nation several times a year. One of the first issues produced by the new government featured reports of an expanded summer voluntary work campaign which sent secondary and university students into the countryside to assist with rural development. The cover had a large, glossy photograph of a railroad coach filled with students and covered with graffiti. The central slogan read, in large letters, "Mary, who conceived without sin, help us to sin without conceiving." Of all the photographs which might have been chosen to illustrate the summer campaign, none could have been more calculated to offend wide sectors of the Chilean populace and the Church. A letter sent to Allende by the bishop of Osorno expressed a typical reaction among practising Catholics to the offending phrase:

> We are talking about an *Educational* magazine, for educators, which on its cover, that is from its very beginning, shows an orientation which is antireligious, antispiritual and antihuman. It is a sign of what the new education is trying to do. (*Las Ultimas Noticias*, 7 August 1971)

One of the milder commentaries referred to this "irreverent inscription" which was "a scandal to those who observe the infiltration of sectarianism into the school system" (*Que Pasa*, 26 August 1971).

Both the substance and the tone of the debate over education between the government and the opposition, as it emerged during Popular Unity's first year in office, were well captured in a confrontation in the Senate on 15 September between Senator Pablo, a Christian Democrat, and Senator Chadwick from the Allendista wing of the Socialist Party (as recorded in *El Mercurio*, 17 September 1971). Pablo started by reminding the Senate of the provisions of the Statute of Democratic Guarantees with reference to education, committing the Popular Unity government to protect educational pluralism and to avoid any official party orientation in the educational processes under its control. He then referred to a text published by the Ministry of Education entitled "Suggestions for Literacy Training."

The literacy program of the new government involved training three hundred chosen adult educators in early March, who then trained approximately thirty thousand literacy workers, mostly secondary and university students, each of whom was in turn responsible for teaching ten illiterate adults. The textbook (actually a pamphlet) to which Pablo referred was a key element in the training process. Of the eighty hours of instruction provided to the initial group, half used this book as the central text. Of the remaining forty hours, twenty-four were devoted to a study of the "national reality" led by MAPU people from the Catholic University's Center for the Study of National Reality.

This campaign was a source of dispute between the government and the opposition from its initiation. *El Mercurio* had warned about the possibility of using the literacy program for political indoctrination in January, two months before the campaign started. The curriculum and selection of students for the first training course were also subjects of intense conflict between the government and the Christian Democrats. Ordinarily, the Center for In-Service Training would have played a central role in organizing such a course. However, its director, Mario Leyton, was a key Christian Democratic officer in the area of education, and he could not legally be removed from his post by the government. The government refused to accept a curriculum outline for the course prepared by the center and rejected assistance by center staff in selecting the students for the seminar. The center then withdrew its official support for the training event. In the words of a foreign observer who was in close contact with center personnel: "It now becomes a pure political event. This is a strong stand by Leyton, and one which he may be hung for later" (private note, 3 March 1971).

In his speech before the Senate, Pablo observed that the textbook in question claimed that its suggestions followed the psychosocial method developed by Freire. He claimed that the Christian Democrats had used the Freirean method in their own work, but had respected its basic tenets, which assumed a dialogue between two equal learners. "A vertical relationship—the imposition of criteria foreign to the consciousness of the subject—is anti-dialogue; it signifies domination and consequently poisoning of the being." He then suggested that a reading of the government text indicated that it was anti-Freire since it involved "systematic political indoctrination and sustained government propaganda, whose objectives are hardly the creation of a critical and reflective consciousness, but rather a fanatical and dogmatic consciousness."[13]

Pablo then claimed that a careful reading of the words of government educational officials, from the sub-secretary downward, indicated that their objectives involved:

1. Taking total control of the educational apparatus of the nation, from the highest executive levels down to the individual school.
2. Direct action upon teachers, students, parents and guardians, and community organizations.
3. The transformation of each educational establishment into a political tool at the service of the general, as well as the educational and cultural, objectives of the government.

Such officials, he said, spoke of the need for a profound educational reform based upon a reform of the society's social structure, of the need for all workers to participate in the formulation of a new Chilean educational policy, of the need to make better use of the nation's human resources for the construction of a new society, "but what they practice is the most scandalous sectarianism toward those functionaries who will not jump onto their bandwagon but maintain their position as non-politicized professionals."

Chadwick replied that the government could hardly be accused of sectarianism in education since it was turning over the control of the system to those who were traditionally responsible for it, the teachers. He noted that the minister of education was chosen because he had been president of the major teachers' union. He then asked the senators to remember that the Popular Unity government was a coalition and hence could not possibly be using education to promote a single party line since no party could be guaranteed the benefit of its own sectarian pressures. Moreover, the president had gone out of his way to indicate that he would comply with the Statute of Democratic Guarantees. "We must have more faith in the word of the Chief of State. And I am sure that he is constantly vigilant to ensure that no abuse is committed."

Pablo replied that "there is a difference between legal reality and the reality we are living." He indicated that while he respected Chadwick's words and believed that they represented his personal position:

> One must recognize the existence of other men, who are unfortunately the majority within the ranks of Popular Unity, and the Senator's own party, whose dogmatic and sectarian positions are both public and notorious throughout the nation. . . . Politics is not simply ideas. It is men of flesh and blood. . . . I am convinced that the educational plans of the Government are infiltrated with ideological orientations. This is what worries me. God grant that in the future men of good will, who seek dialogue, who want change and the transfer of power to popular groups, to the majority, can find a common road in a pluralist society, can find a common equation in which the fight for power is not their only passion, in which they do not seek more and more power in order to silence the voices of others who, being Chileans and patriots with a different conception of the national reality, raise their voices to express their discrepancies.

Chadwick closed the debate by noting that the Christian Democrats also seemed to be divided internally between those who shared many of the government's goals and sought compromise and those who opposed the government on every front, who were as sectarian in their own way as those to whom Senator Pablo referred within the government. He urged the Christian Democrats to engage in a critical self-examination and adopt a position which would allow them and the government "to fight but still live together."

Thus, the two senators reflected the most fundamental political problem the nation faced. There were "two lines," both within the government and within the opposition. Those on both sides who honestly respected each other's positions and who sought compromise within existing institutions in order to effect basic changes in the society constantly found their words contradicted and their efforts blocked by the actions of their more extreme colleagues.

6

The National Congress of Education

The issues which had emerged during the first months of the new regime were fundamental aspects of the debates which surrounded the National Congress of Education and the consultative process leading up to it. Although the government was publicly committed to a broad process of consultation before announcing any major initiatives, the Radicals and the hard-line Socialists within the Ministry of Education had different understandings of the nature and possible outcomes of the national debate. While the commitment to consultation was genuine, growing out of both the general orientation of Popular Unity policy and the distress of organized teachers at not having been consulted during the Frei reforms, the specific tactic of holding a National Congress of Education had been conceived as part of a strategy of opposition rather than of governance. There were many within the Ministry of Education who were frustrated that the implementation of new policy would be delayed by at least a year while the consultative process gradually unfolded. This appeared to be particularly characteristic of those who believed that the consultation should be limited to suggesting ways to implement already determined objectives.

The consultations began with workshop meetings of the teachers in each school in the nation during March, 1971, just before the opening of the school year. These were coordinated by local SUTE representatives, who were to organize the results and forward them to a series of district, regional, and provincial congresses, which would finally culminate in the National Congress, originally projected to be held during October.

In preparation for these initial meetings the ministry provided to all teachers a copy of the decree fixing the school calendar for the year, a brief statement by Astorga noting the importance of the teachers' role in the consultative process, and a skeletal outline of suggested points for discussion (Ministerio de Educación Pública, March, 1971). This agenda clearly reflected a Radical party orientation. It consisted almost exclusively of concrete questions which would have been reasonable items for teachers to discuss under almost any political regime. The topics suggested were:

1. *Society and Education*. The teachers were asked to explore whether the socioeconomic and political situation of the nation made an effective transformation of schooling possible.

2. *Structure of the Educational System*. Under this rubric the educators were requested to estimate the quantitative and qualitative capacity of both the regular and adult education systems to meet the educational needs of their local community as well as those needs at regional and national levels and to discuss the adequacy of the existing structure of the system.

3. *Educational Governance and Administration*. Here they were asked to consider the extent to which teachers had participated in educational policy formation and to provide an estimate of the willingness of educational workers to collaborate in the management of the system. Also included was a discussion of existing and possible future relationships between their school and local community organizations.

4. *The Curriculum*. Discussion under this point was to be focussed on integrating education into the new national project, characterized as "the struggle for an effective national independence, and authentic democratization, and the accelerated development of the nation along the path to socialism."

5. *Human Reality of the Educational Process*. Teachers were expected to discuss the characteristics and problems of the students who attended their school, the status of the school's teachers with respect to economic welfare and social security provisions, career stability, and the like, and the degree of development, organization, and aspiration to change of the local community, especially as these would affect student attendance at school and the community's willingness to improve the local school.

6. *Material and Financial Reality of the Educational Process*. Examination of the adequacy of the existing building and facilities was requested, along with estimation of budget increases necessary to effect improvements.

7. *School Attendance*. Teachers were asked to consider factors which both stimulated and impeded attendance at school in their area (for example, health, nutrition, availability of school supplies and scholarship assistance) with a view to possible modifications of the laws regulating assistance to poor children.

8. *Educational Census*. Suggestions were requested regarding variables which might be included in such a census as well as an evaluation of the willingness of educational workers to participate in a census and to use the results from their own area for local planning.

In his introduction, Astorga indicated that these were suggestions only and that they could easily be modified if a group of teachers thought that would permit them to provide a better diagnosis of the educational and cultural reality of their community.

These school-level discussions were generally held as planned, and without incident, although it was evident that many teachers were not sure what would be done with the results of their labors and that few ministry officials appeared to have any idea of how they would use the products of these consultations. During the March-April period I was asked on several occasions for ideas on how to "systematize and objectify" the results in order to make them useful for the projected discussions at higher levels. After examining some of the reports and noting that they varied greatly both in terms of topics discussed, quality of discussion, and detail, I had to admit that I could think of no simple way to make the information useful for discussions beyond the level of the school from which it came. It appeared to be a classic case of collecting data before giving any careful thought to how it might be used and to what end. Some months later, another non-Chilean working in the Ministry of Education observed in a private letter:

> We have been asked by the Santiago province SUTE Director to help him in "objectifying" the reports he has from the national reality studies. All of this is really impossible, but it was interesting to see that they are trying (belatedly) to objectify data and not just present a program. (Private letter, 20 August 1971)

These observations undoubtedly go a long way toward explaining why there is no evidence that the results of these discussions had any significant influence upon the broader-scale congresses which followed. Rather, these later deliberations were oriented by a series of documents produced by the ministry itself.

THE SIX-YEAR PLAN

The first of these ministry documents was produced in July 1971. It was entitled "General Bases for the Formulation of the 1972 Operational Plan and Frame of Reference for the 'Six-Year Educational Sector Plan' " (Ministerio de Educación Pública, July 1971).

The authors of the document worked closely with the National Planning Office (ODEPLAN) and tried, they claimed, to keep in mind that many aspects of educational policy could not be elaborated until the National Congress of Education process had been completed. The document attempted to provide a diagnosis of the current educational situation, a vision of the major educational problems the government wished to deal with, and a provisional statement of the educational policy of the government. The general educational objectives were specified as follows: 1) democratization of education both through expansion of the system and increasing local participation in educational planning and administration; 2) equalization of educational opportunities, with respect to both initial enrolment and retention in the system; 3) participation of all educational workers in the transformation of the educational system; 4) assistance in the process of structural change which was moving Chile toward a socialist society; 5) establishment of a unified and integrated educational system which would be more closely linked to the socioeconomic and cultural needs of the society; 6) formation of the New Man who would be able to overcome Chile's underdevelopment and cultural, economic, and technological dependency; 7) establishment of a system of permanent education which would help Chilean workers to overcome their cultural disadvantages.

One way to meet these objectives would be through the establishment of a National Unified School which would provide education for all students from first grade through secondary school. Depending upon the community, such a school could be in a single building or in separate buildings serving distinct age groups. It was not clear at this time if a "National Unified School" was meant to be the same thing as the "School for Development" referred to in earlier policy statements. The characterizations were general, but they seemed to refer to something like the consolidated schools already in existence.[1]

Both general goals and specific targets were suggested for each of the levels and types of schooling, along with recommendations for improving special education and adult education and integrating them more fully with the regular educational system and for integrating the pre-service and in-service training available to educators in order to have a "permanent education" system for teachers.[2]

Even though this Six-Year Plan contained suggestions which were for the most part either general or non-controversial, its publication well before the Congress of Education process had been completed (indeed, before it had really started beyond the school level) began to arouse suspicions that the government intended either to ignore or to manipulate the consultative procedures to which it had committed itself. This suspicion even filtered into the government-supporting press. The director of secondary education was asked in an interview reported late in August: "Why do we already have the Six-Year Plan if they have not yet held the Congress of Education, which—they assure us—will determine the educational policy of the government?" He replied that the plan was meant to be just another contribution to that debate.

The more objective and realistic documents which are prepared, the richer and more fruitful will be the debate and the better will be the decisions adopted. . . . The Plan has aroused anger among the reactionaries who are distorting its orientations. The Congress will discuss and decide. I have confidence in the creative support of the teachers, workers, peasants, and youth, who will be the great contributors to this democratic debate, which will be open to all ideologies, although it will not serve as a bastion for those who want to neutralize the basic changes to be produced in this country. (*Ultima Hora*, 23 August 1971)

Such observations did not entirely dispel the suspicion of the government's intentions.

"CONTRIBUTIONS" TO THE CONGRESS BY THE SUPERINTENDENCY

Those suspicions were further aggravated by the appearance of two documents produced by the Superintendency of Education which were labelled, respectively, as the First Contribution and the Second Contribution of the Ministry of Education to the Debates of the National Congress of Education. The first appeared in August; the second, in October.

After the school year started in March, it was felt within the ministry that some sort of position paper or detailed discussion guide ought to be produced to focus discussions at the forthcoming regional and provincial congresses. Originally it was thought that SUTE ought to do this, since the idea for a congress had come from that organization. However, it became apparent that SUTE did not have the capacity to produce such a document since most of its strong leadership had moved to the Ministry of Education. Nor did it have the interest, as it reflected its original status as a collection of traditional trade unions by concentrating its attention upon the economic problems of teachers. In addition, some of SUTE's key members were from the opposition.

It was thus decided to set up a task force within the Superintendency of Education to produce the required position papers. This group consisted of two Socialists, Ivan Nuñez as superintendent and Lautaro Videla as visitor general, plus Hugo Araya representing the Radicals and Gilberto Gonzalez, a Communist from the educational planning office. They operated with no instructions or limitations from the minister or any other group within the ministry. It was assumed that since the team had representatives from the three major parties in the coalition, whatever it produced would be "pluralistic," reflecting the major currents of opinion within the ministry. The task force did not perceive its duty to be to produce a "technical" diagnosis. Much technical work had already been done by the Christian Democrats, and they were aware of the lack of technical training within the new group of officials. What they wanted was a document which would elicit opinions and political judgments.

Three of the four members of the team, Nuñez, Videla, and Gonzalez, had worked in the consolidated school movement. For them, some form of *integrated* education, which would remove barriers between different types and levels of schools and eliminate barriers between the school and its local community was both an "old aspiration" and a basic principle guiding the production of the discussion guides.[3]

The first "Contribution" was relatively brief and was intended specifically to form the agenda for the provincial congresses which were to precede the National Congress (which by now—August—had been postponed to November; it was ultimately held in December). The document clearly represented the ideological and political stance of the government and the Ministry of Education, particularly the hard-line Socialist side (Ministerio de Educación Pública, August 1971). The text, questions posed, and comments made all reflected a view of Chile's educational problems as deriving from the nation's status as a dependent, capitalist, bourgeois society. Moreover, it not only presented a general analysis but also proposed two specific policy measures, the National Unified School and the Law for Democratization of Education as the most appropriate solutions to the society's educational difficulties. There was an immediate strong reaction from members of the opposition who perceived the document as clearly signalling the government's intent to structure and control the congresses so that the "debates" would produce conclusions supporting the government's general objectives and specific policy proposals.

The Second Contribution, aimed primarily at the final National Congress, but appearing while the preliminary meetings were still being held, created an even greater furor. It was much more detailed and contained language which was in many respects much more precise but also, from the opposition point of view, much more extreme.[4] Since this is the most complete public statement of the Popular Unity government's educational policy stance after one year in office and significant portions of this paper are also found in all later educational policy documents, it will be considered in some detail.

The first section dealt with *The Cultural and Educational Problems and Needs of the Chilean People, and the Tasks of the Construction of Socialism*. It began by stating that since the people of Chile had freely expressed their willingness to change, the task confronting them was how to overcome the capitalist order and construct the socialism which was necessary to achieve independence, development, social justice, and full democracy. It was within this context that the congress had to take a stand regarding the future direction for Chilean education.

Following the government's general political position and its many earlier statements, the document asserted that the fundamental cause of Chile's underdevelopment and cultural and educational backwardness was its capitalist regime with imperialist and oligarchical domination. This system could not meet the needs of the people and had brought Chile to a state of profound crisis. Education was one of the fundamental problems which Chilean capitalism was unable to resolve, but it could not be considered in isolation from other social consequences of the crisis. Some of these consequences were: 1) the physical and mental deterioration of an important portion of the population, especially those most exploited, as witnessed by high mortality rates, malnutrition, alcoholism, prostitution, and so forth; 2) social and cultural backwardness of agrarian regions; 3) rural-to-urban migration; 4) high rates of unemployment and professional obsolescence as consequences of a profit-oriented liberal economy; 5) the increasing incorporation, by necessity, of women into the work force, but in inferior and exploited roles; 6) the large number of physically, mentally, and socially handicapped individuals; and 7) a general crisis in the family, leading especially to a lack of care for very young children.

Within this general context, the national educational system exhibited a number of specific problems. Drop-out and repetition rates were very high, and they were associated with family economic status. Various community agencies which played an educational role were neither part of the educational structure nor oriented by educational policy considerations. The various types and levels of schooling within the regular system were also poorly integrated, leading to a great deal of unnecessary complexity which was also associated with the social class position of the student. Educational administration was overly centralized and authoritarian. The education provided was more didactic and intellectual than truly formative and socializing, and it was designed primarily to serve the interests of the dominant sectors of society. The Frei reforms, the report went on, had accomplished a physical expansion of the system, but they had not effected any basic changes because they were not linked with the necessary changes in the overall social structure or with the experience of the Chilean teaching force. After reviewing the efforts of organized Chilean teachers throughout the century to stimulate educational reform efforts, it concluded that "the cultural and educational problems of the Chilean people, and especially those of the working class and the peasants, will be resolved in the construction of socialism, which will in its turn present new challenges to national education."

The second major theme dealt with was *Planning and the National System of Education in the Transition to Socialism.* After discussing the possible mechanisms for integrating educational planning into overall national planning and noting the need to plan both for the regular school system and for an extra-school system of permanent education, the report entered one of its most controversial sections. The theme was the role of schooling in creating the New Man who would live, and could only live, in the new socialist society. Under this rubric it was noted that "the education we will build will not be neutral. . . . The new education will have a political meaning and orientation." Bourgeois education also had such an orientation, it observed, but the dominant classes carefully hid it. It was political because it was an instrument of power, because it was selective, because it operated by deforming consciousness, because it used the efforts of the entire nation to permit a minority to maintain its dominance, because it idealized the capitalist system and hid from view the laws which explained the generation of exploitation and misery, and because it devalued manual labor. "The new education will have a political meaning and a political organization. . .because it will be a function of the overall economic, social, and cultural policy of the Chilean nation, expressed in its historic socialist project, which has a legitimate democratic origin and which we *proclaim to be irreversible*" (emphasis added).

In spite of this, the report continued, ideological pluralism would be maintained. All lines of thinking would be respected, and pedagogical content would have neither a dogmatic nor a single party orientation. "But pluralism cannot be a pretext for the survival of current content. Pluralism cannot be used as a pretext for denying the right of the people of Chile and their Government to replace the liberal bourgeois orientation of current education. It cannot mean the use of the past to blackmail the future. Pluralism, honestly understood, is not incompatible with the socialist definition of the new education."

Within the overall context of the position paper, it was difficult for the opposition to determine just what the limits of an "honestly understood" pluralism might be. Such limits appeared to be narrow and would probably exclude what was most precious to much of the opposition.

The report then went on to state that the formation of the New Man would not be solely the task of the school. Society as a whole would be the school in which the new person was formed, through the struggle to defend and exercise the people's power, through solidarity with other nations in the process of liberating themselves, through struggle to increase production and economic development, through ideological debates and scientific activity, through sports, and through artistic and creative activity.

The third major section was *The Policy of Educational Democratization: An Immediate Response to the Exigencies of a New Education.* A variety of statistics were cited as indicators of the correlation between the social class position of a child and his or her probability of entering into and surviving through the school system. Such a relationship was an inevitable characteristic of capitalist society, and true democratization of education in which all would have the opportunity to develop their capacities could occur only in the context of democratization of the economic system and the political structure.

As conceptualized in the position paper, however, democratization involved more than simple equalization of educational opportunity as part of a general equalization of life chances within the society. It also meant direct participation by all sectors of the community in the governing of their schools as part of a broader concept of participation in decision-making.

Within this double context, a number of general goals and specific policy targets were set, and government actions already undertaken were reviewed. A long list of goals was provided, most of which were so general and repetitive as to be meaningless, for example:

> to extend and diversify services and functions so as to avoid any form of discrimination, especially with respect to members of the working class, peasants, and other marginalized groups;
>
> to contribute to the formation of a new type of man who will be free to develop himself fully in a non-capitalist society, and who will express himself as a personality who is conscious of and in solidarity with the revolutionary process, who is capable of exercising popular power, and technically and scientifically able to develop the economy in a society in transition to socialism, who is open to the creating and enjoyment of the various manifestations of art and intellect, and is in excellent physical condition;
>
> to organize educational work in conformity with the principles of unity, continuity, and diversity, following the laws of individual development and the demands of the process of national transformation, and the scientific, technological, and social realities of the contemporary world.

The fourth and final section of the paper dealt with the *National Unified School as the Representative Institution of the New Education.* The National Unified School was to be the fundamental institution of the new regular school system.

The central idea was to develop a school which was closely linked to its community and in which the traditional divisions between pre-school, primary, and secondary education and between humanistic-scientific schooling and technical-professional schooling would be broken down. As the Six-Year Plan had suggested, such a school could bring all the formerly separate elements together in a single building or, if they were housed in separate buildings, the goal could be achieved by planning for all of the separate units in a locale as a coordinated system. It was recognized that not all of the now-separated elements of schooling could be brought together quickly, but this was not important so long as in the transition period these elements were inspired by the basic principle of the new school, whose "doctrine will be inserted into the process of formation of the new society." The new school would be based on the values of "humanistic socialism and integral democracy" and thus would be entirely different from the traditional school, which was rooted historically in capitalism and was "an instrument at the service of the internal monopolistic bourgeois and imperialistic domination."

Several characteristics of the National Unified School were outlined. First, it would be *democratic* in that it would be integrated into the community and offer to all its members a wide array of educational and cultural opportunities without discrimination on the basis of philosophical belief or socioeconomic position.

It would be *nationalistic*. It would incorporate traditional Chilean values and the "libertarian tradition" of the nation, particularly recognizing the "proletarian struggles for sovereignty and independence which have been virtually ignored in traditional teaching which serves the class interests of the oligarchy." Foreign models and "the negative influence of cultural cosmopolitanism" would be eliminated to avoid "mental colonization." Moreover, such a school would "revive and reactualize the educational experience of the consolidated schools and other experiments at educational integration which previous administrations, bowing to the dictates of traditional education, would not assist."

The new school would be both *unified and diversified*. It would be unified in the sense that the traditional divisions between levels and types of schools would be eliminated. It would be diversified in order to meet individual needs within the overall unity. To this end, the school would not be organized in lock-step age-grade sequences, but in "teaching levels," through which children could proceed at their own pace. Following the pre-school years, there would be a level of basic skills for all, then an intermediate stage in which separate disciplines would be studied, and finally a level of specialization in which various electives and options would be available according to the abilities and career/work interests of the student and the needs of the society.

Such a school would be *productive* since work would be seen not as human exploitation within the capitalist model, but as a means for human liberation, as the way for individuals to contribute not to the enrichment of a few but to the development of their entire society. It would also be *scientific*, replacing traditional memoristic and verbalistic teaching methods with a combination of theory and practice which would produce "rational knowledge of the laws and principles which regulate the actions and phenomena of the natural and social world, making possible a learning liberated from the pragmatism of bourgeois pedagogy."

Finally, this school would be *planned*. Teachers as a collegial body would participate directly in decision-making and administration, and parents and guardians and community organizations would be involved in planning linkages between the school and the community. Its development would not be "the work only of technicians, but a task to be discussed, studied, decided and executed by organizations of teachers, workers, students, parents and guardians, within the general framework of national planning."

It was also noted that this new school would be open all year with flexible hours during the day and week in order to accommodate the particular rhythms of work and life in a given locality. Special teaching posts would also be established within local enterprises incorporated into the social or mixed areas of the economy in order to provide students with direct experience of the world of work.

The position paper closed by observing that "we must underline the experimental quality of the National Unified School. All of its programming will follow a process of planned experimentation. . .whose results will serve the reconstruction of the Chilean educational system. Nobody should hope that the system is going to change by simple legal dispositions or regulations, nor even less should we succumb to the temptation to engage in precipitate action or improvisation."[5]

The release of this document in October contributed substantially to a major dispute already underway regarding the entire consultative process. This disagreement regarding education was part of the broader political fight between government and the opposition, particularly the Christian Democrats, and cannot be understood without reference to the overall political and economic situation as it had developed since Allende's inauguration.

THE GENERAL POLITICAL-ECONOMIC SITUATION IN 1971

Sigmund (1977, p. 128) summarized succinctly the first year of Popular Unity government.

> The tense atmosphere in which it took power did not augur well for the future of the Allende regime, yet it performed surprisingly well during its first year. The climate of violence diminished although it did not disappear; the inflation subsided, and the economy rebounded, producing a generalized sense of prosperity; most of the promised changes in industry (nationalization or state control of key sectors) and agriculture (elimination of large landholdings) were carried out— and all this despite external pressure from the United States and the open or tacit opposition of half the Chilean population. Beneath the

surface, however, were the same economic and political constraints which had limited Frei, now accelerated in their effects and accentuated in their intensity by the polarizing policies of the government and the deepening opposition of the non-Marxist sectors. It was only after nearly a year in office, however, that serious economic problems (inflation and shortages) and political difficulties (solidification of the opposition, particularly on the part of the middle class, and a decline in legitimacy) began to emerge.

One indicator of the early successes of the Allende government was the results of the municipal elections held in April 1971. The Popular Unity candidates received almost exactly half of the votes cast (just over or just under half depending upon whether one excluded or included blank and invalid ballots—government papers excluded them and opposition papers included them!). This represented a substantial increase over the percentage received by Allende in the presidential election, but it also clearly showed that the country was almost evenly split between supporters and opponents of the government. Even though the percentage of votes received by the Christian Democrats declined slightly, to 25.7 per cent, they still remained the single most popular party. (Percentages of the vote received by other major parties were: Socialists, 22.3 per cent; Nationals, 18.5 per cent; Communists, 16.9 per cent; Radicals, 8.1 per cent; Radical Democrats, 3.9 per cent.)

A major concern which began to arise early among the opposition was the use by the government of what were perceived to be quasi-legal or extra-legal means to accomplish its objectives, particularly with respect to gaining control of key sectors of the economy. It was clear from the outset that even though it was a minority in Congress, Popular Unity would be able to get enough support there from other parties to accomplish the nationalization of the copper industry. To reach its goals in other areas of the economy, however, it could not depend upon support from opposition parties and had to use means other than congressional legislation. Since it did not control the *Contraloría,*[6] the government could also not depend upon decree laws. However, the vagaries of Chilean legislative history had provided a resourceful government with a variety of options for taking over enterprises in the sectors noted in the Basic Program. It used its control over wages and prices to drive industries into or near bankruptcy and then took them over. It used government development corporation (CORFO) funds to buy up stock until it had a controlling interest, sometimes after having used other mechanisms to drive the price of the stocks down. Labor disputes with government-controlled unions paralyzed certain other industries, which could then be taken over.

A symbolically important dispute arose around the government attempt to take over "La Papelera," the Paper and Carton Manufacturing Company, which was the only private supplier of paper in the domestic economy and which was headed by Jorge Alessandri. The government considered paper production to be part of the forest industry, which was a natural resource sector over which it should have control. The opposition feared that government control of all of the paper industry would be used to eliminate the opposition press by starving it of its basic raw material, something which had been forbidden in the Statute of Democratic Guarantees. As Sigmund observes, the government development corporation, (CORFO) was

> authorized to buy shares from private stockholders in the company. At the same time, price rises were decreed for the raw materials used by the industry, while price increases were denied to finished paper products—a patent effort to bankrupt the company. The pressures on the paper industry were resisted through the establishment by private shareholders (almost certainly with CIA financing) of a National Freedom Fund to buy shares from any stockholder who wished to sell. This was designed to prevent a takeover by the government through the method used in nationalizing the banks—driving the price of the stock down by threats of nationalization and then offering to buy it at a price well above that offered on the market. (Sigmund, 1977, p. 157)

These methods for taking over industrial, commercial, and financial enterprises were formally legal, even though the opposition saw them as illegitimate. In rural areas, however, a wave of clearly illegal land seizures was taking place at the same time. In some cases these were spontaneous takeovers of land by peasants. In others, they were evidently led or encouraged by the rural arm of MIR. Although the government did not officially support these moves and publicly disclaimed responsibility for them, it did very little to stop them (indeed, there was little it could have done without sending troops in against peasants—and in some cases students—who were its own supporters, albeit more radical than the government itself.)

Opposition fears that the Allende government's promise to use only legal means to accomplish its ends was a limited commitment and that it would resort to non-legal and, if necessary, violent methods were encouraged by the selection of Carlos Altamirano as secretary general of the Socialist party in January 1971. Altamirano was the leader of the revolutionary wing of the party, and his accession to power was supported by Allende. Allende's support appeared to be rooted not in his personal convictions but in his dislike of the outgoing secretary general, Aniceto Rodriguez, but Allende's stance contributed to doubts regarding his "real" intentions. These doubts were further fueled by a well-publicized interview between Allende and Regis Debray, a popular disciple of Che Guevara, which was published early in 1971 (*Punto Final*, 16 March 1971, pp. 25-63). Allende insisted to Debray that he favored the legal route and that the Chilean historical circumstance made such a stance the only realistic option open to those who wished to install a socialist society. However, he also observed that his differences with the revolutionaries were only "tactical" and that traditional legality had to be observed "for the moment."

The tension within the coalition between the hard-line and the soft-line proponents continued to increase. The Communist party consistently supported Allende's "legal" or reformist position (to the point where there were occasional armed confrontations between MIR and the Communist youth brigade, the Brigada Ramona Parra). At its biennial convention in July 1971 the Radical party endured a further rupture over this issue; five of its seven senators and seven of its nineteen deputies left to form a new party (the Party of the Radical Left), which was soon voting with the opposition. They claimed that the party was adopting policy positions which were too clearly Marxist and which were alien to the traditional ideological orientation of the party with its commitment to democratic parliamentary institutions and the preservation of an area within the economy of private ownership of the means of production. This action, combined with the splits during the convention in 1969, meant that "the official Radical Party thus had lost or expelled its last three presidential candidates and seen its 1969 congressional delegation reduced from nine senators to two and from twenty-three deputies to twelve" (Sigmund, 1977, p. 152). This further weakened the already tenuous position of the Radicals within the governing coalition and increased the difficulty of the relations between the Radicals and Socialists within the Ministry of Education.

All of these developments were pushing the Christian Democrats into a position of firmer opposition to Popular Unity. The Tomic position, not too far removed from that of Allende, had been weakened but not completely discredited by his poor showing in the presidential election. In the December 1970 meeting of the party's national assembly, a long debate developed between those who believed the party should support Allende except where there was a clear difference and those who believed the party should adopt a stance of "constructive opposition," while supporting the government where appropriate. The difference was one of degree, but it was a sign of the conflict which became sharper as months passed. In December, a compromise position was reached, but by the May 1971 meeting of the party's national council, the policy of "constructive opposition" was endorsed, and one could see the first attempts by supporters of Frei to move toward a new alliance with the National Party in the hope of repeating in 1976 the victory of 1964. Two months later, in a fierce debate between the left and right wings of the party, the former lost. The position adopted noted that while the Christian Democratic party was still willing to support Popular Unity in many areas, it condemned the government's "totalitarian and exclusive spirit" and accused it of "intransigence, sectarianism and hatred." The party also announced that it would introduce bills to limit the power of the government to circumvent the legislature and to protect small businessmen and farmers from arbitrary government seizure of their enterprises.

One consequence of this was that a small group of the most left-leaning members of the Christian Democratic party withdrew and joined with the major figures within, and founders of, MAPU, who were unhappy with the increasingly Marxist stand of their own party, to form a new party called the Christian Left. The more important consequence was the introduction by the Christian Democrats in October of a constitutional amendment which would have carefully defined the "three areas" of the economy and drastically limited the government's freedom of action in taking over private firms. This led to the acceleration of attempted negotiations between the government and a Christian Democratic party whose opposition position was continually hardening. (These negotiations continued until the day before the coup two years later.)

An important indicator of the hardening attitude was a long speech delivered in the Senate in September by Renan Fuentealba, who was identified with the moderate or Tomic wing of the Christian Democrats. He accused the government of "sectarianism and antipluralism," citing attacks against freedom of the press (in other words, the Papelera controversy) and freedom of education, and claimed that in spite of repeated attempts by his party to reach an understanding with Popular Unity the actions of the government were forcing the Christian Democrats to take a harder line. He accused Allende of playing "a double game." "The Fuentealba speech was an important turning point, since it indicated that groups within the Christian Democratic Party that were not identified with its right wing were now in favor of stronger opposition to the Allende government." (Sigmund, 1977, p. 158).

Crowning the events of that Chilean spring were massive street demonstrations by university students protesting what they claimed to be oppression and sectarianism in the universities and the famous "march of the empty pots" which brought thousands of (mostly middle-class) housewives into the streets banging on empty cooking pots to protest increasing inflation and food shortages. The demonstration produced several dramatic and well-publicized incidents of street violence against the marching women.

CONFLICT OVER THE CONGRESS OF EDUCATION PROCESS

The Christian Democrats were not totally opposed to the idea of a massive national consultation on educational policy, nor did they object in principle to many of the specific ideas advanced by the government. With respect to the idea of a widespread consultation, Ernesto Livacic, subsecretary of education during the Frei regime, noted:

> Ideas are applied progressively, especially those like participation which are relatively new. Broad consultation, of which they now speak, is a logical progression from consultation with qualified representatives which we have been having for almost twenty years now. Through the National Council of Education, created in 1953, education is the only sector of national development which has an organization with community participation to advise the government regarding policy. There teachers, parents, the universities, private education, and the productive sector are represented. It does lack students, and they should be incorporated. (*Que Pasa*, 18 November 1971)

Livacic observed that every aspect of the Christian Democratic educational reform had been discussed and approved by that council and thus denied that it had been imposed "from above," although "this does not mean that a massive consultation would not be even better."

Within this context, however, the opposition attacked the government on two fronts: 1) the nature of the "agenda" being set for the congresses by the government documents; and 2) attempts to control the representation at the congresses and the procedures within them to ensure outcomes supporting government policy goals.

Given the general philosophical position of the Christian Democrats and their educational policy position as discussed in Chapter 2, it is hardly surprising that the party found much of the hard-line socialist rhetoric in the government documents objectionable. In their responses to the government position papers, members of the party tended to reassert their own value positions regarding education and to defend their own reforms, while admitting that much remained to be accomplished. (See, for example, the pamphlet entitled "Focusing on the Agenda of the National Congress of Education," which was also published in the journal *Presencia*, which reflected Christian Democratic thought (Partido Demócrata Cristiana, undated).

One of the most common themes was the claim that although the tone of the language suggested revolutionary socialism, the terms used were not clearly defined, so one could not be sure just what the government had in mind. In mid-November Livacic observed that:

> no one has told us, in the name of the government, what they understand by the New Man. With such a lack of clarity regarding the basic values underlying an educational reform, it is not surprising that there

are discrepancies. The term socialism has many connotations, and there are distinct socialist experiences. They say, and there is no reason to deny it *a priori*, that this will be the Chilean road to the construction of socialism, but up to now we do not know what it is going to be. Nor have they defined the extent to which education is going to be transformed into a simple echo of a political and social system, or, as we educators, and specifically we Christian Democrats, think, the extent to which education will be a very significant tool in the construction of a new Society. (*Que Pasa*, 18 November 1971)

With reference to the ENU proposal specifically, the Christian Democrats claimed that its reference to "socialist humanism" was also unclear and that the proposal was so vague and grandiose as to be impossible to implement. From what they could deduce regarding the proposed curricular content for the new school, they concluded that it would be antipluralist and would produce not critical individuals whose creative capacity would be the tool of their own liberation, but "cookie cutter men." Eduardo Jara, director of the educational department of the party, complained:

The problem with the government men is that they want everybody to think, live, and react "as socialists." Education for them is an instrument to create consciousness and the Ministry is an administrative organism placed at the service of ideological and political action. They thus commit a crime against the child; creating a fanatical consciousness. (*Que Pasa*, 18 November 1971)

As with the idea of a national consultation, the Christian Democrats also did not, in principle, oppose the proposed law for the democratization of education. Although its details were not spelled out in the ministry's final "Contribution" to the congress process, the idea that it would involve local and regional educational councils was clear. In a general sense, this was consistent with the "communitarian" thrust of Christian Democratic thinking. Indeed, the party had established various forms of local councils in non-educational areas during its six years in power. They proposed that the existing National Council of Education be supplemented by a system of internal school councils and local and provincial councils. The one thing they insisted upon was adequate representation of all interest groups in such councils.

Indeed, at this time, concern over the representativity of such councils was far more important than disagreements over the vaguely defined content of such proposals as that for the National Unified School. If membership in the various proposed councils was structured to provide an automatic majority for government representatives, then it would not matter what the official national policy was. "At the local level they could do whatever they wanted" (interview with Mario Leyton, 4 December 1978).

The same reasoning led Christian Democrats to the position that their most fundamental concern about the consultative process occurring from September to December 1971 was the issue of the representativity of the various congresses and the extent to which they would be controlled by Popular Unity forces in order to guarantee the result desired by the government (interview with Mario Leyton, 24 November 1980). Throughout these months Christian Democrats complained that the combined representations of SUTE, controlled by Popular Unity parties, and the National Workers' Federation (CUT), along with other groups which were guaranteed participation, assured that the government would have a majority in almost all important congresses, particularly the provincial congresses and the final National Congress. They objected to a representation for private education which was far less than its actual proportion of the total enrolment in the Chilean educational system. They asserted that when local and provincial congresses were held, schools which were not likely to be favorable to the government's position somehow received information too late to permit effective participation, that only those community groups whose positions were likely to be "convenient" for the government were invited to participate, that in most of the congresses minority voices were silenced by manipulation of the rules, and that minority reports were not permitted. (See interviews with Eduarda Jara and Ernesto Livacic in *Que Pasa*, 18 November 1971. Livacic did recognize that in some cases the provincial and local congresses had been held without problems, though this was not true in the majority of cases.)

On 7 November Senator Tomas Pablo summarized these complaints and concluded:

> The mechanisms employed up to the moment indicate that they have not wanted to support a meeting which authentically represents all of the groups which make up the school community of our country. Rather, the objective has been to make of Chilean education a political instrument, in spite of the Constitutional Guarantees. . . . In truth they wish to use education as a vehicle of a steely ideological dogmatism, violating the letter and the spirit of the Constitution. (*El Mercurio*, 7 November 1971)

Five days later, *El Mercurio* explicitly linked the educational congress process to the general political dispute in the society.

> The marxist instrumentalization of education cannot be viewed with indifference in a country living in our current circumstances. Not only

are the followers of this ideology concerning themselves with conscious-ness-raising of adults in various ways but, working for the future, they are trying to monopolize education in our country. The National Congress of Education is directed to this end, since from this Congress will come directives which will begin to be implemented in March of 1972. (13 November 1971)

There is no question that the local and provincial congresses were highly politicized. Most resulted in emotional disputes between government and opposition forces, typically leading to walkouts by opposition groups. The government-supporting press consistently noted instances of support for the Popular Unity position and downplayed disruptions; the opposition press vigorously reported the disruptions and breakdowns. Some representative examples are noted below.

On 25 September the congress for the city of Valparaiso was held. Representatives of private education, students from ten public secondary schools and secondary students from private schools all withdrew, along with a large number of parent and guardian association representatives, complaining of biased representation, late delivery of the agenda, and a biased agenda (*La Prensa*, 28 September 1971). After all these withdrawals, the main conclusion of the congress was that "the national system of education should have as its essential goal to contribute to the formation of the *new man of the socialist society*" (Vivallos, 1978, p. 189).

The Valparaiso provincial congress, held a few days later, encountered similar difficulties. Private school representatives accused the organizers of "using the assembly only for proselytizing." The organizers rejected the charges, claiming that they had invited representatives of the local bishopric to participate in the debates. Nonetheless, many representatives walked out (*La Tercera*, 4 October 1971).

On 17 October *El Clarin* reported that the congress for the First Educational Sector of Santiago was about to start "With the slogan, 'Toward socialism, we will build the new Chilean education.' " The same meeting was broken up by a massive walkout of Christian Democratic and independent delegates, who listed the standard complaints about poor representation of many sectors and political management of the event, adding that the votes of the plenary session were completely unrelated to the agreements reached in working commissions. "They were changing and misinterpreting the themes according to political party positions" (*La Prensa*, 22 October 1971).

Ten days later *La Tribuna* reported on another provincial congress under the headline "Creation of the National Unified School: Popular Unity Deals the Final Blow to Freedom of Education."

The Ministry of Education took off its mask in the Provincial Congress of Education held the 16th and 17th of this month in Puerto Montt, dealing the final blow to free education in the nation. The irregularities committed by the "new men" in this congress provoked the massive withdrawal of the great majority of the democratic delegates and of those who will defend to the utmost the liberty of education. . . . But the pretences of the government reached their climax when Sr. Victor Brahm asked to speak. The Marxists cut off the microphone, provoking the massive walkout of the delegates at the event; thus the government supporters who were left could approve whatever stupidities they wished, and share among themselves the administrative positions. All of this was directed by the Ministry of Education, which sent Hernan Moreno to supervise the "behavior" of the government supporters and to ensure the consummation of Marxist totalitarianism in the different levels of education. (*La Tribuna*, 27 October 1971)

All of these disputes, both in substance and reporting, were represented almost perfectly in the last and largest provincial congress to be held before the National Congress; that of the province of Santiago, the most populous in the nation, held in late November.

On 27 November *Las Ultimas Noticias*, representing the opposition view, reported as follows:

Only delegates from the government line are participating since last night in the Provincial Congress of Education. . .which started yesterday morning. . . . Around 9:00 PM the following groups walked out of the meeting: Federation of Private School Teachers, Federation of Private School Parents and Guardians, Federation of Private Schools, Federation of Public School Parents and Guardians, Federation of Private School Students, Federation of Public School Secondary Students, Federation of Students of the Catholic University, Mothers' Centers, Neighbourhood Assemblies, the Christian Democratic group, and others who had been asked to participate in the provincial event.

After citing the usual complaints, the article noted that the Federation of Secondary Students of Santiago (FESES) had withdrawn because it received "credentials with falsified seals and the signatures of ghost representatives from the government in FESES, since the government sectors have not yet named their representatives to the directive committee of the organization."[7]

On the same day *La Nacion*, the official government paper, reported the opening speeches of the Popular Unity representatives in detail but did not even mention the walkout. Another view of the walkout was taken by *La Ultima Hora*, which represented the revolutionary wing of the Socialist Party.

> In a preconceived attitude, Christian Democrats and fascists of the ultra-right walked out of the Provincial Congress of Education. . . . The organizing commission for the event has multi-party representation and Christian Democracy is represented there. This commission had unanimously agreed regarding the voting procedures for the first plenary session. However, when the Christian Democrat-rightist sector lost the first vote they used the voting system as an excuse for walking out. The president of the Organizing Commission, Wilfredo Fuentes, pointed out to *Ultima Hora* that the attitude of these sectors follows a preconceived national level plan, and that nothing justified the walkout of delegates who were nominated by their organizations to represent them in the Congress. . . . The event continues normally today, in spite of the sectarian and antidemocratic attitude of the minority sector of Christian Democracy and the right.

In contrast, *El Mercurio* provided on the same day a long, fact-filled, and generally accurate report of what actually had occurred during the turbulent first day of the provincial congress. (*El Mercurio*'s version has been verified by the personal reports of several participants from various political affiliations.) The first problem was long delay in granting credentials to delegates while what the delegates referred to as the "political bureau" met for hours behind closed doors. This committee consisted of four representatives from each of the Popular Unity parties plus four Christian Democratic representatives (who felt themselves outnumbered). This resulted in a postponement of the opening plenary session from 3:00 PM to 6:30 PM. Finally, Fuentes, president of the organizing commission, announced that the plenary session would start even though the process of granting credentials was not yet completed, and the organizing commission could not yet present its report. He proposed that they leave pending until the next day (Saturday) the report of the organizing commission and begin by approving the rules, the agenda, and the working schedule. He then asked for a vote.

Popular Unity supporters agreed, waving their credentials in the air. A Christian Democratic spokesman insisted they could not vote if they did not have the report of the organizing committee and hence did not even know how many delegates there were. Moreover, the president of SUTE himself had assured them that credentials were still being granted. Many other delegates agreed, and it was decided to wait another half hour. At 7:30 PM they started again, and the same impasse occurred. Finally, at 8:30

a member of the organizing commission read a brief résumé of its findings and the debate on basic rules and agenda began. It was agreed that each side would have three speakers, each limited to three minutes of speaking time. At this point the meeting began to disintegrate. Students representing the various parties entered the hall, waved banners, and shouted approval or protest depending upon the political affiliation of the speaker. "Then came the moment in which from all sides, from the Government sector, from that of the opposition, and from those who were completely independent, the debate was raised from the educational to the political level. . .with everything breaking down into face to face arguments, even though it did not arrive at the point where 'the blood flows to the river.' " Then the massive walkout occurred. "Representatives of Popular Unity and of the opposition agreed that the Provincial Congress was poorly organized, which was perhaps one of the factors which led to the breakdown." In a personal letter a colleague summarized all of the reports he had received from participants as "too much politics and too little organization" (3 December 1971).

Both sides drew lessons from this event for the forthcoming National Congress. *El Mercurio* editorialized:

> The sectarian pressure of the popular Unity and CUT is the exclusive cause of the breakdown of the Provincial Congress of Education just held in Santiago. . .[which shows] the true character and objectives of the forthcoming National Congress of Education, to be held in the middle of next month. . . . [It] proves that the intention of Popular Unity has been to tie up the sectors not committed to Marxism in a process in which the minority is deprived of all possibility of modifying a precooked plan, and deprived of all opportunities to express its point of view. . . . They form a prefabricated majority which can be called on to block any suggestion inconvenient to their ends. Of a total of 610 delegates, 265 were from SUTE and CUT, plus 60 from state organizations. In contrast, the quota for parents and guardians was only 26 representatives. (29 November 1971)

The Communist party's *El Siglo* replied a few days later:

> Faithful to their seditious line, the reactionary sectors have been launching these days an intensive publicity effort to distort the character of the Congress and sow alarm and fear among parents with the phantasm of the implantation of a national system of education which will be totalitarian, dogmatic, rigid and intolerant of the beliefs of others and the "values of civilization and culture." This offensive is one of

the many variants of the campaign of terror with which sectors committed to imperialism and the oligarchy are trying to paralyze the march of the people toward the realization of the goals chosen by their own free will. . . . With an exclusionary class criteria they have tried to establish that workers organized in CUT have nothing to say in the National Congress of Education. . . . [This] reveals the reactionary position of the bourgeoisie who appear to consider education as an essentially technical function, but really conceive of and defend it as a privilege reserved for the social sectors with the greatest incomes, which ensures their survival as a directive class. (12 December 1971)

However, if the Communist party was not happy with the attitude of the opposition, it was also not impressed with the official Ministry of Education position. In a commentary in *El Siglo* (27 November 1971), Francisco Villa Lezana observed that the official goal of the forthcoming National Congress, "To propose to the Popular Government a new educational conception which will be consonant with the perspective of the transition toward socialism," far exceeded the real possibilities of such a meeting. Such a new conception would require "hard research work" with people from many sectors and with many skills participating. After reviewing the agenda for the congress and the various ministry documents provided as supports, he stated:

It appears that they have considered fundamentally the sociopolitical aspects which have to be taken into account for the formulation of a future educational policy. But the analysis of the "internal dimension" of education, pedagogical work itself, appears to have been rather overlooked. We believe that any educational policy will lose its effectiveness if in the schools they continue working with methods, techniques, and procedures which are authoritarian, memoristic, repressive, and purely theoretical and individualistic. . . . It is also essential that the analysis of what we understand to be the transition to socialism is carried out with reference to the internal dynamics of education itself, since, although it is true that the educational system is a superstructural form, it has a degree of autonomy that obliges us to undertake an internal analysis.

In its emphasis on the need for careful research in order to develop an educational policy and its concerns with the inner workings of the school, the Communist party continued to be much closer to the position of the Radicals than that of the hard-line Socialists within the Ministry of Education.

STUDENT AND TEACHER ELECTIONS

Just as these disputes over the educational consultative process were beginning to reach a crescendo, two highly politicized and widely publicized elections in the educational sector were held. The first was for the president and members of the central committee of the Federation of Secondary Students of Santiago (FESES). Five slates of candidates contested the election: 1) Popular Unity, including the Communist and Socialist parties, MAPU, and the Christian Left; 2) the Christian Democrats; 3) the Revolutionary Students' Front and Radical Revolutionary Youth (basically MIR); 4) the Independent Movement of the Radical Left; and 5) the National Party and Radical Democrats.

For both government and opposition the election was symbolically important. Reflecting their general line regarding education, Christian Democrats claimed that the government had been attempting to turn the secondary student organization into a political instrument to further its own ends. In their view, FESES should not only be concerned with political problems, but also with cultural, sporting, artistic, social, and educational aspects of students' lives, and it should not simply be a mouthpiece for government policy (See *La Prensa*, 25 September 1971). For students who supported the government, the two central elements of their electoral campaign were "participation by students and consolidation of the educational revolution" (*El Siglo*, 27 September 1971). They spoke of the need for major reform of the educational system with full participation of teachers, administrators, and students and claimed that the Christian Democrats had no moral authority to speak on behalf of students since they had "oppressed students and the people for the six years of the Frei regime" (*La Ultima Hora*, 29 September 1971).

The election was originally scheduled for late September, but it had to be postponed until 6 October because of serious disagreements regarding the eligibility of many schools to participate. Each side accused the other of trying to exclude schools likely to vote against it and to include unqualified schools likely to be in its favor. A number of schools were taken over by students in protest against their exclusion from the official eligibility list. Government and opposition accused each other of being responsible for school occupations and for provoking acts of violence and vandalism. However, moderate government-supporting students such as the Young Communists also complained of the "infantilism and irresponsibility of the ultra-left" (primarily MIR) whose violent behavior provided a propaganda tool for the opposition (*El Siglo,* 6 October 1971).

Christian Democrats accused government officials of openly intervening in the campaign on behalf of Popular Unity candidates. Guillermo Yunge, the Christian Democratic candidate for FESES presidency, stated "I denounce publicly the Director of Secondary Education, the Intendent of Santiago, and the President of FECH [the University of Chile student federation] for openly intervening in a process in which only secondary students should be involved" (*El Mercurio*, 29 September 1971). He claimed that Jorge Espinoza was providing official Ministry of Education credentials to Popular Unity candidates, which permitted them to enter schools and give campaign speeches in any class (see *La Prensa*, 2, 3, and 4 October 1971). Yunge also asserted that one of the Popular Unity candidates was actually a university student and that several, including Alvaro Alarcon, the Popular Unity presidential candidate, were "free students of the Ministry of Education," a legal designation which permitted them to be classified as students even though they were not actively attending any particular school. (FESES regulations at that time permitted such individuals to hold office in the federation [*Ercilla*, 6 October 1971].)

Popular Unity students replied that such charges were "irresponsible" and part of a "hate-filled propaganda campaign" and that Christian Democratic students were making use of their own party's machinery in their election efforts (*La Ultima Hora*, 3 October 1971, and *Puro Chile*, 5 October 1971).[8]

The official results of the election provided a clear victory for the opposition students. The votes received were as follows:

	Percentage of Votes
Popular Unity	36.7
Christian Democracy	41.5
Revolutionary Students' Front and Radical Revolutionary Youth	8.5
Independent Movement of the Radical Left	0.5
National Party and Radical Democracy	7.8
Null or blank	4.8

Christian Democracy was clearly the most potent political force among these urban secondary students. Excluding the null or blank ballots, 52.4 per cent voted for an opposition group, with 47.6 per cent supporting Popular Unity or other left-wing parties. Yunge attributed his victory to the fact that most students understood that one should have a student movement which served the students and not the government. He also claimed that his party's campaign against sectarianism persuaded many students to participate in the elections who had previously not felt themselves represented by extremist groups (*El Clarin*, 9 October 1971). In spite of their campaign complaints about politicization of the student movement, the victors were quick to attach wider political significance to the election. In

Yunge's first press conference after the results were known, he was accompanied by a group of well-known directors of the Christian Democratic party. He asserted that the results indicated support not only for his program within FESES, but also support for the national policies of the party. The opposition press attached particular importance to the results since FESES was the *public* school federation, and the students involved therefore came primarily from working-class and lower middle-class backgrounds, where one would have expected strongest support for Popular Unity. This was particularly important because in just a few more years these students would be old enough to vote in national elections (*La Tercera*, 10 October 1971). *El Mercurio* noted that this was one more in a series of defeats for government supporters in elections within student associations, unions, professional colleges, and other groups, which ought "to convince the Government that its methods are not exactly arousing enthusiasm among the Chilean citizenry" (8 October 1971).

Some government spokesmen claimed that they attached little importance to the results, since only a few schools were involved (*La Tercera*, 10 October 1971), but most agreed that the election "was one of the most important political events, which captured the attention of the entire nation" (*El Clarin*, 8 October 1971). Although some of the explanations for the defeat referred to such things as Yunge's good looks attracting female voters (*Ahora Santiago*, 13 October 1971), most attributed it to: 1) the fact that many students were only recently incorporated into the national political process and were therefore not sufficiently politicized, being easy prey to the "anti-communist" and "anti-Marxist" slogans of the opposition; and 2) the lack of unity among parties of the left (see *La Ultima Hora*, 8 and 10 October 1971; *La Nacion*, 10 October 1971; and *El Siglo*, 9 and 10 October 1971). While there had been an official "Popular Unity" slate, the candidates and press of each constituent party had devoted most of their efforts to promoting their own party's interests, and no agreement was reached with the ultra-left students who received about 8 per cent of the total vote. Even after the election, the Socialist Youth, in an official declaration which lamented the "fatal" lack of unity, could not resist observing that of all the votes cast for Popular Unity slate, 60 per cent were for Socialist Party candidates (*El Siglo*, 10 October 1971).[9]

During November, another widely publicized and symbolically important educational election was held for president and directors of the newly formed SUTE at both the national and provincial levels. This was the first time that members would vote for the leadership of the combined union rather than for the separate groups of which it was composed. Although every party produced and fought for its own separate slate of nominees, the issues, charges, and countercharges between government and opposition were almost identical to those in the FESES campaign.

The process of counting votes from all areas of the nation took some days and was surrounded by complaints of irregularities. Finally, Sergio Astorga, brother of the minister of education and a Radical, was elected national president. He announced that early in December the newly elected national directors would meet for the "definitive establishment" of the organization and that they would make preparations for a national meeting to be held just after the National Congress of Education (*Puro Chile*, 14 November 1971). The final results of the voting, by party, were as follows: (*El Mercurio*, 16 November 1971)

	Percentage of Vote
Radical Party	36.8
Christian Democratic Party	30.2
Socialist Party	20.3
Communist Party	11.5
MAPU	1.1

The government press hailed these figures as a great victory for Popular Unity. Two patterns, however, were particularly noticeable. The Radical party maintained its predominant position within the teaching ranks, receiving more votes than all other Popular Unity parties combined. However weak that party had become in other aspects of national political life, it was still a key force in education. Second, the Christian Democrats, who had controlled none of the separate unions which formed SUTE, had now become the second most powerful party among the teachers, being only about six percentage points behind the Radicals and well ahead of the Socialists and Communists. (SUTE included only *public* school teachers. Christian Democrats were overwhelmingly predominant among private school teachers.)

THE NATIONAL CONGRESS OF EDUCATION

The National Congress of Education finally convened on 13 December and continued until 16 December. After the turbulence and heated arguments of the preceding months, the congress was almost anticlimactic in its relatively calm and orderly deliberations. The Christian Democrats had threatened to refuse to participate if the experience of provincial congresses was repeated. However, they agreed to participate fully after intensive negotiations provided what they regarded as satisfactory guarantees regarding the agenda and procedures. The proposed Law for Democratization of Education, which was the issue that most concerned them, was removed from the agenda. Additionally, since the official voting represen-

tation in the congress was clearly "loaded" in favor of government sup-
'porters, the opposition was guaranteed the right to present minority or
alternative reports and have them published as part of the official proceedings. On the day the congress began, the education department of the Christian Democratic party issued an official proclamation announcing their
decision to participate fully while remaining alert to any attempts by government supporters to distort the proceedings (*La Prensa*, 13 December
1971).

The congress suffered from many of the same administrative and organizational problems which had impeded serious deliberation in the earlier
meetings. The entire first day was taken up with organizational and administrative work. The 996 official voting delegates who were finally registered were divided into four working commissions, each of which had too
many participants to permit substantive debate. Moreover, the leaders of
the organized teachers, who had been expected by the government to be
the main intellectual force in the meeting, were concentrating most of their
energy on organizational details arising from the results of SUTE elections
in November and on preparations for the SUTE conference to be held just
after the National Congress. As a result, the actual work of preparing reports from the several commissions fell to small groups who relied almost
entirely on previously prepared ministry documents. The participants had
available to them almost none of the results of the local, regional, and
provincial meetings, there was very little discussion or debate, and votes
generally followed party lines.

Each of the four commissions was assigned one of the major themes
outlined in the "Second Contribution" prepared by the ministry. The first
commission thus dealt with *The Cultural and Educational Problems and
needs of the Chilean People, and the Tasks of the Construction of Socialism*. Two reports were prepared. The first represented the majority view
and was essentially a condensation of the text of the ministry's "Second
Contribution" on the same theme. The minority report reflected the Christian Democratic viewpoint. It suggested that it was incorrect to think of
Chile solely as a backward or underdeveloped nation, since it was univer-
sally recognized as one of the most advanced Latin American societies,
particularly in the area of education. This did not, however, indicate that
Chile had no problems. "We are still far from the cultural advances of
other countries such as those of Western Europe, the United States, the
Soviet Union, and some nations of Eastern Europe" (*Revista de Educación*, no. 36, 1972, p. 107. All quotes from the proceedings of the National Congress which follow are from this source.) But the alternative report
rejected any explanation of this backwardness which was "merely economic." While condemning capitalism, "both the individualist and the State
variety" (p. 107), it advanced several other explanations of Chile's lack of

advancement. The society suffered from a lack of unity, aggravated by the government's partisan attempts to divide the nation into antagonistic social classes "which it will be impossible to harmonize later" (ibid). Such a situation was even worse when many who had access to government power put the interests of their own particular ideology or political party above the interests of the society as a whole. Excessive bureaucratization and centralization and a tendency to copy foreign models rather than relying on the creative capacity of the Chilean people were also noted. All of these factors made it impossible to arrive at a national consensus regarding educational or social policy.

With respect to education, the minority report emphasized the primordial right of the family with respect to the growth and formation of the student. It suggested that education should help individuals free themselves from all forms of dependency and alienation. It asserted that education was not neutral but committed to man himself and not to some determined ideology or system. The individual was the subject and object of his or her own development, which could only occur in "intimate community" with others. But integration of oneself with the community could only be the result of a freely taken individual decision.

The alternative report addressed itself, at its conclusion, to the concept of socialism.

> At the present moment we recognize the validity of socialism as the channel for the social and educational process, so long as it is understood in terms of liberty, respect for the human person in all its variety and diversity, especially in the educational area, exercise of the critical and creative sense, social solidarity, institutionalized participation of the community, respect for pluralism, and the development of structures which enable man to not be affected by either state or private ownership of the means of production. (p. 108)

Another commission focussed on *The Policy of Educational Democratization: An Immediate Response to the Exigencies of a New Education.* It also produced two reports, a majority one which faithfully repeated the main ideas in the government's discussion guide and a minority alternative which reflected the Christian Democratic line. This minority report contained a strong defense of private education, emphasizing that the state was not the only agent of education and that it should neither monopolize education nor insist that all schools follow a single ideological orientation. It also rejected the proposition that the mass media should be monopolized by the state.

The most fundamental difference between the two reports, however, was in their understanding of the role of the state in the process of participation and democratization. The majority report placed great emphasis on the participation of the state, representing the people, as the most effective guarantee of democratization. In contrast, the minority report emphasized the direct participation of the community and insisted upon limitations on the power of the state to impose its will upon dissenting groups. This difference related to the even more basic question of the legitimacy of a minority government such as Popular Unity and reflected deep differences in the understanding of the role of the state.

Although Popular Unity forces regularly referred to themselves as the government "of the people," it was clear to all that the most they could claim was that half of the population (as expressed in the municipal elections early in the year) supported them. The stance of the other half ranged from worried neutrality to violent opposition. Within this context, a predominant attitude within the government was that they could and should use the instruments of the state available to them to consolidate and spread their power. This was well captured in the slogan which terminated MAPU's contribution to the Congress of Education documentation: "TO CONVERT VICTORY INTO POWER AND POWER INTO SOCIALISM" (MAPU, 1971, p. 6). Such an attitude was anathema to those in the opposition who regarded the Popular Unity government as representing at best a substantial minority with no legitimate right to impose its worldview on the majority. On the day the National Congress opened, *El Mercurio* clearly stated this opposition view (13 December 1971).

It is not true that the country aspires to and believes in revolutionary change. A sector of it, committed to Marxism, will adhere to this point of view, but there are other sectors of the citizenry which repudiate it. It would be very grave if the new education, as it is called, supports revolutionary changes founded on the belief that the majority of the nation wants them. This is an error that should be quickly eliminated, above all because there are clear constitutional provisions forbidding the political manipulation of education in our nation.

Another commission dealt with *Planning and the National System of Education in the Transition to Socialism*. This group developed a single report, which also closely followed the relevant section of the ministry's position paper. What appears to have made consensus possible, however, was the elimination of the highly controversial portion of the "Second Contribution" dealing with the political orientation of education in forming the New Man, which had been seen as a considerable limitation on the meaning of educational pluralism. The offending text was replaced by the following phrases:

The formation of this new man is the great social task which we are going to complete before the twenty-first century arrives. For this we need a new education. This new education will not be opposed to the practice of ideological pluralism. We respect, and will respect, all manifestations of thought. The new education will not have a single-party or dogmatic orientation in its content. It will have a scientific orientation, and will seek the formation of personalities able to investigate and construct for themselves their own conception of the world. (p. 110)

The fourth commission dealt with *The National Unified School as the Representative Institution of the New Education.* As with the commission just discussed, this group produced a single report. It was also very similar to the section of the "Second Contribution" which discussed the National Unified School. However, attached to it was a qualifying motion, advanced by the National Association of Parent Centers and the Federation of Private School Parents and Guardians and approved by a majority vote of the commission. The qualifying clause read as follows:

As parents we are the primary and undeniable educators of our children, and we delegate this function to the school, integrating ourselves into the educational process through the School Community. Therefore, it is not society which delegates the educational function to the school, but *parents as individuals.* As such, we have, and will defend, the right to search for the type of school and/or education we desire for our children. We conceive of the School Community as the organic integration of all the social estates *committed to* the educational process. This School Community would consist of the following basic groups or estates: 1) parents and guardians; 2) students; 3) teachers; 4) auxiliary school personnel; 5) community organizations if they are actively collaborating in the process (such as unions, mothers' centers, neighborhood centers, etc.) but only if they are providing educational support, and not simply because they exist. We advocate an education which liberates people, which seeks their integral development, as well as the development of a critical spirit with reference to the various alternatives provided to them. We recognize that to some degree education has been classist, and we advocate an equalitarian education (equal opportunity for all), which would mean that it should be free of cost. The National Unified School ought to be based on the formation of these School Communities, one for each establishment. (p. 124)

Approval of such a motion by the majority of government representatives on the commission represented a significant move away from the hard-line position found in the documents produced by the Ministry of Education.

Thus, the published reports from the National Congress of Education represented what the government had officially promised and what the opposition had fought for: pluralism and compromise. In the two commissions where a single report was presented, the documents showed considerable softening of key ministry arguments. The other two commissions, in which such consensus could not be reached, produced majority and minority reports, clearly reflecting the opposing worldviews of the participants.

But if the work of the commissions produced a certain sense of compromise between government and opposition, that feeling was eliminated in the final plenary session. After the formal presentation of the various reports, several concluding speeches were delivered. The most important of these was by Ivan Nuñez in his capacity as superintendent of education. In attacking the minority (Thesis B) reports, he outlined the position of the revolutionary socialists in the Ministry of Education more clearly and succinctly than in any of the previous documents and speeches produced by this group. The speech was perceived by the opposition and by the soft-line members of the Ministry of Education as representing what the hard-line Socialists wanted to do with education. Given both the occasion and the content, it was a political landmark. After an introduction which referred to the pleasure of seeing this long-hoped-for meeting coming to a conclusion within the context of a national transition to socialism, Nuñez continued:

> It would be very easy for us to succumb to the romanticism of unity, to succumb to the romanticism of a dry pluralism; it would be very easy to try to reach agreement through pretty phrases, through common ground. However, we believe that this Congress was called together to contribute to an ideological conquest, to contribute to an effective clarification of the real and concrete problems we have to face. It is for this reason that, although we could subscribe to many of the phrases, much of the verbalism, of Thesis B, we see ourselves obliged to clear the field, to clearly identify the modes of thought represented here, so that, later, history can tell us who was right.
>
> They speak to us of a liberating education which is committed only to man, an education which is neither subject to nor committed to any system or ideology, but thereafter they display for us an ideology which underlies the kind of education which they, the comrades of Thesis B, want to maintain in this country. We claim that education has to have an ideological foundation, and that it is a good thing that we are discussing what will be the ideological foundation for the new education we are going to build. . . . It appears to us that the ideology of Thesis B is juggling with reality, is hiding reality. We respect the

thinking, we respect all the workers who are here, we respect them as workers, we respect them because we know that there are no oligarchs here, nor imperialists, nor big businessmen; we respect as persons these workers who have come to this Congress. But we do not respect their ideas, and we think they are in error, and it is right and legitimate and pluralist for us to say that they are in error. Who is in favor, we ask, of hiding the fact that in this country, and in humanity as a whole, there is a class struggle. Who is in favor of trying to make us believe that there is a real national unity. . . . [Here he was interrupted by shouts from the audience.]

We are exercising our legitimate right to discuss, to feel, indeed to identify and criticize the ideas of those who are opposed to us. We believe we have earned this right, that this right reflects a new democracy which is growing, a democracy in which we workers can express our point of view. It is probable that a little while ago if we had expressed these same thoughts in public we would have been subject to legal sanctions, or we would probably have been thrown in jail. We say that it is not possible to have national unity with Edwards,[10] that it is not possible to have either unity or dialogue with Benevente, the large landowner who killed Hernan Mery,[11] that it is not possible to have unity with the people who killed Schneider. It is possible, and we desire, to have unity with you workers, with you students, with you comrade teachers, but not with those who still have power, not with those who are cheating us, not with those who are introducing to the people ideas such as we have seen here. And we claim that classes exist, and that classes have antagonistic interests, and that classes also fight in education, even though through third parties. We claim that it is impossible to assume some kind of national unity when there still exist in this country profound contradictions that have not been overcome, and will not be rapidly or easily overcome, when there are antagonistic interests and ways of life that are different. Thus we have to take a stand, to indicate what side we are on in these lifeless societies, because this is the reality, the side we are on, the stand we take. Chile is an abstraction; what are concrete and real are social classes, and a majority which is exploited and humiliated.

Thus, we have indicated our educational position, we have delivered it clearly and in writing. We accept responsibility for what we have said, and for what we are going to do. We invite this National Congress of Education. . .to join us in the work we are beginning, to overcome the interests that would divide us, to overcome those who would camouflage reality, to overcome those who consciously or unconsciously are representing the past, who are representing a capitalism which has been liquidated by history, but who are still hiding behind a verbalism we have thought it useful to denounce. Nothing more. Many thanks. (pp. 124-25)

Thus ended the National Congress of Education and the Popular Unity government's attempt at widespread consultation regarding educational policy.[12] The process had contributed more to sharpening and clarifying divisions, both between the government and the opposition, and between factions within the government, than it had contributed to the formation of a national agreement regarding educational policy. Given the general political situation, such an agreement would have been impossible to achieve, for the educational disputes were central to the arguments regarding the fundamental legitimacy of the Popular Unity regime itself. Given the over-all political situation, it was remarkable that the working commissions of the National Congress had managed to reach a degree of accord, or at least an "agreement to disagree." It was even more characteristic of the time that even that minimal degree of accord was immediately ruptured by Nuñez' speech. The next question was, what would the government do with the results of this massive effort at consultation?

7

Educational Calm Amid Growing Politicial Crisis January to October, 1972

During the first months of 1972 it appeared that the government was going to do nothing with the results of the National Congress of Education. Disputes over educational policy virtually disappeared from the pages of the mass media as the public's attention was focussed on other aspects of a growing political and economic crisis.

In January, two key by-elections were held, one for a vacant senate seat representing the provinces of Colchagua and O'Higgins, the other for a position as deputy from the province of Linares. This was the first test of electoral strength since the municipal elections nearly a year before. The Popular Unity candidates lost in both elections. In one sense this was not surprising since the seats had previously been held by the opposition. However, careful comparisons with the results of the municipal elections indicated that Popular Unity had lost support (in the range of five to ten percentage points) everywhere, including locales with heavy concentrations of miners, industrial workers, and peasants who had directly benefited from the massively increased land reform.

Allende's immediate response was a cabinet reorganization to attempt to broaden his base of support. One consequence was that Mario Astorga was replaced as minister of education by Antonio Rios Valdivia, who had previously been minister of defense. Rios Valdivia was a Radical and a retired teacher at the military academy. He had achieved a reputation as an excellent teacher, and almost all of the high-ranking officers in the armed forces were his former students. This close connection with the military gave him a power base outside of the traditional political party structure. In early February he announced that his four initial goals would be:

1) to sharply increase teacher salaries; 2) to build more schools; 3) to eliminate party appointments in the ministry and replace them with appointments based solely upon merit; and 4) to reform the Ministry of Education administratively.

The by-election defeats were also a major subject of discussion during a meeting of representatives from all the parties and movements in Popular Unity held in early February in El Arrayan, a suburb of Santiago. The meeting was intended as an exercise in self-criticism and analysis of the accomplishments and problems of the first fifteen months of the regime. The results were published in *El Mercurio* on 10 February. Much of the document was devoted to recapitulating the achievements of the government and establishing general targets for the future in the various policy sectors.

One thing which was very evident was that *educational* policy change had low priority within the government's program. In the closely printed text the only mentions of education were three sentences referring to enrolment increases during 1971 and the following statement in the section dealing with tasks for the future: "We also have to redouble our effort to reach goals already established for the benefit of children and young people, and to undertake new efforts in the field of education, sport, culture, and the active participation of youth in the process in which we are living. It is urgent to multiply the number of nursery schools." This was not exactly a ringing endorsement of the conclusions from the National Congress of Education, held just over a month before with so much media attention!

What was most important about the meeting, however, was that it showed that splits within Popular Unity were becoming more serious. The official report recognized that disagreements between parties in the coalition were still a major problem. The first substantive paragraph began:

> The analysis carried out made clear, once again, the agreement of all the parties of Popular Unity with the central programmatic objectives. Nevertheless, it is recognized that this basic agreement has not yet been translated into a unified organization for practical work nor into modalities of common labor which overcome strictly party interests.

A few paragraphs further, the report continued:

> It is clear that our labor is incompatible with sectarian attitudes and procedures, whose persistence was recognized as another notorious deficiency which has to be corrected. . . . We propose to eliminate the sectarianism which has been seen in the relations between the parties of Popular Unity itself, which slows down the common work and leads to unjust types of competition in the recruitment of party militants

and attempts to parcel out sectors of public administration, socialized enterprises, and spheres of influence.

The major internal problem involved the deepening split between the two sectors of Popular Unity: 1) the hard-line wing which favored rapid radicalization of the revolution and which now included MIR (not officially a member of the coalition, but cooperating), the revolutionary wing of the Socialist Party, led by the party's Secretary General, Senator Carlos Altimarano, and MAPU (except for its founding leaders who had split to join the Christian Left); and 2) the soft-line wing, still favoring gradualism and legality, which included the Communists, the Radicals, and Allende's sector of the Socialists (Sigmund, 1977, p. 167). The Communist party produced an analysis of the by-elections which strongly attacked the hard-liners as being responsible for the defeats. MIR responded with a position paper blaming the Communists. These internal documents were leaked to *El Mercurio*, which published them along with the official report.

Another consequence of the by-election defeats and the El Arrayan meetings was an agreement among the coalition members that for the March 1973 elections they would form an electoral confederation to nominate single Popular Unity candidates for each congressional seat, rather than allowing each party to have its own candidates. An agreement was then negotiated with the opposition to permit each side to present such a combined list in those elections. This formalized in the electoral process the increasingly polarized state of the society as a whole.

As Chileans returned from their summer holidays, the central political issue was the problem of legal control of government takeovers of economic enterprises and formal clarification of the limits of the three areas into which the economy was to be divided: the area of social property, the area of private property, and the mixed area. In February, the constitutional amendment to limit the government's behavior in taking over private enterprises proposed by the Christian Democrats a few months earlier was approved by the Congress. It immediately became lost in a complex tangle of legal and constitutional arguments between government and opposition. The fundamental difficulty, however, was a stalemate between the legislative and executive branches. Since the opposition controlled the legislature, it could effectively block any law proposed by the government of which it disapproved, which would include almost any initiative really important to the government. This forced the government to resort to precisely the quasi-legal means to which the opposition objected. The opposition, on the other hand, could pass almost any bill in the legislature, as it did with the constitutional amendment on the areas of the economy, but it lacked the two-thirds majority required to override a predictable presidential veto.

Negotiations outside of standard institutional channels were the only way out. As noted in Chapter 2, such negotiations, managed by "honest brokers" from centrist parties, had been a traditional feature of the long-standing stability of the Chilean political system. The increasing polarization evident in the early months of 1972, with the legitimacy of the government and its program at issue, made such negotiations more and more difficult. Centrist negotiators from both sides increasingly found their efforts thwarted by their more extreme colleagues.

Early in the year, the radical minister of justice, Jorge Tapia,[1] negotiated an agreement regarding the limits of the three areas of the economy with the Christian Democrats.[2] The hard-line elements of Popular Unity promptly rejected the compromise. With this failure of negotiations, both sides turned increasingly to the politics of mass mobilization in the form of large demonstrations and counterdemonstrations in the streets, plazas, and stadiums of the nation, with both government and opposition trying to show by the number of bodies demonstrating that they had the greater degree of popular support. These demonstrations were frequently accompanied by street violence. According to Augusto Pinochet, in an interview conducted after the military coup, it was at this time, in April 1972, that the general staff of the armed forces first began to discuss the political situation and concluded that the "conflict between the executive and the legislature will not have a constitutional solution" (*Ercilla*, 12 March 1974).

Meanwhile, throughout 1972 the economic situation was deteriorating rapidly. Industrial, mining, and agricultural production were all dropping dramatically. At the same time, the money supply was continually increased to support the redistributive policies of the government and to save large firms taken over by the government from bankruptcy caused by inefficient management, labor indiscipline and the chaotic policies of the government. In combination, these factors led to shortages of basic consumer goods and a rapid rise in the rate of inflation. By mid-1972 long line-ups for such essential items as bread, cooking oil, meat, kerosene for heating homes, babies' diapers, and so forth were becoming a standard feature of Chilean life. During 1971 the inflation rate had been held to about 22 per cent; for the period January 1972 to January 1973 it was 180.3 per cent (Valenzuela, 1978, p. 65).[3]

Faced with growing political and economic crises, the parties of Popular Unity held another "self-evaluation" meeting in early June in another Santiago suburb, Lo Curro. Here the confrontation between the two wings of the coalition was even more apparent and more bitter. After long debate, "the conflict was resolved with the triumph of the Communist party strategy, which included a policy of wage and price adjustments and a new attempt to negotiate a common definition of the Social Property Sector with the Christian Democrats" (Tapia, 1979a, p. 49).

Negotiations, at first secret but later made public, between Jorge Tapia and Renan Fuentealba, leader of the centrist faction of the Christian Democrats, began immediately. They were able to reach substantial agreement on most of the major conflicts between the government and the opposition. Some issues remained unresolved, and implementation of the accords would have involved careful compromises within the legislature, but as Valenzuela notes:

> Nevertheless, fundamental issues were settled. These issues were at the core of the primary disputes between the government and the largest opposition party and their resolution would have helped to defuse much of the confrontation. Even if elements on both extremes, Right and Left, had balked, an agreement by the Center could have gone a long way toward consolidating a process of change, albeit more gradual. (1978, p. 76)

But once again an agreement reached by moderate, centrist elements from both sides was rejected by the extremes. Each side blamed the other for the failure. Conservative Christian Democrats and their colleagues from the more rightist opposition were the first to publicly reject the agreement and hence bear most of the responsibility for the failure. It does not seem likely, however, that even if the opposition had agreed to support the results of the negotiations, the hard-line elements within Popular Unity would have been prepared to accept them, for the government side had already moved further than had the Christian Democrats in attempting to reach a compromise. With this failure of negotiations, the political style changed from mass mobilization with occasional confrontation to naked confrontation with no institutional checks.

> No longer would it be a matter of increasing bargaining stakes by filling more corners of the Plaza Bulnes or more seats in the national stadium. The clear message of the aborted negotiations—that resolution of the Chilean crisis could only come from winning or losing decisively in the 1973 congressional elections eight months later—led to an unprecedented effort by a multitude of political actors to prove *actual* as opposed to potential power capability. Political mobilization became political confrontation. As early as August, 1972 a rash of confrontations took place between the government and its supporters and groups on both the Left and Right. (Valenzuela, 1978, p. 78)

These confrontations continued to grow in intensity until what became known as the "October crisis" paralyzed the nation. It started on 11 October in the remote southern province of Aysén, where independent truckers went on strike in protest against an announced plan to establish a public trucking enterprise on the grounds of inefficiency in the private sector. They claimed that their problems were caused by the government's own mismanagement, which made it impossible for them to acquire spare parts. They were joined by the national truckers' federation, and the strike soon spread to shopkeepers, merchants, professional associations, and large sectors of the organized peasantry. At its height it was estimated that the strike involved 100 per cent of transport, 97 per cent of commerce, 80 per cent of the professions, and 85 per cent of peasant cooperatives, involving between six and seven hundred thousand citizens (Sigmund, 1977, p. 186). It was very much a middle-class strike, seeming to give vent to long pent up frustrations of the key middle sectors of society, who, according to a poll published shortly before the strike, felt themselves to be the group most adversely affected by the Allende government's policies (*Ercilla*, 13 September 1972). The confrontation had now passed completely outside of normal institutional channels, and traditional negotiation procedures were failing to resolve the national crisis, which was worsening day by day during October. The government could do nothing to stop it, and the opposition parties could not control or contain it (Tapia, 1979a, p. 50). "The politicians had had their day. There was only one other institution which could fill the political vacuum and make it possible for the 1973 elections to take place at all. That institution was the Chilean military" (Valenzuela, 1978, p. 80). During the last week of the month, Allende reorganized his cabinet, bringing into it several key military figures. Although this resolved the immediate problem, it marked as well "the beginning of the end of civilian rule" (Sigmund, 1977, p. 187).

Bringing the military into the cabinet also had an important effect upon the balance of forces within the government since it strengthened the moderates. Expansion of the social property sector, using the methods to which the opposition had been objecting, was sharply curtailed. Moreover, "the government adopted a conservative stance toward the organizational capacity of important working-class and popular sectors. Not only was popular mobilization neither taken advantage of nor institutionalized but, on the contrary it was gradually dismantled. As a result, new conflicts between the Communist and Socialist parties appeared within the coalition" (Tapia, 1979a, p. 52).

EDUCATIONAL POLICY FORMATION EARLY IN THE YEAR

Against this background of deepening conflict, the educational policy formation process slowly unfolded during the first months of 1972. At first little was done within the ministry to follow up on the reports of the

National Congress of Education. The El Arrayan meeting had not suggested any desire on the part of the government for major educational policy change, and such change was not among the stated priorities of the new minister of education.

Reflecting the objectives of the minister, a major study was undertaken of the administrative systems within the ministry, which ultimately produced some significant improvements. However, at its inception this study suffered from the internal sectarianism which the El Arrayan meeting had condemned. The idea was strongly resisted by Communists and Socialists and was not enthusiastically received by all of the Radicals. The person in charge of the project within the ministry, an Allendista Socialist, had tried for more than a month to get an interview with the director of secondary education (now Aida Migone, another Communist who had replaced Jorge Espinoza early in 1972) in order to get permission to distribute questionnaires in the ministry. She refused to see him. It was also impossible to get approval for such a study within the planning and budget office. Assistance was requested from Unesco to bring in a team of outside advisers. It was only when the team was structured to represent the interests of all major parties that the administrative study was approved. One member of the team requested from Unesco was the dean of the Polytechnical University in Moscow. In the words of the project organizer, "When the Communists heard this they applauded, and were suddenly interested in the project. To satisfy the Socialists I brought in a socialist from Spain. To satisfy the Radicals I requested a Belgian sociologist who was a kind of radical. That's how it was."

Meanwhile, Nuñez, who interpreted the majority reports from the National Congress of Education as "recommendations," could not get Rios Valdivia to take action on them. As Nuñez saw it, the new minister was an old man who "had his own rhythm." He did not appear to understand fully the role of the superintendency of education and, therefore, of Nuñez; he told Nuñez that if he had been still at the Ministry of Defense he would have thought of the superintendency as his general staff. But "it was hard to get close to him, and to get him to take the decision to move on substantive changes" (interview with Ivan Nuñez, 15 December 1980).

Finally in May two internal commissions were formed to develop concrete policy propositions regarding: 1) a Decree for Democratization of Education; and 2) the National Unified School. The ministry's desire was to get the local, regional, and national councils foreseen under the idea of democratization into place and then turn to implementation of the new kind of school. This is precisely what the Christian Democrats most feared: that the government would establish, under the rubric of democratization, councils which it could control and then use these to implement whatever other policies it wished. Therefore, Nuñez, Araya, and Gonzalez, three of the four men who had prepared the ministry's position papers for the National Congress, were assigned to the first commission, and lower level officials from the planning office and the Center for In-Service Training were assigned to the second. The idea was that when the high-level team finished its work on the Decree for Democratization, it could then move on to the National Unified School proposal and take advantage of the preliminary work already done by the second commission.

As they started their work, each commission had available not only the reports of the National Congress and all of the background papers from that event and the preceding lower level congresses, but also two documents prepared as summaries of the congress results. One was written by Hugo Araya, the other by Roberto Balocchi, a Socialist from the educational planning office. Both of these were more nearly *interpretations* than *summaries*; each reflected the position of the party its author represented.

Araya saw his document, which was entitled "Immediate Measures for Democratization for the Year 1972 Derived from the Conclusions of the First National Congress of Education," as a kind of detailed appendix to the document he had written just before the inauguration, taking into account the deliberations in the National Congress (interview with Hugo Araya, 8 May 1981). Reflecting Araya's ideological position, it referred to the new society to be constructed as a form of "democratic socialism" and asserted that educational change was not simply a response to societal change but an integral part of the change process. Some forty-five concrete measures were proposed, divided into those which required a change in law, those which required a new decree, and those which could be implemented under existing laws and regulations. With reference to democratization of education, he proposed that a system of regional, provincial, local, and school councils be quickly established by decree but suggested that the same decree should change the structure of the school system by adding an additional year to primary education (which had never been discussed at the National Congress). Araya also asserted that the National Unified School concept would take years to implement through careful experimentation. He suggested that implementation start by: 1) naming all of the existing consolidated schools as National Unified Schools; 2) allowing local directors of education to propose to the government the formation of "educational complexes" which would involve a planned linkage of already existing educational facilities in a given locale, urban or rural; and 3) establishing such "consolidated" or "linked" schools in each agricultural area expropriated by the agricultural reform agency.[4]

Balocchi's document, on the other hand, was a clear reflection of the hard-line Socialist position. Even its title was indicative: "Synthesis of the Reports of the Commissions of *and the Contributions to* the First National Congress of Education" (emphasis added). It was indeed more a summary of the controversial position papers prepared for the National Congress than of the congress itself. Although it referred to "socialist humanism" as the ultimate goal, it constantly used the word "revolutionary" when referring to education. Education's goal should be the "formation of a revolutionary consciousness" or "ensuring an ideological development capable of creating the new man, in solidarity with his class, and committed to the goal of revolutionary transformation of society. . . . In a society in which the workers have achieved political power, education has the revolutionary task of supporting the conquest and consolidation of economic power and total power." Although it claimed to reflect opposition thinking as expressed in alternative reports from the National Congress, these were edited in such a way that phrases central to the opposition view were removed from direct quotations. For example, in reporting the opposition alternative from the first commission of the congress, Balocchi eliminated a reference to "respect for pluralism" and the phrase which stated that education should not be committed "to a determined ideology." In addition, the document suggested that the Ministry of Education should have complete control over mass communications media and that private education should be totally absorbed by the national system. Both of these propositions were violently opposed by non-government forces.

The commission charged with preparation of the Decree of Democratization worked quickly and had a first report ready for the National Council of Education in June. Before it could be seriously discussed, however, there was another change in ministers as part of a cabinet reorganization.

ANIBAL PALMA BECOMES MINISTER OF EDUCATION

The new minister, Anibal Palma, was a dramatic change. Rios Valdivia had been the epitome of a traditional education minister in Chile, a powerful representative of a previous generation. During his brief tenure, he had issued decrees insisting that secondary school boys had to have their hair cut relatively short and that girls had to wear skirts which came down at least to their knees—this in an era when long hair in the Che Guevara style and mini-skirts were much in fashion among the young whom the government was trying to recruit. Allende wanted the new minister to be young and dynamic, someone who would provide a new image and who could work well with students. He also wanted someone who, like Rios Valdivia, did not have a history of association with the internal bureaucratic disputes within the ministry, but who also had a reputation for being able to move items from discussion to action. The new person also had to be a Radical.

Palma had been serving as sub-secretary in the Ministry of Foreign Relations, and in this post he had made a favorable impression. He had forcefully represented Chile at the meeting of the Organization of American States where revelations regarding ITT's attempted intervention during the period between the presidential election and inauguration were discussed, and he had played a key role as government spokesman during meetings of the United Nations Commission for Trade and Development in Santiago. He had been a student leader as a young man and later a university professor. As a powerful figure within the Radical Party and within the government, Palma was generally aware of the educational issues, but he was chosen for his personal characteristics and his friendly relationship with the president. As Palma understood it, his job was not simply to represent a new image and establish good working relationships with activist students, but also to start moving the agenda of policy issues which had been discussed and, in the ministry's view, agreed upon, at the National Congress of Education (interview with Anibal Palma, 12 December 1981).

Although the commission which prepared the proposal for a Decree of Democratization was urging that it be quickly approved and promulgated, Palma agreed to demands in the National Council of Education that all the organizations represented there be given time to study and comment upon the proposition. No action would be taken until all sectors were heard from. Again the problem of ministerial credibility arose—could the minister's stand be taken seriously given the position of other powerful figures in his organization? Palma had to restate his position publicly on several occasions. For example, on 29 June, in a speech to the annual meeting of the Parents and Guardians Association of Las Condes (the wealthiest municipality in Santiago), he noted:

> We have no intention of putting into practice any project of this nature until we have the opinions and participation of all interested sectors. Thus we have given copies of the project to FESES, to SUTE, to various parent groups, and to all those who are committed, like yourselves, so they can analyze it and give us their observations, with the absolute security that all sectors will be heard and all opinions considered, because in matters of this sort neither sectarian nor exclusivist criteria can be applied. . . . If there are sectors that want to politicize this problem, I say don't do it; there is no political interest in this matter. We want the opinions of all sectors, and we will not take any precipitate steps, because if there is any matter where it is worthwhile to wait and consult all sectors, it is in anything that has to do with education. (Palma, 1972a)

In spite of the increasingly tense political climate, the discussion which ensued within various groups and in the National Council of Education was calm and deliberate. Objections to various aspects of the proposed decree were put as "observations," with the understanding that they would be seriously considered. The Permanent Committee of Private Education, which represented the interests of those who had potentially most to lose as a result of changes in government policy, produced for the National Council a document of only three pages, two of which simply summarized the decree. The third page contained a series of rather gently worded requests for clarification of terms and concepts as they might relate to private education and, finally, the observation that, "given the various instances of decentralization announced in the document, and agreeing with the basic idea, Private Education claims its just right to be truly and proportionally represented wherever that is appropriate" (Comite Permanente de la Educación Particular, 1972).

By this time, members of the National Council of Education were finding themselves increasingly confused by the array of documents, alternative documents, and replies to documents which were coming to them, all purporting to relate to the results of the National Congress. These reflected the debate that was ongoing *within* the government. Ernesto Livacic, the dominant opposition spokesman in the council, has noted that this proliferation of documents made work very confusing. They never knew which documents, from where, would be brought forth for discussion until receiving agenda material shortly before a meeting. For opposition members, it was difficult to get a clear idea of the central thrusts of the emerging government policy, or indeed to discern if there were such thrusts (interview with Ernesto Livacic, 24 September 1982). The council therefore decided to establish a small committee with equal representation from government and opposition to go through all of the reports and documents and try to identify points of agreement which might form the basis for widely acceptable changes in education. The committee consisted of Araya and Videla from the government side; from the opposition, there were Livacic and Bernardino Silva as a representative of private education. The group's nine-page report (Consejo Nacional de Educación, 1972), which was discussed and approved by the council in late July, was a model of brevity and careful compromise. The last two pages were concise but faithful representations of the central disagreements between government and opposition reports in the National Congress. The preceding seven pages, labelled "points of agreement," quoted those parts of the government alternative reports least likely to offend the opposition and developed a conception of society and education which clearly reflected the joint views of the reformist wing of Popular Unity and the centrist wing of the Christian Democrats. For example:

The socialist society, especially that based on socialist humanism, is opposed to all types of oppressive alienation and exploitation of people, opposing therefore both capitalist individualism and any form of totalitarianism. It organizes all economic goods for the service of the integral development of the person as a function of the common welfare. The socialist society to which we aspire has the following characteristics: free, formed by persons who are protagonists of history, democratic, critical, pluralistic, perfectible, and solidary. In this socialist society there must exist an equilibrium between the value of the person and the society as a whole, so as to fall into neither individualism nor sectarianism.

While awaiting the results of these consultations, Palma undertook several policy initiatives which were designed to indicate that the government intended to move ahead with reference to democratization and the National Unified School, but in directions which he assumed, correctly as it turned out, to be non-controversial. In early July a decree was issued which provided a foretaste of the democratization principle. Student and parent representatives were permitted to participate in meetings of the teachers in a school when they were discussing non-academic matters. This degree of participation in decision-making had already been accomplished in many schools, including many private schools. The measure encountered no opposition whatsoever. Even the most right-wing opponents of the government could not object seriously to a decree which extended to the entire system something which was already being done in the elite schools their own children attended.

A national campaign for maintenance and repair of schools was also announced. It was clear to the ministry that the number of schools in badly deteriorated physical condition was so large that the government could not possibly finance repairs and maintenance out of its own budget. Therefore, a system was established which permitted responsibility for upkeep to be assumed by local school communities, consisting of teachers, students, parents, community organizations involved with education, and local industry. This system tapped directly into the definition of school community which had been advanced by the National Association of Parent Centers and the Federation of Private School Parents and Guardians in the fourth commission of the National Congress of Education. An extensive publicity campaign was mounted, and the national organization of construction firms, business enterprises, and other groups quickly became involved in this attempt to bring all elements of communities into connection with their local schools.

As an early signal of the National Unified School (ENU) idea, two "superior institutes of education" were established. These used the facilities of existing secondary-level technical-professional schools to provide post-secondary short courses in technical occupations, high-level executive secretarial skills, and the like. They were designed to be the first of a nationwide system of institutions which, it was hoped, would take some of the pressure off university enrolments. Again, there was no significant opposition.

THE POLITICIZATION OF STUDENT TURBULENCE

Just as the process of deliberate but rapid policy formation under Palma's leadership was beginning to gain momentum within the ministry, the shift to confrontation politics resulting from the failure of the negotiations between Tapia and Fuentealba in June produced a qualitative change in the nature of student activism. A series of dramatic confrontations in the nation's secondary schools occurred which were occasions of extensive and highly partisan media coverage. Once begun, they occupied almost all of the new minister's attention and within months drove him out of office. This was particularly ironic since one of the reasons Palma had been chosen as minister was precisely his predicted ability to deal equally with politically active students.

School takeovers and often violent street demonstrations by secondary students were a longstanding feature of Chilean life. Such incidents had increased in number during the Popular Unity regime, but qualitatively they were little different from student activities during the Frei government. As an example of the frequency of such events, in the last two months of the 1970 school year and the first four months of the 1971 school year the Santiago press reported a total of eighty-six separate school occupations or student strikes, and not all incidents, especially those occurring outside of Santiago, were reported. This was a reasonably typical number.

Since part of Palma's mandate was the improvement of relationships with students, as soon as he was installed as minister he held a series of meetings with their leaders in an attempt to establish working relationships which might avoid conflict. During these initial conversations, which he perceived to be productive, he offered space and facilities within the ministry of education to all of the student federation leaders. FESES,[5] controlled by the Christian Democrats, was the only federation which refused this offer, saying that they already had their own headquarters and did not need additional space.

In late July Palma left the country to attend an international meeting. At the time everything in his jurisdiction seemed to be quite calm. He returned in early August to discover that what had at first seemed to be another routine takeover of a school by a faction of its students was very rapidly becoming politicized. The school was Liceo No. 13 for Girls in Santiago. The issue involved had started about a year earlier as an internal dispute. This particular school had functioned very well for many years with a well-respected director and team of teachers. Although not one of the few "great" schools, it had acquired a substantial reputation. A year earlier the director had retired, and a provisional director was named to serve until the cumbersome bureaucratic process for selection of a permanent director could be completed.[6] The provisional director, Mirta Castillo, had applied for the permanent post, along with many other candidates, but Palma had not yet made his decision.

From the first day she entered the school, there had been continuing conflict between the provisional director and a large faction of the student body. The school had been occupied briefly on several occasions during the year. However, FESES leadership was actively involved in supporting this latest occupation, which began on 3 August, and opposition political figures were beginning to come to the school and make public statements in support of the occupying students. Their demand was simple: that Castillo not be appointed permanent director. She was a Radical (although the opposition press sometimes labelled her a "Communist" or "Marxist"). To Palma, however, the problem within the school appeared to be basically interpersonal: a vocal and politically active group of students simply could not get along with this particular person. On several occasions the student leaders told the minister: "Appoint a Communist, appoint someone from MIR, but just don't appoint Señora Castillo."

Palma met with the students and told them that he would judge the case solely on its merits after having carefully examined all of the credentials of the short-listed candidates. But he said that he would only do this after the students had returned the school to its normal functioning. This was an extremely important point to the minister, since he did not want to appear to be making a decision under student pressure. In his view, this would have created a damaging precedent, which would have been demoralizing for and rejected by all of the teaching force, whatever their political affiliation. If he allowed this particular promotion to be decided, or appear to be decided, on the basis of pressure, then ultimately no teacher's career would be safe. Moreover, when he became minister, Palma had publicly promised that all educational appointments would be based solely on merit.

Palma then met with the parents of the students who had taken over the school. He explained his view of the situation and what he could and could not do. They agreed to try to persuade their children to stop the occupation, but the parents were unable to move them.

After examining all of the credentials, the minister determined that the best candidate was Señora Castillo. Since the students were clearly not prepared to leave the school, he announced his decision and published with it a comparative analysis of the credentials. The opposition (by now this had become not just a student issue but a major public political issue) then shifted ground, arguing that the short-list itself had been manipulated so that Señora Castillo would be the obvious choice, in spite of the fact that the key man in the ministry process for generating the short-list was a well-known member of the National Party. As the occupation went on, an increasing number of students and their parents began to express concern that if the situation were not soon resolved, they would lose the entire school year. Public tension increased. On 29 August, FESES declared an indefinite strike for all liceo students until the conflicts in several liceos, but especially Liceo No. 13, were resolved. Violent street clashes ensued between FESES supporters and counterdemonstrating students who supported the government.

The next day, Palma announced his solution to the problem. Very near to Liceo No. 13 was a boys' liceo which had empty space, Liceo No. 8. He proposed that it be converted into a coeducational school and provided with facilities (desks, teachers, equipment) for those students from Liceo No. 13 who wanted to finish their year. Those who firmly supported the strike and were willing on principle to risk losing the year could remain occupying the Liceo 13 building. Close to 80 per cent of the students took advantage of the minister's solution and began attending classes in the new locale under the direction of Señora Castillo.

Yunge then accused Palma of strikebreaking and of attempting to divide the student movement. The strike called by FESES continued, with more and more street clashes between pro- and anti-government students, leading on 2 September to incidents so violent that practically all commerce and public transportation in central Santiago were brought to a halt, with 150 students arrested and many injured.

The violence continued, sometimes in the streets, sometimes centering on a particular school. Palma was convinced that the opposition was trying to force him to send in the police to dislodge students with the hope that a student would be seriously injured or killed, thus creating a martyr who would serve as a rallying symbol against the government. Palma moved the annual week-long school holiday for Chile's National Day (18 September) forward to start on 11 September, hoping that this would let the situation calm down and avoid the danger of serious injury to students. (Information regarding the Liceo No. 13 events is taken from an interview with Guillermo Yunge, 4 December 1981; an interview with Anibal Palma, 12 December 1981; interviews with Mirta Castillo and Patricia Toledo, the leader of the occupying students, published in *Chile Hoy*, 17-23 November 1972, p. 9; and almost daily reports in both the opposition and government press between early August and late September 1972.) However, when classes resumed on 20 September, another liceo became the focus for even more serious disturbances.

The center of dispute this time was Liceo No. 12 for Girls, also in Santiago. Students had started occupying the school early in September before the mid-month holiday. Here the problem was essentially the same as in Liceo No. 13. A respected director had retired and a provisional director had been appointed. However, in this case the provisional director had not applied for the permanent post. And this time the students wanted the inspector general responsible for the school, who was one of the short-listed candidates, to be named director. The opposition appeared to be particularly interested in ensuring that another of the final candidates, a Socialist, not be appointed. (Here too the short-list had been established by the usual procedures, but Palma had not yet had the opportunity to examine the credentials and make his decision.)

Palma met with the students and with the parents and guardians committee and outlined to them the same position he had held with respect to Liceo No. 13; that because of the precedent it would set, he would not accede to student pressure. He offered to give all of the background documentation regarding the three final candidates to a committee of parents, teachers, and students so that they could evaluate the credentials with him. He also recommended that a plebiscite among the students be held, a suggestion which was rejected by the leaders of the occupying students. An indication of the highly politicized nature of the conflict was that on the same day that Palma met with the students and parents, Friday, 22 September, the presidents of both the Senate and the Chamber of Deputies visited the school to interview students and issue public declarations condemning the government's intransigence.

As the minister saw it, the situation here was even more complicated than that in Liceo No. 13. It was now so late in the school year that it was not possible to organize a new school to provide an option for the students who were not supporting the occupation. Combined with the Liceo No. 13 incident and other less-publicized school occupations, this presented the government with a serious dilemma. If they used the police to dislodge the occupying students in order to protect the right of the others, there was considerable danger that a student would be seriously injured. This would have been particularly damaging since this was a *girls'* school. On the other hand, if the government did not do something about the continuing occupation, with all of the political activity and publicity surrounding it, their inaction would contribute to a growing image of a regime which lacked the power and authority to enforce order in so basic an institution as education, in which almost every family in the nation had a stake.

Within hours of Palma's meeting with the students and parents, the situation escalated to a critical level. In the middle of the night of 22/23 September, the school was assaulted by a group of government-supporting students, apparently including some young people who were not students. There was considerable violence and destruction of property; seventeen of the students who had originally occupied the school were injured, and some had to be taken to hospital for treatment. This particular school was situated in the midst of a large apartment complex which had been built by the previous government, and most of the residents were supporters of the Christian Democrats. The minister arrived in his own car to find the school surrounded by a large crowd of students, parents, neighbors, journalists and politicians, who had apparently also been roused from their beds. They were in an ugly mood. At the door of the school he announced that he would take personal responsibility for the school, that he would place it in the charge of the inspector general and give her whatever authority she needed, and that he would ensure that it was protected by the police so that no one else could enter. He then went into the school with the inspector general and repeated his message to the young people there. He then walked back to his car, expecting to be assaulted by the crowd at any moment.

When Palma returned home, he phoned Allende and arranged for a meeting early in the morning. In spite of their friendship, Allende was extremely angry. This was another "scandal," and Palma, as minister, was responsible for it. The president instructed him that he must resolve the problem quickly and arrange to appear on a national radio and television network to calm public opinion.

That afternoon the opposition press was full of front-page stories about the incident, referring in large headlines to the "massacre" of students for which the government was responsible. Particularly damaging in terms of propaganda were reports that the attacking students had taken a small dog which served as a mascot for the students who had originally occupied the school and had decapitated it and placed its head on the director's desk as a sort of trophy.

A meeting was scheduled for the next morning (Sunday) between Palma and a committee of two parents, two teachers, and two students. Shortly before it took place, a group of the students who had assaulted the school on Friday night came to Palma's office in the ministry and brought with them the by-now famous "decapitated" dog, alive and well. They were instructed to go into an adjoining room and wait for a call. The representatives from the school arrived, and Palma proposed again that he would give them all of the credentials of the final candidates and allow the group fifteen days to evaluate them. After that, he would consult with the school committee and base his final decision upon the usual formally established criteria. The committee agreed. Palma then pointed out that this was exactly the formula he had proposed earlier. If they had accepted the original proposition, none of the recent events would have occurred, and no one would have been injured. This led to an angry exchange, which culminated in accusations regarding government students who were so bestial as to decapitate a small dog.

Palma replied by questioning them closely on the incident. The replies were uncertain, but the committee insisted that it must have happened, that a pool of blood had been seen, that no one had seen the dog. In the midst of this exchange Palma discovered that one of the students, a girl of fifteen or sixteen, had been responsible for the mascot. She was obviously extremely upset. The minister then called in the students in the adjoining room. They placed the dog ceremoniously on the minister's desk, and Palma asked the girl if this was the animal in question. She admitted that it was and broke into tears. After this, everyone was satisfied and the meeting ended with good feeling. They all went out into the hallway outside of the minister's office where they encountered a large crowd of journalists, with microphones and television cameras. The representatives from the school announced that the issue had been satisfactorily resolved and that the dog had been found. (*El Mercurio* referred the next day to a dog which was "identical to" the one which had been decapitated!)

Palma then reported the resolution of the crisis to Allende. He also said that he was going to appear on radio and television that night to explain his actions and announce his resignation. Allende asked him to reconsider, but after what he remembers as a highly emotional and rather disjointed presentation, Palma did announce his resignation (Palma, 1977b). The impact was great. The next morning large numbers of students who supported the government were in the streets demonstrating in support of the minister and appealing for him to continue in his post.[7] On the following Wednesday, Allende formally rejected the resignation, noting that he had consulted the *Contraloría* and had received the advice that the minister's actions in the school crisis of the past month had been within the law.

Thus, the immediate issue was resolved, but Palma's position was difficult. His strong stand against student political interference in the career advancement of professional educators and the solutions he had devised for the incidents in Liceos 12 and 13 had won him wide support from teachers and ministry personnel of all political affiliations. At the same time, he was identified as the educational leader of a government which had been unable to maintain order in the schools. In this sense, the opposition campaign to use students to create an image of anarchy in a fundamental social institution had been successful.[8] As part of the continuing attack on the government which culminated in the October Strike, the opposition laid formal impeachment charges against Palma and three other ministers. At first Allende wanted to resist, but he finally had no choice but to replace Palma as part of the cabinet reorganization which ended the October crisis.[9] (The account of the Liceo No. 12 incident is based upon interviews with Anibal Palma, 12 December 1981 and 25 May 1983; an interview with Guillermo Yunge, 4 December 1981; interviews with other sources; and daily media coverage through September and early October.)

THE DECREE OF DEMOCRATIZATION

In the midst of the political turmoil with which Palma had to deal during August and September, the National Council of Education continued quietly discussing the document "Proposal for a General Decree of Democratization" (Ministerio de Educación Pública, July 1972), which had been placed before it by the commission of Nuñez, Araya, and Gonzalez, and receiving representations from the various groups who had been asked to comment upon the proposal. After seven meetings between 25 July and 12 September the council suggested three major changes to the commission's proposal: 1) that private education be provided with a degree of representation in the various councils which more nearly reflected the proportion of students it served; 2) that the implementation be on an experimental basis until the end of 1974, after which there would be an evaluation which would lead to a law rather than a decree to establish the mechanisms for democratization; and 3) that a clause which expanded the representation within the National Council of Education and changed its name to "The Council for Education Development" be eliminated.

The government was not obliged to take these recommendations into account. The decree which had established the National Council in 1953 referred to it as a consultative body. Previous governments, particularly the Christian Democrats, had used it as an agency for testing ideas and sensing the probable reaction to them, but the experience of the Frei regime's educational planners had indicated that a government which ignored the council's recommendations was likely to find itself in difficulty (Schiefelbien, 1975). Even the Statute of Democratic Guarantees did not *require* the government to be bound by the results of free and pluralistic discussion of its policy initiatives. It only insisted that no educational policy measure be adopted without such discussion.

A comparison of the text of the original proposal submitted to the National Council with that of the decree signed by Palma and then Allende in late October (*El Mercurio*, 6 November 1972) indicates that some of the recommendations were accepted. A slight increase in the representation of private education was included, although nothing like what was requested in the brief submitted by the Permanent Committee of Private Education. The final decree referred to creating several levels of councils of education with an "experimental character," but it did not fix a deadline for evaluation. The proposed clause which would have changed the nature of the National Council of Education was eliminated.

The decree which was finally signed authorized the creation of councils of education at three levels: 1) *local* councils, one for each legally recognized community in the nation; 2) *provincial* councils, one in each of the nation's twenty-five provinces; and 3) *regional* councils, one in each of the ten educational regions into which the nation had been divided for administrative purposes. These councils were to be subject to the National Council, and like it they were to have the authority to "advise" and "collaborate" with the formal educational bureaucracy in the planning, implementation and evaluation of educational policy at their corresponding levels of jurisdiction.

At each level the councils were to have representation from the following agencies or organizations, the number of representatives varying with the level of jurisdiction:

The National Planning Office (ODEPLAN)

The Ministry of Health

Local universities or local branches of universities

The National Federation of Workers (CUT)

Peasants' Community Councils

Parents and Guardians Associations (from both private and public education)

Student federations (from both private and public education)

The National Union of Educational Workers (SUTE)

Neighborhood Councils

The National School Assistance Commission

The National Pre-School Education Commission

The Corporation for Educational Construction

The Industrial Development Corporation

The Ministry of Public Education.

The National Council of Education was also empowered to hold a National Congress of Education every two years along with preliminary meetings at the local, provincial, and regional levels, following the model of the consultation in 1971. These congresses would serve as forums for debate, but not for decision-making.

In addition to the councils, the decree authorized the establishment of three local-level organizations: 1) the council of educational workers; 2) the school community council; and 3) the school directive committee. The council of educational workers was to be an advisory committee at the local school level, which would deal primarily with pedagogical and administrative affairs of the school, and would include all employees from the administrators and department heads down to the para-teaching personnel and maintenance workers. Such committees already existed in many schools, but they involved only teaching personnel. The school community councils were to include representatives from the council of educational workers, the parents and guardians association of the school, the school's student federation at the secondary level, local unions (if affiliated with CUT), and other community organizations. They were charged with the responsibility of identifying local educational needs and resources and finding means to bring them together. The school directive committees were to work with the director of the school (whose responsibilities were also outlined in the decree) in interpreting, evaluating, and applying the recommendations of all of the other councils without prejudice to the legal authority of the school director and subject to national, regional, and local planning, and the "existing legislation and regulations, and complementary instructions from the Ministry of Education."

This careful outlining of constraints upon the one level of council which appeared to have some actual executive authority reflected a fundamental tension between the ideological commitment of the Popular Unity government to popular participation at all levels and the concern among professional educators, who were the government's power base in the area of education, for safeguarding what they understood to be their professional prerogatives and autonomy. The preamble of the decree attempted to allay fears that the authority of teachers and their administrative superiors would be usurped by noting that the various councils "would not affect the legal powers and responsibilities of the educational executive authorities, nor would they go beyond the framework of national, regional or local planning, nor would they interfere with the professional work of the teaching force."

This possible loss of professional autonomy was of concern only to teachers and educational administrators. The balance of membership in the various councils raised a much more general political issue, which had been foreseen by the Christian Democrats a year before during the disputes preceding the National Congress. If these councils were to have any power at all, they were clearly weighted in favor of the government. Combining representatives of government agencies and unions controlled by the government (SUTE and CUT), the government controlled twelve of the eighteen places on the local councils and nineteen of twenty-five places on the provincial and regional councils. This could be a serious problem, however, only if the councils had executive and directive rather than simply advisory power. It was on this issue that the *Contraloría* rejected the Decree for Democratization the following January, claiming that the powers given to the councils would indeed make them executive authorities outside of the legal chain of command within the Ministry of Education. Constitutionally, such a change in pattern of authority required congressional legislation rather than executive decree. Two months later, in March 1973, the government submitted a revised decree to the *Contraloría* (Ministerio de Educación Pública, March 1973). Even though the revision did not really alter the attributions of the various councils to which the *Contraloría* had objected, the new version was allowed to take effect in April. However, by that date the entire nation was engulfed in a much more critical debate over the government's other educational policy initiative: the National Unified School.

8

The Internal Fight Over the National Unified School

On 2 November 1972, Jorge Tapia was formally installed as minister of education. As he and Anibal Palma rode together to the ceremony, Palma said "Jorge, I'm leaving you a project that is going to make you famous." He was referring to the National Unified School proposal, the latest draft of which Palma had not seen.

Tapia, a relatively young but well-known professor of constitutional law, was coming from the post of minister of justice. He had been a central government figure in the negotiations leading to the Statute of Democratic Guarantees and in the failed negotiations with the Christian Democrats the previous June. He was perceived by many key officials within the Ministry of Education as having little experience in or knowledge of the field, but he felt confident of his ability to master this new portfolio. He had spent a year in the United States in 1968 studying then-current educational theories and techniques. He had read and thought a great deal about the general question of education's role in a society such as Chile. He was aware of Philip Coombs' argument (1968) that continued quantitative expansion of formal education would exacerbate educational or social problems in developing nations rather than solve them and that qualitative changes were required. He had also been impressed by the general approach of the soon-to-be-published Faure report, *Learning to Be* (Faure et al., 1972) and had examined a number of other Unesco documents and position papers regarding education.

When Tapia returned from the United States, he participated with a group of faculty members in the School of Law who were developing and experimenting with new forms of instruction in law. This experience led him to the view that one could not seriously consider the role of university education without also analyzing the system of education below it. Although he had not known, until Palma mentioned it, that the Ministry of Education was actively preparing a specific ENU proposal, he was not surprised. As a prominent minister and as a central figure within the Radical party, he was familiar with the controversies which surrounded the National Congress of Education process and was aware in a general sense of the debates regarding the need for a major educational reform. He also had experience with some staff members of the Center for In-Service Training and had confidence in them and its director, Mario Leyton, even though Leyton was a Christian Democrat. He expected to be able to rely heavily upon them in implementing any major educational reform.

Tapia was also perceived by many of his new colleagues as a forceful personality who had acquired, through some of his actions as minister of justice, a reputation for being strongly opposed to the hard-line wing of the Socialist party which was so influential in the Ministry of Education. Indeed, Tapia arrived at his new post "prepared to fight with the extremists" (interview with Jorge Tapia, 10 December 1981).[1]

In spite of his reputation, the new minister quickly gained the respect of many of his senior officials. They saw that he had a good grasp of the basic policy issues, asked good questions, and learned quickly. They welcomed his attention to policy questions and his refusal to become involved in lower level bureaucratic political maneuvering. He quickly established a set of ad hoc groups to avoid delays in the decision-making process. Tapia understood himself to have two basic assignments: 1) to calm the student turbulence which had created Palma's major problems, and 2) to move a number of items off the policy agenda and into implementation. The first and most important of these policy issues was the proposal for the National Unified School.[2]

THE NATIONAL UNIFIED SCHOOL PROPOSAL: THE INTERNAL DRAFT

The draft proposal which Tapia soon saw was prepared by a National Unified School Commission. This was actually the second committee to work on the proposal. The first had started work at the same time as the Commission for the Decree of Democratization and had worked quietly during the May-August period producing a number of draft documents and analyses, among them a complete draft of a new Organic Law of Education which went well beyond its mandate (Balocchi, 1972b). Following the original plan, as soon as work on the Decree of Democratization was completed, a higher level commission was formed to work on the ENU proposal. This commission was charged with bringing a complete draft proposal to the ministry's coordinating committee as soon as possible. Members of the ENU Commission, which was chaired by Ivan Nuñez, were chosen to represent the political parties in the coalition and the various areas of education. There was great diversity in individual opinions regarding many aspects of the proposed policy, and there were occasional clashes between strongly held views. Nonetheless, participants do not recall this group as an arena into which "official party positions" were introduced—this occurred later. The commission started work in September and had a complete draft ready for examination soon after Tapia assumed office.

The draft closely followed the propositions embodied in the position papers prepared by the Ministry of Education for the National Congress of Education and the government alternatives among the reports produced by it (Ministerio De Educación Pública, December 1972).[3] It began by observing that all of humanity was witnessing a struggle between two antagonistic economic systems and conceptions of life: capitalism, which was facing a profound international crisis, and socialism, which had shown in just a few decades its ability to overcome the contradictions of capitalism and produce a just, humane, and classless society. The educational crisis in Chile was a reflection of the general crisis of capitalism, and significant educational transformation could only occur as part of a change to a socialist society. Since Chile had freely opted for a transition to socialism, it was the task of education to create the New Man who would both create and live within the new type of society. Throughout its twenty-seven pages, and particularly in the first two sections which referred to the educational crisis of Chile and the educational program of the Popular Unity government, the document quoted liberally from the Basic Program of Popular Unity, Allende's speech at the inauguration of the 1971 school year, and previous government educational documents. To understand the proposal and the arguments it produced both within the government and between the government and the opposition, it is necessary to consider three different aspects: 1) the technical or structural recommendations, 2) the schedule for implementation, and 3) the underlying ideology and rhetoric.

Technical or Structural Recommendations

The concept of "permanent education" as it was developed in Unesco publications, particularly the Faure Report (1972), was a central feature of the proposal. Under this rubric, the national educational system was defined as consisting of two areas: the area of regular education and the area of out-of-school education.[4] The first involved the existing formal system of pre-school, primary, and secondary schooling. The second included all adult education programs and activities provided by the Ministry of Education or by other agencies of government, universities, religious and community organizations, the military, and commercial and industrial enterprises, which would be integrated gradually with the services provided by the regular system using the various broadly representative councils established by the Decree of Democratization.

The National Unified School itself would involve a reorientation and restructuring of institutions within the area of regular education. The ENU was characterized, following earlier government documents, as: National, Unified, Democratic, Productive, Integrated with the Community, Scientific and Technological, Diversified and Planned. The emphasis was to be on *polytechnical education*, breaking the existing barriers between mental and manual labor, and giving all students direct experience with the world of work available to them in their community. *Integration* of existing levels and types of schooling and of schools with their local communities was also a central idea of the proposal.

Throughout the twelve years of primary and secondary schooling, the curriculum was to be divided into three areas of study: *a common plan*, to which all students would be exposed; an *elective plan*, which would allow freedom of choice to students; and a *specialization plan*, in which students would prepare themselves for a particular field of work. The eight years of primary school were to be divided into three cycles. During the first years, all students would study a common curriculum, not divided into subject-matter areas. Here, the objective was to build a foundation of basic skills and understandings. This cycle was to be followed (at a point not specified in the report) by a stage in which some subject areas would be studied separately. Then in grades seven and eight, there would be full differentiation of the curriculum into separate subjects of study.

In grade nine, in addition to a set of common plan and elective plan subjects (the subjects to be included in the common and elective plans were not specified), each student would be exposed systematically to the major fields of work available in the society. (These fields of work were also not identified.) Throughout the year, students would rotate from one field to the next, receiving both a general technological and theoretical orientation and direct experience through compulsory practical work and opportunities for voluntary labor. In grade ten, while the common and elective plans continued, each student would choose one field for specialization. Continued study and practical work experience through grades eleven and twelve would lead, at graduation, to a certificate as a Middle Level Technician in the chosen field. The certificate would not only note the levels of formal achievement in both theoretical and applied aspects of the field, but would also list the voluntary work the student had undertaken and would include a general evaluation of his/her aptitudes, abilities, attitudes, and interests. Provision was also made for an additional year of study to qualify for more complex specializations. Throughout the program of study, emphasis would be on continuing evaluation and vocational guidance, and provision was made for reentry into the formal system if a student had to leave school for economic or other reasons.

In order to integrate the various types and levels of schools, all public schools at the primary and secondary levels in a given locale, corresponding to the area of jurisdiction of a Local Council of Education (as established in the Decree of Democratization), would be brought under a single administration. Each unit would be called an Educational Complex or a Unified Local System, with provision for school and school-community planning at both the level of the individual school and the educational unit, subject to the provisions of regional and national plans. In areas where there were few or no existing schools, mainly small rural communities and marginal urban settlements, provision was made for the establishment of Complete School Units in which all levels and types of schooling would be housed in a single building.

Schedule for Implementation

It was proposed that implementation begin in the 1973 school year, which was to start the following March. For the first year the following specific propositions were advanced:

1) Creation of a First Integrated Year. This was to be a two-year transition arrangement which would provide a common curriculum for grade nine classes in all types of secondary schools while longer term curriculum changes were planned.

2) Experimentation with various means to incorporate productive work into the classroom.

3) Establishment of a program of intensive curriculum development for the new system, focussing particularly on grades one, four, seven, eight, and ten, which were to be changed in 1974.

4) Experimentation in various localities with the formation of educational complexes.

5) Designation of existing consolidated schools as complete school units, in order that they could serve as pilot projects for this form of implementation.

6) Evaluation, at the end of the school year, of the first integrated year efforts.

Specific targets were listed for each of the following years, leading to complete change in the educational system by 1976.

Underlying Ideology and Rhetoric

A careful reading of the ENU Commission's proposal indicates clearly that the ideological position taken as a background for the specific educational reform propositions was that of the hard-line Socialists within the

ministry rather than that of the Radicals and their supporters. In its opening paragraphs, the document referred, for example, to a transition to socialism through "a radicalization of class conflict" and to a need to overcome economic underdevelopment "in a revolutionary fashion." It spoke
of the "national and revolutionary meaning" of the program of the Popular
Unity Government and of the "authentically humanistic and revolutionary
character of the socialist community we want to build." It also condemned
the ideological "neutralism" of education and called for a fight "against
individualism" (pp. 2-4).

Radical party documents, in contrast, rarely used the word "revolutionary," referred to class conflict as a phenomenon which could be overcome
through democratic parliamentary means, emphasized the necessary ideological "pluralism" of education, and warned against *both* individualism
and state totalitarianism. The contrast between the ENU Commission report and the Radical party position can be seen best in a document entitled
"Democracy and Education," written by Hugo Araya and approved as
an official policy document by the Radical party annual convention held
in November 1972, at the same time the ENU Commission document was
circulating in the Ministry of Education (1972b). This paper referred to
the fundamental conflict in society not as a Marxist confrontation between
capitalism and socialism but as a contest between individualist liberalism
(of which capitalism was an economic expression) and democratic socialism, defined as a condition in which "all of the community would play an
active and decisive role in directing the society, which would be translated,
in the economy, into an equitable distribution of the wealth generated by
productive labour." Throughout the paper the word "socialism" was consistently associated with "democratic" or "democracy." Although the
specific technical and structural proposals in Araya's paper for a "unified" school were similar to those in the ENU Commission report (indeed,
reflecting the general Radical position, they were more detailed and precise than the proposals in the government document), it was carefully noted
that education should avoid ideological "exclusivism" and that schooling
must serve both individual and collective goals.

Finally, it should be noted that although the ENU Commission report
frequently referred to specific proposals as experimental, Nuñez' introductory statement labelled the report as the "definitive version" upon which
the official decisions would be based.

THE POLITICAL FIGHT WITHIN THE MINISTRY;
POSITIONS, PERCEPTIONS AND STRATEGIES

As soon as Tapia read the ENU Commission report, he was alarmed.
His immediate reaction was that the ideological rhetoric would be very

damaging politically to the Popular Unity government and that the proposed timetable for implementation was logistically impossible. He quickly circulated the document to a group of individuals in whose judgment he had confidence of varying political affiliations within and without the government. All of these "private advisors" (as the minister called them) who were outside the formal decision-making channels in the ministry confirmed his judgment that the proposal represented a potential political disaster. Thus, within days of assuming his post, Tapia was confronted with a serious dilemma.

The arguments against the ENU proposal were powerful. The ideological rhetoric was so extreme and inflammatory that it could have the effect of gratuitously providing the opposition with a "battle flag" to rally support at a time when, in the view of moderate elements within the government, the position of the regime had just been strengthened by the outcome of the October crisis and the outlook for success in the March elections was quite bright. Indeed, Tapia perceived the ENU proposition as an attempt by the hard-line Socialists, who had been defeated in the Lo Curro meetings of the Popular Unity parties a few months previously and who had lost even more ground with the inclusion of military officials in the government at the end of October, to force the Ministry of Education into creating a political "explosion" which would so radicalize public opinion that the government would be forced to abandon its reformist line and adopt a revolutionary strategy.[5] The extreme Marxist analysis in the document also contradicted the position of his own party. Moreover, Tapia interpreted the proposal as a violation of the Statute of Democratic Guarantees he himself had helped to negotiate with the Christian Democrats two years before. To support them would place him in an impossible position.

Added to these difficulties were the problems of implementation. The proposed starting date was just four months away, yet there were no estimates of the possible costs of the proposed reforms, nor even preliminary assessments of the actual availability of opportunities within either socialized or private enterprises for the sort of direct productive experience envisaged in the polytechnic education proposals. Indeed, the Radicals and many of the Allendista Socialists had been consistently arguing that the data available in the ministry regarding the scale and functioning of the system were so incomplete that an educational census and/or the creation of an ongoing "educational data base" system were essential before a major reform could be implemented.[6] This was in spite of major improvements in data collection and analysis undertaken in the educational planning office during the Frei regime. As Araya noted, "We didn't even know for sure how many teachers we had" (interview with Hugo Araya, 8 May 1981). It is indicative of the difference in ideological positions and conceptions of policy-making within the ministry that when Tapia asked those in the superintendency who were supporting the ENU proposal why they had not undertaken the technical analyses he saw as essential, they replied "We don't have to worry about that. We have the power to do it." These same individuals presented to Tapia, along with the ENU report, a series of draft decrees for immediate implementation, "ready for my signature" (interview with Jorge Tapia, 10 December 1981).

On the other hand, the main technical or structural elements of the proposal were viewed by the minister as valuable. He saw the ENU scheme as having the potential for 1) providing a much greater degree of democratization of the educational system, 2) producing an educational system which would be linked to a non-dependent style of national development, 3) preparing children to adapt to new technologies, and 4) educating children not only for earning a living but for self-realization. These were important goals, although they were long-term in nature.

But *something* had to be done quickly. Even without detailed financial analysis, it was evident that the ministry was facing precisely the kind of inevitable cost-growth problem which Coombs had forecast for developing nations generally (1968). (Many of the key figures in the ministry from the various parties were familiar with Coombs' analyses.) The Frei reform had substantially increased the flow of students through the primary educational level. This had already resulted in increases in the number of students entering secondary school, and available forecasts indicated that the secondary enrolment ratio would grow even more over the next several years. Moreover, Popular Unity policy had already produced sharp upturns in the proportion of secondary level entrants who opted for technical-professional education, where the cost per student was even higher than in the traditional liceos. It could easily be foreseen that in a few years the increased flow of students through the secondary level would produce a marked rise in applicants for enrolment in university, where costs per student were even higher.

Enrolment reductions were not a viable option. "We could not have gone to the President with a proposal to reduce the number of students" (interview with Ivan Nuñez, 15 November 1981). Therefore, some way had to be found to divert the flow away from the traditional secondary-school-into-university route and send the graduates into the labor market. But these students had to enter the world of work with marketable skills, which were not typically provided by secondary level *liceos* or technical-professional schools. Also, because of the pledge to hold a National Congress of Education, and the slow follow-up thereafter, the first two years of the new regime had been lost as far as educational reform was concerned.[7] If new policy was not put into place in 1973, financial pressure would become intolerable before the end of the government's six-year mandate in 1976.

This analysis of the problem was widely shared within the ministry, as was the perception that an appropriate solution would necessarily involve some form of polytechnical education along with better integration of the schools and a move toward a "permanent education" concept along the lines suggested in then-popular Unesco documents.[8] Thus, there was little serious disagreement regarding the technical or structural recommendations in the ENU report. Rather, the disputes centered on the other two aspects of the report. With respect to the implementation schedule, there were two issues: 1) Was if feasible to begin implementation in March 1973, given the lack of technical back-up studies? and 2) Considering the increasingly polarized state of Chilean society as a whole, could any kind of major educational reform be introduced without causing significant political damage to the government? There were strong disagreements regarding these questions, but the most heated disputes dealt with the ideology and rhetoric in the proposal.

The minister perceived his own ability to resist the ENU proposals as limited by the fact that he was new to the ministry and that he was dealing with adversaries who had been thinking in detail about the issues for a long time. This difficulty was aggravated because the ENU document was presented to him as a proposal with a long history, deriving from at least fifteen years of thinking within the organized teaching force (SUTE and its predecessors) and having the imprimatur of the National Congress of Education. "If it were just some document that Ivan Nuñez and a few other people had dreamed up, I could more easily have said: 'Ivan, take this back to your desk and think some more about it' " (interview with Jorge Tapia, 10 December 1981). Thus, despite his misgivings, Tapia did not feel free simply to exert his ministerial authority and stop the document immediately.

Moreover, Nuñez, as superintendent, was formally responsible for policy formulation within the Ministry of Education. Tapia could not easily by-pass him, but neither could he realistically ask Nuñez to produce a document which expressed Tapia's very different ideological position. Tapia saw himself caught between two distinct opposition groups: the *internal* opposition, from the extreme left, which strongly supported the ENU Commission report in its current form, and the *external* opposition, the Christian Democrats and the extreme right, who were sure to reject the report outright if it was not altered.

Under these circumstances, the minister's objectives were to maintain the structural proposals while softening as much as possible the ideological rhetoric and to extend the timetable for implementation to allow for pilot projects and needed technical studies. He also wanted to ensure that whatever document finally emerged was clearly identified as coming from the superintendency, for discussion in the National Council of Education, rather than from the ministry. This would allow him a freer hand to negotiate with the external opposition, using any still-objectionable aspects of the proposal as bargaining counters.

The coordinating committee of the ministry became the central arena in which the battles over the ENU proposal were fought. This entity had remained relatively inactive until Palma became minister, and it became very active as soon as Tapia took over. It was supposed to provide general political direction for, and routine policy coordination within, the ministry. It consisted of the heads of the major administrative divisions, supplemented by enough other high-ranking officials to provide balance between the three major parties. It was, thus, an example of the plethora of interparty check and balance mechanisms which effectively made coherent policy formulation and implementation impossible throughout the government.

The membership of the coordinating committee at that time was as follows: for the Radicals, there were Tapia, Fresia Urrutia as director of primary education, and Hugo Araya as technical secretary of the superintendency. The Socialists were represented by Waldo Suarez as sub-secretary, Ivan Nuñez as superintendent, and Carlos Moreno as director of technical-professional education. From the Communist party there were Aida Migone as director of secondary education, Juvencio Valle as director of libraries and museums, and Lucindo Saavedra, from the libraries division, who acted as secretary for the group. Three others who were not formally part of the committee but who participated regularly in its deliberations were Andres Dominguez, a young sociologist from MAPU who served as a sort of roving policy analyst within the ministry, Sergio Arenas, the Radical head of the planning and budget office, and Lautaro Videla, as visitor-general. Other officials would participate when an item relevant to their area of jurisdiction was being discussed.

Debates within the coordinating committee regarding the ENU proposition illustrate the complexity of the policy formulation process within the Popular Unity government—indeed, within any multiparty government in crisis. The outcome was the result of a combination of individual characteristics and positions, official party positions (not always clearly reflected in the actions of individual members), and perceptions of others' positions as colored by a long history of interactions among the individuals and their parties.[9]

Among the Radicals, Tapia and Araya were the main actors. Urrutia was so occupied trying to administer the largest branch of the ministry that she was able to play only a minor role in broad-scale policy debates. All of the Radicals agreed with the structural changes embodied in the ENU proposal, but they were all opposed to the timing and the ideology in which they were embedded.

Their degree of commitment to the structural recommendations, however, and their degree of opposition to the other aspects of the proposal varied. Araya, for example, was strongly in favor of the structural change recommendations. This was hardly surprising since they were very close to ideas he had been promoting in his own documents, including the recently approved official party position paper. Although he observed several serious technical weaknesses in the ENU Commission documents (for example, by his analysis, the implementation schedule for 1973-76 would have some cohorts of students passing through three different curricular systems within four years) which had to be corrected before it could be approved, he was sufficiently committed to the basic technical propositions that he was prepared to negotiate and compromise on the problems of rhetoric and timing in order to get needed reform in place quickly. At the same time, a number of other Radicals within the ministry were strongly opposed, arguing that the entire idea should be scrapped and that in the political climate of the moment, introduction of any major educational change would invite disaster.

This division of opinion within the party produced mixed and confusing signals to the rest of the coordinating committee. Several members saw the Radicals, correctly, as internally divided, while others saw them as the main cohesive source of opposition to the ENU proposal, and one member understood them to be the strongest supporters of the proposal. In particular, there were widely varying perceptions of Tapia's personal position. Nuñez, who had endeavored to convince the minister of the need for this type of reform, saw him as neutral—as playing the role of a good chairman who listens to all sides, asks pointed questions for clarification, and keeps the discussion orderly. Migone understood him to be ambivalent, but basically in favor of the proposition. She saw him as a strong man who was trying to impose his will on other factions of his own party. Videla, on the other hand, saw the minister as strongly opposed to the proposal. Thus, the supporters of the ENU Commission's recommendations constructed their arguments and strategies with widely different understandings of who their opponents were and the nature of their objections.

The Communists within the coordinating committee were not enthusiastic about the proposal. They understood the political dangers. Since education, following orthodox Marxist analysis, was not a high priority area for policy change in the view of their party, which was by far the most disciplined, cohesive, and pragmatic unit within the government, they did not see much point in risking a major political confrontation over it. It was assumed by several other members of the committee, however, that they would not be prepared to oppose it openly. One participant noted, "They could not afford to be seen to be less revolutionary than the Socialists." Tapia was sure that they had already entered into an agreement with the Socialists to support the proposal. In spite of this, two participants have indicated that they suspected that without major concessions to the opponents' objections, the Communists would ultimately refuse to support the proposal.

It was clear that the primary supporters of the ENU proposal were the Socialists. Nuñez was the major advocate. He had chaired the commission which had produced the proposal, and it reflected his policy direction and the ideology which he had been promoting in both written documents and within the councils of the government since well before the National Congress of Education. He was commonly referred to by his colleagues as "Mister ENU." Not all members of his party shared his enthusiasm. Waldo Suarez, for example, had seen some of the technical and political problems. He had quietly informed a small group of Allendista socialists in the ministry, who also had serious misgivings, that they should be ready to devote themselves fully to the preparation of an alternate proposal which would be more widely acceptable. Suarez' responsibility, as sub-secretary, was administration rather than policy formulation, and he did not openly oppose the ENU report during the coordinating committee debates. Carlos Moreno and his staff in the directorate of technical-professional education also had strong reservations. From their own experience, they saw a number of serious technical problems with the implementation of the polytechnical education proposals—namely, staffing, equipment, supervision, and site location. They also appeared to several other committee members to perceive the ENU proposal as likely to alter beyond recognition a style of schooling to which they had developed strong personal and bureaucratic loyalty.

The internal division among the Socialists led one participant in the debates to conclude that the Socialist party was actually formally *opposed* to the ENU proposal and that Nuñez was arguing for it only because he was so instructed by Tapia. Another participant has described his attempt to follow the arguments in the committee as like "being in a Jai-Alai match, with the ball moving rapidly and coming at you from unexpected directions. It was *very* confusing."

This left Videla and Nuñez as the active proponents of the ENU report. The reaction to the proposal among their colleagues in the coordinating committee ranged from unenthusiastic support with reservations, through insistence upon alterations, to adamant opposition. Faced with such a situation, the proponents continued to fight hard for the proposition and refused to accept suggestions for modification. The explanation of their insistence upon implementing the report under such conditions involves a mix of personality characteristics, personal history, pragmatic understanding of the Chilean schooling system, technical analyses, and ideological commitments.

Nuñez and Videla were both powerful and strong-willed men, skillful and fiery public speakers and debaters. They had long and generally successful experience in the often vicious in-fighting within the Socialist party. They were accustomed to taking strong public positions and defending them. Note, for example, Nuñez' final speech at the National Congress of Education and their joint actions at the Socialist party's National Congress in Chillan just a few years previously.

They also shared a long history of personal commitment to the pedagogical and social principles underlying the ENU proposal. This commitment had its roots in their experience in the consolidated school in San Miguel, where Videla had served as Nuñez' mentor. Both recall those years with a great deal of fondness and refer to them as fundamentally formative in their understanding of the power of an integrated and polytechnic type of schooling closely linked with its local community. They had subsequently fought for more than a decade to have those principles incorporated into the policy positions of their own party and the teachers' unions. During the 1960's, Nuñez worked as an investigator in the Educational Research Institute of the University of Chile, winning a competition for appointment to a professorship early in 1970. During this time, he was involved in a study of the problems of financing locally administered community schools within the Chilean fiscal and administrative system. This gave him an understanding of the logistical and administrative obstacles and potentials for expanding the San Miguel experience throughout the nation. In his role as visitor general, travelling throughout the country, Videla had acquired extensive pragmatic understanding of the difficulties facing local community schools within the highly centralized Chilean educational system. At the end of 1972, after spending two years carefully and doggedly maneuvering their ideas through a long public consultative process and a bureaucratically cumbersome Ministry of Education, they were not likely to give up easily.

In addition, being even more familiar than Tapia with Coombs' arguments, they were genuinely alarmed by the impending fiscal crisis caused by the rapid expansion of enrolments. Having lost two years already, further delay to avoid a possible immediate political uproar would inevitably create for the government another type of political crisis a few years later which would also necessarily disrupt the lives and plans of many students. As responsible educational authorities, they felt they had to press for quick implementation.

Finally, there was a strong ideological commitment. Despite their efforts to modify somewhat the hard-line position of the Socialist party at the Congress of Chillan, they were firm adherents of the revolutionary socialist position within the party and the government. Following the slogan "Advance without Compromise" ("avanzar sin transar"), they would not be satisfied simply with modifications or improvements of previous reforms or with solving technical and fiscal problems caused by rapid educational expansion. As a matter of political commitment, a reform had to be introduced which would advance the "socialist project" as they perceived it. At a time when the government appeared to them to be paralyzed and mass mobilization politics had been abandoned, they saw the ENU proposal as a means of recruiting support among those portions of the middle sectors they thought to be susceptible to mobilization for the Popular Unity government.

With reference to Tapia's belief that the objective was to create a political "explosion" which would force the government into a more revolutionary position, Nuñez insists that the intent was to *mobilize* rather than *radicalize* popular support. Indeed, he notes that the Socialists in the coordinating committee thought that the project they were proposing would help government candidates in the forthcoming March elections, allowing them to refer in their campaign speeches to the government's new initiative in education.[10] "If we suspected what was going to happen, we would never have done it" (interview with Ivan Nuñez, 21 September 1982). Videla, on the other hand, avers that he recognized all along that there would be a violent reaction to the proposal, but that he felt that such a reaction would in itself serve to mobilize middle-sector support for the government (Interview with Lautaro Videla, 19 March 1981). In any event, their joint commitment to the revolutionary socialist line led Nuñez and Videla to the position that the ideological content of the ENU proposal was absolutely essential. They would, if need be, accommodate the objections within the ministry regarding technical matters and details of the implementation schedule, but they could not surrender with respect to the fundamental necessity of placing the reform proposition squarely within their conception of the crisis of ideological confrontation and class conflict which Chile was experiencing.

With this sort of intransigent insistence upon the ideological content of the ENU document by one group and equally committed resistance to its inclusion by opponents also within the government, it quickly became apparent that the dispute was so basic a reflection of the fundamental conflict between the revolutionary and reformist currents within the Popular Unity coalition that it could not be resolved within the coordinating committee. Tapia's strategy was to delay as much as possible, hoping that Allende would be forced to intervene and impose a compromise which would at least allow him to soften the ideological rhetoric and alter the implementation schedule. As the stalemate within the coordinating committee became absolute, the Socialists took to walking out of meetings in an attempt to force the issue to a conclusion. Finally, they complained to the central committee of their party regarding the refusal of the Radicals and Tapia to agree to a much-needed educational reform. Representations were made to Allende regarding the problem. Opponents of the proposal had also been meeting privately with the president to alert him to what they saw as a grave danger to the survival of the government itself.

Just before Christmas, Allende called a special meeting of the coordinating committee in his offices. After listening to all the arguments, he insisted on the need to avoid these paralyzing partisan disputes within the government and reminded them of the vital need not to alienate the Church and the military. Without discussing the details of the arguments he had heard, he commanded them to keep working until they had a report which 1) could be announced by Tapia at the end of January, in order to permit at least partial implementation in 1973, but which 2) would have the support of all of the parties in Popular Unity.

THE FINAL ENU PROPOSAL

The coordinating committee then appointed a small group of four individuals to rewrite the ENU proposal in a form which would satisfy the conditions of Allende's compromise. The individuals chosen had to work fast since the deadline was only one month away. They also, of course, had to represent the contending political forces within the ministry. Nuñez was chosen as the Socialists' best educational theoretician and writer. Araya played the same role for the Radicals. Tapia, as minister, was also included. The fourth member was Andres Dominguez, from MAPU, who was seen as representing an intermediate position between the opposing camps. He was known to have a talent for writing with clarity; he had often served as a speech writer for Tapia. The fact that a Communist was not appointed indicates that party's lack of enthusiasm for educational reform.

Inclusion of Dominguez as a member of this small group added a significant new theoretical element to the mix of ideas regarding educational policy. MAPU had responsibility for the directorate of adult education and had some influence in the Center for In-Service Teacher Training, but, except for Dominguez, it was not an important element in the rest of the ministry. MAPU had recently lost its founding members to the Christian Left. Those who remained accepted a Marxist analysis of the historical roots and current nature of Chile's problems. However, they did not believe that the needed social changes could be accomplished through structural alterations imposed from above. Drawing upon the communitarian socialist philosophy of Christian Democracy, from which they had broken just before the 1970 election, MAPU members believed that significant change could only start at the base level, with small groups of individuals becoming empowered to take control of their own communities. Such a process, spreading gradually upward, would eventually result in a long-lasting and deeply penetrating change in the entire social system. In the field of education, they consequently believed that changes in structure or ideology imposed from above would accomplish nothing. Their preferred strategy was to work with small groups of teachers in local communities, helping them to understand how to link their own school to the particular social problems faced by the community from which their students came and to modify their teaching methods so as to provide children with a sense of control over their own lives and their environments. They could then effect local level changes independent of the dictates of a central authority which could not possibly understand the particular problems of each community.

There was, in this view, no such thing as "the child." Children lived in very different realities, and changes in education had to grow out of and be adapted to them. This analysis actually fitted closely the experience of the consolidated schools which were the concrete historical antecedent for the Socialists' educational program. But MAPU members did not believe, as did the Socialists, that one could translate that experience into a uniform national program. Rather, such schools had to grow organically out of the experience of individual communities and their schools.

Consideration of the MAPU view highlights a fundamental contradiction within both the Socialist and Radical positions as well as a basic similarity. Both parties dealt at great length in their educational documents with the need for participation by teachers, parents, students, and community groups in the formulation and implementation of educational policy. Yet, the participation was consistently defined in terms of membership in organized groups extending from the local community level to some central authority. Propositions for implementing participation consistently referred to the *national teachers union* (SUTE), student *federations*, parents and guardians groups which had *national organizations*, and labor unions which were members of the *National Workers Federation* (CUT). The contradiction between the desire for central (state) control and uniformity, on the one hand, and the possibility of locally idiosyncratic development, on the other, was neither fully recognized nor resolved in either party. Both ended up opting for a centralized "statist" view. For the Socialists, this derived from a Leninist preoccupation with power and the historical Marxist conception of a dictatorship of the proletariat as expressed in a single uniformity-imposing national party. For the Radicals, it grew out of the "Teaching State" concept. Both positions reflected a lingering, not usually recognized and often strongly denied, inheritance from the traditional Mediterranean corporatist emphasis on a tutelary state. The disagreement between the Socialists and Radicals dealt with the *content* of the "discourse of the State."

Dominguez shared the MAPU view and was, therefore, opposed in principle to the ENU proposal, in either the Socialist or the Radical version. He saw it as having the "smell of the school" and representing an unfortunate combination of the longstanding desire of the left-wing teachers' unions to impose a uniform ideology on education and the highly centralizing and control-oriented "Teaching State" tradition of the Radicals. He thus found himself in the position of being asked to help edit and modify a document with whose underlying principles he disagreed. Under these circumstances, his objective was to use his writing skills to tighten the analysis and clarify the ENU document, inserting the MAPU position wherever he could.

The objectives of the other members of the group reflected their previous arguments. Tapia wanted to alter the implementation timetable, and he particularly wanted to eliminate what he perceived to be the worst excesses of revolutionary Socialist rhetoric. Nuñez' primary objective was to preserve as much as possible of that ideological position to which he was committed. Araya shared Tapia's objectives, but he was also interested in improving the technical and structural aspects of the proposal. It was from this mix of different personal histories, ideological positions and objectives that the final document emerged.

The actual rewriting was undertaken by Nuñez, Araya, and Dominguez, each of whom took responsibility for certain sections of the original document. They worked individually and met frequently as a group to share and compare ideas. Tapia's role was to check the emerging draft and keep everyone on schedule. By mid-January, they had a preliminary draft, which was presented to the full coordinating committee. Although the document was still incomplete, the committee authorized the editing group to produce a final version without having to seek additional formal approval. This would ensure that the deadline could be met. This deadline had not been chosen arbitrarily. Ministry officials wanted to have the final proposition in the hands of members of the National Council of Education before they left for their summer holidays, so that they could read it carefully during February and be ready to discuss it in early March, before the school year began. This schedule was essential if there was to be any hope of starting implementation at the beginning of the 1973 school year.

Although Allende had insisted that the new version be acceptable to all of the Popular Unity parties, at no point in January was formal approval sought from the central committees of any of the parties. Within the overall crisis the government was facing, educational policy did not have a high priority, and most members of the coordinating committee perceived themselves as having the confidence of their parties. In addition, such consultation would have produced further delay. It was also not considered necessary to keep Allende or the central coordinating committee of Popular Unity informed regarding the details of the emerging policy proclamation.

The president occasionally asked the minister if he was having any difficulty "managing this thing," to which he replied that there were no problems. (This lack of detailed communication with higher authorities is not as strange as it might at first seem. Nuñez, Dominguez, Araya, and Tapia were all closely associated with their own party central committees.)

While this rewriting was taking place, the concern regarding the political impact of the original document had been strengthened by the fact that in early January the ENU Commission report had been leaked to the opposition press. The tone of the newspaper report provided a foretaste of what to expect if the hard-line rhetoric were not eliminated. This also led the editors to pay careful attention to the whereabouts of each copy of each preliminary draft on which they were working.

In an article headlined, "Confidential Report: 1973: Popular Unity Will Implement a Marxist Plan in Education," *La Prensa* strongly attacked the ENU Commission document, quoting extensively from it. It noted that "The agreed intention to apply a Marxist scheme in Chilean education can be seen in the new educational program elaborated by the planners of the Government of Salvador Allende, which *La Prensa* has acquired." It also noted that "along with open references to the sectarian political character they want to give to Chilean public education, and following the models applied in Cuba, they are insisting that students, in addition to their own activities, MUST WORK 'in order to convert them into active builders of the new society.' " Radical party opposition to the proposal was also reported, along with a "fierce fight" between Tapia and the Socialists, but the article suggested that it appeared the Socialists were prepared to move the reform forward in spite of the opposition within the ministry (9 January 1973).

In an editorial commentary three days later, the same newspaper claimed that the objective of the implementation of ENU "is nothing other than a contribution, with a new type of ideological instrument, to the installation of Marxist socialism, through indoctrination and training of Chilean children and youth in the acceptance and practice of collectivist forms of living." It also emphasized the "notable similarity between the model sponsored by the Chilean Socialist Party and the educational models of Popular China and Cuba." The editorial finally observed: "In the fulfillment of this great objective of instrumentalizing education and placing it at the service of its own official ideology, Popular Unity is playing one of its most decisive cards in the consolidation of Marxism in Chile" (12 January 1973.)[11]

The final editing of the new version was completed on the last Sunday in January beside the swimming pool in Tapia's garden. At this juncture, the minister intervened forcefully and pointedly, insisting on the elimination or alteration of a number of phrases and passages which were still, in his view, too revolutionary or simply unclear, with Araya occasionally joining in to demand further softening or clarification of the language.

The final document which emerged was, as had been intended, a compromise between the contending views within the ministry and the government. While the Radicals managed to eliminate or soften much of what they regarded as the worst excesses of revolutionary rhetoric, the basic elements of the hard-line Socialist analysis, which were essential to Nuñez, were nonetheless maintained. Dominguez was able to insert some aspects of the MAPU position into the text. The structural change proposals and the implementation schedule were technically improved. Moreover, one month of concentrated editing by a small group of skilled writers produced a document which was much clearer and better organized than the ENU Commission report.

Nuñez wrote the introduction to the final document. It was no longer labelled the "definitive version" of the government's proposal which would serve as a basis for official decisions. Rather it was described, as Tapia had wanted, as a report from the superintendency, "for the consideration of" the National Council of Education and, through it, the wider community (Ministerio de Educación Pública, February 1973, p. 1). The intention of the presentation of the document was "to open the debate," to "motivate and orient discussion" within the national community. Moreover, any attempts at school reorganization undertaken in 1973 were clearly labelled as "experiments." It was also noted that the National Unified School proposal was only part of a broader educational policy which would be outlined in a set of complementary discussion papers and a forthcoming speech by the minister of education. The new introduction significantly modified the finality and apparently compulsory character of the ENU Commission report.

The first section of the final report, which was drafted by Nuñez, was entitled "A National System for Permanent Education in a Society in Transition to Socialism." It began by observing that "the strategic perspective which illuminates the new educational policy assumes the construction of a *humanistic* socialist society, based on the development of productive forces, on overcoming economic, technological and cultural dependency, on the establishment of new relations of production, and on authentic democracy and social justice guaranteed by the effective exercise of power by the people" (p. 2, emphasis added). The addition of the modifier "humanistic" represented a significant concession, since the phrase "humanistic socialism" was understood by important sectors of the opposition to refer to some non-Marxist form of socialism (interview with Ernesto Livacic, 24 September 1982). The principal theme of the first section was the concept of "permanent education." In spite of the modifier "humanistic" which was introduced into the first sentence, the development and definition of this major theme clearly reflected Marxist socialist analysis. There would be a national system which would provide educational attention "from birth to old age" (p. 2). Permanent education was to be understood as *"education of the masses*, by the masses and for the masses, in a society of the socialist type, in which the community progressively organizes itself to assume collective responsibility for educating its members, while the regular institutions of schooling, which up to now have maintained a species of very costly educational monopoly for the dominant minorities, are slowly overcoming the barriers that separate them from concrete social life" (p. 2, emphasis in original). Such education would be "the only viable response to the needs of a society in a revolutionary transition" (p. 2).

The identification of two areas of education, regular education and extra-school education, was maintained with a few modifications. The National Unified School was still to involve a new form of organization of the existing institutions of preschool, primary, and secondary education in the area of regular education in order to eliminate the barriers between them, which reflected the "existing class contradictions." A significant change was introduced into the statement of the objectives of the area of regular education. In the original version, this area was to provide general and polytechnical education in accord with the capacities and interests of the individual and "the possibilities and needs of the collectivity" (p. 8). In the final report, this area of education was to respond only to the "psycho-biological needs of the students" (p. 2); all reference to the "collectivity" was eliminated. The definition of the extra-school area was not fundamentally changed. However, a more flexible and experimental conception of planning for programs and institutions in this area was introduced along with the possibility of obtaining formal academic credits for university admission through extra-school educational experiences, including work experience.

The second section, "Basic Principles," was drafted by Dominguez. It was a reorganized and more coherent presentation of analyses of the Chilean educational reality which had been scattered in various parts of the previous report. The analysis of the structural crisis of Chilean education was presented dialectically as a series of nine contradictions, some of which reflected traditional socialist understandings, and a few of which reflected the MAPU emphasis on base level non-centralized planning. For example:

2.1 The contradiction between the growing process of socialization of economic, social and political relations (a product of such factors as industrialization, urbanization, the demographic explosion and the scientific-technological revolution), and the inability of a classist and individualistic educational system to respond to the educational needs which this process brings with it, but rather to continue promoting an anachronistic capitalist ideology.

2.3 The contradiction between the powerful fight which is freeing the people to make of Chile an effectively democratic society in which power is exercised by the great majorities, and an educational system designed to reproduce a class society and its consequent system of domination of the majority by a minority and the exploitation of man by man.

2.8 The contradiction between the needs for organization, planning and administration implied by the development of a democratic society, and the centralized, authoritarian and compartmentalized character of the educational administrative system, which favors the development of verticalist bureaucratism which strangles popular potential and the consideration of the particular needs of each region, which acts as a brake upon the expansion and improvement of services, and which limits the development of the regional and local potentials of the system. (pp. 3-4).

The third section "Characterization," was drafted by Araya. It maintained the eight characteristics of the National Unified School outlined in the ENU Commission report and found in previous documents for which Nuñez had been responsible: National, Unified, Diversified, Democratic, Productive, Integrated with the Community, Scientific and Technological, and Planned. However, the Radical influence was clearly evident. For example, in the introduction to the section, a reference to the "revolutionary process" was dropped. The definition of "national" eliminated mention of "emancipation from ideological, cultural and economic colonialism" and replaced it with "strengthening our identity and sovereignty." The definition of "Democratic" kept the emphasis on community participation, expansion of opportunity, and elimination of discrimination within the schools found in previous versions, but added the phrase: "in addition, the education provided will be based on the best democratic traditions of the people of Chile" (p. 5). Most importantly, two new characteristics were added, "Humanistic," whose connotation has been noted above, and "Pluralistic," defined as follows: "because it will not be a vehicle for the imposition of a doctrine, but will rather try to make of education a liberating process in which students grow and form their own manner of thinking, through a creative pedagogy which critically and scientifically confronts reality" (p. 5).

The following section, "Objectives," was drafted by Dominguez. The most important change was in the first sentence. In the ENU Commission report the first general objective of ENU was "to contribute to the process of construction of a socialist society" (p. 14). The new version referred to ENU as "inserted in the process of construction of a socialist, *demo-*

cratic and humanistic society'' (p. 6, emphasis added). The rest of the section was a more precisely worded and more logically ordered presentation of the content found in the initial document.

These four sections occupied the first seven pages of the sixteen-page final report. The remainder dealt with structure and implementation. Araya was responsible for redrafting this portion. The major structural elements introduced in the ENU Commission report were maintained, although the text was expanded, providing more detailed and precise descriptions of the various components of the new type of schooling. The implementation schedule was also altered to eliminate problems Araya had identified in the original schedule, and the starting date for the first experimental applications was postponed three months, to June 1973. The one significant substantive change related to private education. The original document contained only one sentence on this theme, simply noting that private education would have to adopt the new scheme, which could easily have been read as effectively eliminating private schooling. The final version made the same general claim, that private education would have to adopt the curricular content and structure of ENU, but preceded it with the statement that such education would ''maintain its current administrative structure and all its rights and obligations'' (p. 11). It then indicated that, to assist private schools in implementing the new plans, they would be provided by the state with many services previously granted only to public schools, such as free texts, technical assistance, and in-service training of teachers (private school teachers had been complaining for some time that they had no access to such training). Beyond providing such incentives, a number of possible mechanisms was suggested by which private schools could, if they wished, integrate themselves into the educational complexes to be formed in their locales ''without losing their quality as private establishments'' (p. 11).

When the final text was agreed to by the four editors at the end of that January Sunday, mimeographed copies were quickly produced and sent by mail to all members of the National Council of Education, although most did not actually read it until they had returned from their vacations. The sub-secretary was given responsibility for producing one hundred thousand copies as quickly as possible for nationwide distribution. This massive distribution (no educational reform proposal had ever been so widely circulated in Chile) was meant to indicate that the government truly wanted a national discussion regarding the proposal. It was also hoped that if the document were widely available before the March election, it could be used as campaign material by Popular Unity candidates. The printed version was not, however, available until early March.

Tapia was extremely annoyed by the delay. He was sure that after they were produced, the printed copies were kept in the ministry for at least two weeks before being sent out, which he saw as a maneuver to sabotage their work (interview with Jorge Tapia, 23 May 1983). This was a plausible belief, as Waldo Suarez, the sub-secretary, had and freely used a great deal of administrative power. He often refused to authorize decrees or forward documents he did not approve of by simply allowing them to sit on his desk (including on at least two occasions personnel appointments sponsored and pushed by the president himself). However, the delay could as well have been the product of endemic bureaucratic slowdowns, which were particularly troublesome during the vacation period.

Whatever the cause of the delay, it was not until mid-March that the final official ENU report became widely known. It quickly generated an extraordinary public debate.

9

ENU as a Political Disaster: March 1973

As discussed in Chapter 7, both government and opposition forces were looking to the congressional elections in March 1973 to provide some resolution to the political crisis and institutional stalemate which had developed during 1972. The confrontation between the two major lists of candidates, the Popular Unity Federation and the Confederation of Democracy, which included all opposition parties,[1] was very stark and produced an electoral campaign which reached unprecedented depths of vituperative name-calling. During the campaign the opposition confederation generally presented a united front, defining the election as a final and decisive plebiscite on the conduct of the government. The extreme right forces were calling for a two-thirds majority in the two houses of Congress. This would permit the impeachment of the president, which they saw as the only alternative to armed confrontation. Simple electoral arithmetic made such an outcome highly unlikely, since only half of the seats in the Senate were open for election, and the more moderate opposition groups aimed for a substantial electoral majority which, they hoped, would send a clear signal to the government that it had to alter its course.

A series of electoral victories within education during the previous November encouraged opposition hopes for a decisive victory. FESES elections had once again produced a defeat for government secondary students, when Miguel Salazar, another Christian Democrat, was elected president of the federation, succeeding Guillermo Yunge. Popular Unity students, who had a majority in several other smaller secondary student organizations, refused to accept the results, and formed what amounted to a separate, government-supported federation, but the results were clear. Within the Catholic University, a "non-political" slate of students who were sympathetic to the extreme right National party also won a student election. In the Technical University Federico Santa Maria, in Valparaiso, a prominent Christian Democrat was elected as rector. Even in the University of Concepción, known as a particularly left-wing institution, the opposition gained the rectorship. Combined with the results of earlier contests for leadership of student federations and rectorships, these results in November meant that only the State Technical University was led by government supporters.

During the election campaign, Popular Unity forces were badly and publicly split. The Communists, Radicals, and Allendista Socialists appealed strongly for support from the middle sectors, frequently asserting that strong support for the government was needed to avoid civil war. The Altamirano wing of the Socialist party, on the other hand, continued to insist on the need to intensify and accelerate the class struggle in the nation. Historically, governing parties had lost ground in mid-term elections. Generally, therefore, government supporters hoped that they would not lose too much ground with respect to the municipal elections in 1971 and that their electoral percentage would at least not fall below the level which had won the presidency for Allende in 1970.

Voter turnout on 4 March was heavy, including some seven hundred thousand people who were voting for the first time owing to the recent enfranchisement of illiterates and young people between the ages of eighteen and twenty-one. Although both the government and the opposition ran single lists of candidates, the party affiliation of each candidate was listed on the ballot. This permitted calculation not only of overall support for each side, but electoral support for each party. Combining votes for deputies and senators and eliminating blank and invalid ballots, the results were as follows:

Government Forces		*Opposition Forces*	
Socialist Party	18%	Christian Democratic Party	29%
Communist Party	16%	National Party	21%
Other parties	10%	Other parties	6%
TOTAL	44%	TOTAL	56%

As one might expect, each side interpreted the results differently. Popular Unity spokesmen compared the results to the 1970 presidential elections, when Allende had received only 36 per cent of the popular vote, and emphasized that the results were better than any pre-election estimates and better than those achieved by any previous government in mid-term elections. The opposition compared the results to the 1971 municipal elections, when the government had received almost exactly half of the votes cast, and stressed the fact that the opposition percentage was almost equal to Frei's winning vote in 1964, which had generally been considered a landslide victory.

The most interesting comparison was to the results of the 1969 congressional election. In that contest, the parties which formed Popular Unity had received 43 per cent of the vote, a result which was almost identical to the 1973 outcome. The government gained two seats in the Senate and six seats in the Chamber of Deputies because of changed voting patterns in some electoral districts, but in spite of all of the events of the intervening four years, there had been practically no overall shift in voting patterns for or against the governing coalition. Even the moderate opposition took this as evidence that Popular Unity was still a minority government which did not have the legitimate authority to impose radical political and economic change on a majority which opposed it. Nonetheless, the unexpectedly high vote in favor of the government candidates (optimists within the government estimated that Popular Unity candidates would receive no more than 42 per cent of the vote—interview with Jorge Tapia, 23 May 1983) gave an important psychological boost to Popular Unity.

However, the most significant aspect of the election results politically was that they did not resolve the institutional crisis. Rather, they exacerbated the confrontation between government and opposition and strengthened the extreme elements on both sides. As Valenzuela has observed:

> The eagerly awaited congressional elections did not clear the political air. Instead, they gave renewed impetus to forces eager to accelerate the process of confrontation. The strong showing of the Socialist party within the Popular Unity coalition was interpreted by many as clear evidence that working-class Chileans were ready for an acceleration of the revolutionary program. By the same token, many opposition elements, concerned about the preservation of the status quo and prevailing institutions, saw the election as a signal that the rules of the game were no longer adequate to protect their goals and interests, and that unconstitutional means would have to be employed to curb the government. Violent and seditious acts escalated; military officers plotted. (1978, p. 87)

Within the government, the gap between the reformers and the revolutionaries widened, and Allende continued to vacillate. As a consequence of the election, he had to restructure his cabinet yet again. The extreme left had never been happy with the appointment of military officers to cabinet posts to resolve the October crisis. At the same time, these "constitutionalist" military officials were under increasing pressure from the now more powerful elements in the officer corps who favored a military solution since the political defeat of the government was impossible.

Faced with the situation, Allende appointed a new civilian cabinet drawn from moderate elements within Popular Unity. This was a somewhat conciliatory gesture toward the opposition. However, at the same time, the government decided to use a "decree of insistence" (signed by all members of the cabinet) to overrule a decision of the *Contraloría*, which had refused to approve the takeover of forty-three industrial plants occupied during the October Strike. This move was seen by the Christian Democrats as a totalitarian attempt to expand the social property sector unconstitutionally, and it brought to the forefront once again the conflict regarding the definition of the three areas of the economy which could not be resolved among the normal institutions of government, the presidency, the legislature, and the *Contraloría*. But the increasingly bitter and mistrustful relations between government and opposition made it even less likely than before that a settlement of the impasse could be negotiated outside of the formal institutions.

It was in the midst of this ever more tense political confrontation that the debate over the ENU Report erupted. In every respect a singular and extraordinary debate, it both reflected and fatally intensified the fundamental conflicts which had been developing in the society since September 1970. Hernan Vera, one of Chile's most eminent educators, who was sent by the Organization of American States for whom he was then working to advise and assist the government in the implementation of this reform, described the debate this way:

In the midst of the very confusing post-electoral period through which the country has been living, this very widespread debate brought with it violence without precedent with respect to an educational affair, a debate and violence which contributed to making the situation even more confusing. In addition to its extraordinary expression in the streets, the debate had one most unexpected characteristic: it was practically unilateral, and in the best of cases it was a debate among the deaf.[2] In effect, it was a debate between the report—unable to rebut or answer— and the minister—who had to be everywhere at once—on the one hand, and, on the other, the Cardinal, the Bishops, the Armed Forces, professional colleges, student centers, parent centers, teachers' councils, municipalities, cities, political parties, etc. While the report and the minister were dutifully aided by the official means of communication, the opponents and critics used profusely all of the means of mass communication. Adverse opinions of institutions and individuals generally received no response from institutions or individuals who supported the government. (1973, pp. 7-8)

Once started, events moved rapidly; so rapidly that many of the key participants have great difficulty remembering when important meetings were held, who participated, what was discussed, and what decisions were reached. Within the government, the already inchoate decision-making apparatus involving a variety of committees with overlapping membership and agendas, each trying to cope with the unresolvable internal conflict between hard- and soft-line elements, broke down almost completely under a barrage of concentrated attack. The opposition seized upon the ENU proposal as an issue which not only united its own forces but also brought into the fight the two major institutions which had previously maintained public political neutrality: the Church and the military. Popular Unity was unable to rally its forces in defense of the educational reform proposal. The psychological momentum derived from the results of the congressional election quickly dissipated, and by the end of April the government had retreated almost completely.

In this debate, the mass media played a particularly important role; they have to be treated as a separate set of actors operating outside of traditional institutional political channels. Valenzuela has described their role very well.

The media, which saturated every corner of the small country, became the principal exponent of the most extreme views. It was hard to separate the real battle from the symbolic battle of the newspapers, radio and television screens. Events were exaggerated and distorted. Lies and character assassination were the order of the day. Everything took on political significance, and even the most insignificant event became a crucial and more ominous turning point. Opposition papers, and in particular the influential *El Mercurio*, which had received large sums of money from U.S. intelligence,[3] were particularly skillful in rallying the vast array of opposition groups and organizations. For the most part the wielders of information acted independently of the political leadership, and their strident accusations and counter-accusations contributed to further polarization in the already volatile atmosphere. With the erosion of regular bargaining channels, leaders on each side were forced to rely more and more on a medium which did not always convey with accuracy the positions of leaders on either side. Symbolic politics increasingly replaced "real" politics, further undermining the possibility of creating institutionalized channels for accommodation. Leaders of the Popular Unity government and of the Christian Democrats both expressed their despair at the excesses of their respective media organizations. (1978, pp. 79-80)

The development of the debate will be dealt with here in as nearly chronological a fashion as is possible. The literature regarding this crisis is replete with neat summaries of the positions taken by various political actors and groups. In reality, these positions evolved almost day to day in the heat of an unpredictable and complex dialectic. They did not spring fully formed into view. Arguments developed bit by bit in response to what one's opponents were saying and doing. What key players said at any particular point was different from what they might have said a few days previously.

The debate also has to be reported in detail if it is to be understood at all. The symbolic importance of some phrases changed almost daily, and they varied dramatically depending upon the public political position of the person who used them.

THE DEBATE OVER ENU BEGINS

The process started quietly enough. On 6 March the Ministry of Education sent a circular to the directors of all schools in the nation which noted that the government planned to begin the implementation of basic changes in the national educational system in 1973. (Circular No. 15-12-14). It noted that the ENU Report had been delivered to the National Council of Education for discussion and designated the period 8-23 March for teachers to discuss and analyze the report and to plan their year's teaching activities taking the report's propositions into account. Two days, 16 and 17 March, were set aside for provincial seminars, which all school directors were obliged to attend, where they could clarify doubts and problems arising from discussions in their schools. School directors were also to inform their parents' and guardians' centers as quickly as possible regarding the National Unified School plan. The circular noted that while the month of March was set aside for debate, some preparatory measures would be implemented before all of the legal provisions were in place. Among these advance measures, specific mention was made of a new curricular plan for the first year of study within technical-professional schools which would be the subject of a separate circular.

Shortly thereafter, the director of professional education sent the circular (which became known as Circular 13) to all the schools in his jurisdiction. It authorized school directors to implement immediately the First Integrated Year proposal, if, in their judgment, after consultation with their school community, local circumstance such as enrolment pressure, lack of staff, or lack of equipment suggested that it was a pedagogically useful alternative to the traditional plan of studies.

At about this time, as Chilean officials returned from their summer holidays, a set of technical commissions began to work seriously. Their task was to prepare the complementary supporting documents called for in the

ENU Report and to develop the detailed curriculum proposals necessary for full implementation of the reform over the next several years. To facilitate their work, these commissions were given a great deal of office space in the Gabriela Mistral Building, a massive new structure in central Santiago which had been built to house the recently completed UNCTAD conference.

On 10 March the first public attack against the now widely distributed ENU Report was published, in the form of an official declaration from the Federation of Students of the Catholic University (FEUC), which became one of the strongest and most vocal critics of the National Unified School proposal. In this initial statement (*El Mercurio*, 10 March 1973), FEUC touched upon several of the main themes in the opposition attack against ENU: indoctrination, lack of pluralism, totalitarianism, imposition by a minority who assumed themselves part of an historically inevitable process of change, and unconstitutionality.

> Behind an empty claim of "pluralism" the report attempts to convert Chilean education into an instrument of political conscientization at the service of Marxism. All of its text shows that it confuses the concept of "education" with that of "indoctrination."

The declaration then quoted from the ENU Report such phrases as "the process of transition to socialism," "moulding new generations of Chileans," and "the process of revolutionary change" and observed:

> No one can fool themselves about what such language means in the mouth of a government of overwhelming Marxist-Leninist orientation. Abusing the concept of "life-long education," and attempting to eliminate all possibly divergent influences, it attempts to place Chileans— from the cradle to old age—under the mental monopoly of a dogmatic State, constructed on the concepts, values and categories of Marxist thinking. In common with all regimes of a totalitarian inspiration, the current government appears to believe that its arrival in power is historically irreversible. Thus, it is attempting to capture the future of the nation as though it were the property of a particular ideological conception, changing the Chilean educational system at its roots to mould it to political designs.

FEUC then claimed that the proposed educational reform violated both the spirit and the letter of the provision of the Statute of Democratic Guarantees, which insisted that "The education provided through the national system will be democratic and pluralistic. It will also be modified only democratically, after free discussion in competent agencies which represent all lines of thought." A reform of the sort proposed by the government could only be implemented by a law passed by the Congress, not simply by government decree.

> Nobody can convince anyone that a complete change in the Chilean education system can have as a sufficient base of support the very general point of view of a questionable National Congress of Education, the approval of a government agency such as the National Council of Education or a vague discussion in the future in *some* community organizations. Given the gravity of what is under way, the most serious attempt to implant totalitarianism in Chile, FEUC calls on all democratic sectors of the nation, especially those most closely linked with education, to form a great National Command to defend educational liberty and to fight against the government's model of the National Unified School.

It was clear from this initial attack that Tapia's efforts to soften the rhetoric of the proposal had not had the intended effect. The revolutionary socialist conception was still clear in the first few pages of the report, and there were still enough inflammatory phrases to provide targets for the opposition. Moreover, adamant opponents of the regime could not be convinced that phrases such as "pluralism" or "humanistic socialism" were anything other than camouflage for the real intentions of the government. Such belief was encouraged by the fact that the leaked ENU Commission Report, with its even more extreme language, had been circulating among some sectors of the opposition. Even among moderate opposition forces and those middle sectors who were still relatively neutral, the problem of who to believe became even more difficult as the dispute between the two lines within the government deepened and Allende continued to vacillate.[4]

On the same day that the FEUC attack appeared, a three-day conference at the Center for In-Service Training for 130 central and regional officials of the Ministry of Education finished. The objective of the seminar was to give them a detailed understanding of the report whose implementation was about to begin. An extensive report on this seminar in *La Nacion* two days later was the first significant discussion of the ENU Report in the government press. Several aspects of the article are instructive. First, there was neither mention nor response to the already evident opposition attacks. Second, the discussion almost completely ignored the several pages of revolutionary socialist analysis used in the ENU Report as justification for the proposal, and, instead, it emphasized that the project closely followed Unesco recommendations and had its roots in the consolidated school tradition in Chile. "This is a mandate from the United Nations for which Chile is already prepared" (12 March 1973). Third, the article contained several examples of sloppy journalism, failing to check data and getting elementary facts wrong, for which the government-supporting press was notorious. For example, of seven individuals highlighted in the article as forming the central planning team which had developed the ENU proposal, only two had played a major role. Similarly, a follow-up editorial in *La Nacion* referred to a speech from the minister to accompany the ENU proposal, which would be delivered "in the near future." The speech in question had been delivered by Tapia six weeks previously, on a nationwide radio and television network.

EL MERCURIO BEGINS ITS ATTACK

El Mercurio then began what became the most concentrated and carefully developed campaign against the National Unified School proposal. On 13 and 14 March it published the ENU Report in full, accompanied by an editorial attack on 14 March. The editorial, entitled "Educational Conscientization Increases," picked up and expanded upon the central themes of the FEUC attack. It began by noting that "education and culture are fields of battle for Marxism. In this terrain the offensive is even more profound when it appears to pass unnoticed by the common citizenry." It then condemned what it referred to as government attempts to infiltrate and control the mass media, particularly the production and distribution of new school texts which reflected a Marxist orientation. From this theme, the editorial passed to ENU itself, referring to its obvious "Marxist-Leninist inspiration" and claiming that this "totalitarian ideology" was going to be imposed "from birth to old age." Various phrases from the report were quoted to demonstrate the "Marxist concepts" hiding behind words such as "humanism" and "authentic democracy." "One must read from these words, then, that the new educational policy will be inspired by the ideal of the construction of a Marxist-Leninist society." Moreover, this new policy was to be implemented without any basis in law.

The theme of totalitarian indoctrination was then linked with the question of legitimacy.

> How then, after the triumph of the democratic majority on March 4th, can the government morally impose an educational policy, that is to say, influence the children and adults of Chile, based on a totalitarian Marxist ideology? . . . These observations show that the so-called National Unified School is not so much a new educational policy as it is a system of ideological infiltration into all sectors and ages of the population. The idea promoted by Popular Unity is to convert the

Ministry of Education into a species of Ministry of Propaganda, à la Goebbels.

A few days later, Nuñez replied to this editorial with a ferocious personal attack on the editor of *El Mercurio* and the paper itself in a letter to the editor which the paper was obliged by law to publish (20 March 1973). Indicating that he was acting on special instructions from the minister, Nuñez noted that all of the school texts which the government was distributing had been approved by the previous regime and related to programs of study established before 1970. The texts were neither new nor Marxist in inspiration. "As frequently happens, *El Mercurio* is lying, in the style of Goebbels which its editor had the opportunity to learn in the decade of the 30's." He then asserted that the ENU proposal was not his personal document, but that it reflected longstanding aspirations of the educational community as expressed through the National Congress of Education. "You ought to consult the reports of the Congress, as published in the *Revista de Educación*, No. 36, so that at least in this area you can forget the lessons of Herr Goebbels."

Nuñez responded to the charge of illegality by noting that *El Mercurio* was hiding the fact that the superintendency of education was charged by law with the responsibility of proposing new educational policy and that the ENU Report had been submitted to the National Council of Education, which was the legal route followed by previous governments. He asserted that the editor should not be "scandalized" by the fact that the proposal assumed the construction of a humanistic socialist society. "*El Mercurio* forgets that all previous reforms were based on a conception of national development which correponded to the political definition of the regime in power. . . . Why is it that something which was legitimate in the regime of Mr. Alessandri is not legitimate in the administration of comrade Salvador Allende?"

Nuñez then referred to the charge that ENU was going to be imposed upon the Chilean people as an "impudent lie," noting that no previous educational reform proposal had ever been subjected to such wide discussion before its implementation. "All previous reforms have been implemented by simple decrees. There have never been local, provincial and national Congresses of Education, nor have technical documents been widely distributed for study and discussion by teachers at the local level before being transformed into decrees."

Finally, he replied to the "birth to old age" complaint, noting that "permanent education" was a concept recommended by Unesco and that there were still many illiterate or poorly educated adults in Chile. Moreover, in a forum sponsored by a United Nations agency regarding the Faure Report, the editor himself had recognized that these were serious problems. "*El Mercurio* should clarify why it is opposed to pre-school education and education of adults." He concluded by charging that, "The 'fear' of *El Mercurio* is nothing other than one more scheme in its sectarian and politicized fight against the legitimate and necessary transformations which the educational community is demanding."

Rene Silva Espejo, the editor of *El Mercurio*, published an immediate reply, noting first that he would ignore the tone and language of Nuñez' letter and deal only with the substance. He began by conceding that the paper had been wrong about the textbooks, that they had indeed all been approved before 1970. "But we are certain that the editorial policy of the government will tend to substitute this fund of pedagogical culture for another which corresponds to 'the process of creation of the National Unified School, inserted into the process of construction of a democratic and humanist socialist society.'. . . If the present line continues the day will come when the educational process, including textbooks, will be immersed in an official ideology." He asserted that whatever the government might claim about widespread consultation, it was its clear intention to implement the National Unified School in any case. Given the reaction of the opposition to the National Congress process and the opposition to the ENU Report which was already beginning to swell, the government could hardly insist that its proposal had widespread public support even within the teaching force. There was no evidence that the proposal "corresponds even vaguely to a general agreement."

Silva Espejo admitted that the law authorized the superintendent to propose educational policy, but suggested that this did not oblige him to do so, particularly when a proposal clearly lacked careful technical preparation. The editor agreed that previous reforms had been proposed by the superintendency, discussed in the National Council of Education, and then implemented by decree. Moreover, they had obviously been based upon each regime's general political position. But none of these previous reforms had provoked such widespread disagreement, nor had they represented such a fundamental change, transforming education into a "mere tool" for constructing a closed social model. In addition, none of Nuñez' predecessors had been in such a rush to implement their reform propositions immediately. "The fundamental criticism directed against the educational concepts of the current government is that their application will lead to a closed dogmatism, to the systematic exclusion of everything which differs from official truth." This criticism was based not only on the current Chilean situation but on the history of other nations "which were democratic and pluralistic, but ceased to be so with the implementation of the Marxist Unified School." It was for this reason that the editor had claimed, in the United Nations forum cited by Nuñez, that the history of socialist educational reforms which forced minds into a fixed ideological mould demonstrated they were far removed from the basic Unesco principle of "emancipating the minds of the new generations."

This exchange was a clear example of the "debate among the deaf." It also illustrates the degree of interpersonal animosity, even hatred, stimulated—or perhaps crystallized—by the ENU proposal.[5]

Meanwhile, the attack against ENU continued. On 15 March Pedro Ibañez, a prominent National party senator, declared that:

> The Marxist goal of establishing a monolithic type of education in the name of the National Unified School, designed to conscienticize all Chileans, particularly the youth, is the worst of all the abuses committed by Popular Unity. . . . I am confident that an act of this nature will open the eyes of those who haven't yet realized that we are under a communist regime which is implacably taking into its hands all the instruments of power in our society. (*El Mercurio*, 15 March 1973)

On the same day, Antonio Carkovic, from the Center for In-Service Training, published a long article in *El Mercurio* which developed a new set of arguments (15 March 1973). Carkovic observed that while the theoretical foundation for the ENU proposal was clearly Marxist, it was a very traditional form of Marxist thought which had already been "demolished" by Marcuse. It would be "myopic" to criticize the proposal only with reference to its outdated theoretical base. Rather, it suffered from three serious technical-pedagogical defects. First, no technical reasons had been given which would justify the desire of the government to implement rapidly a total change in the educational system with its "evident risk of chaotically disarticulating the operation of the existing system." This was an accurate charge. Neither the ENU Report nor any of the statements by government officials had outlined in detail the analyses of enrolment pressure and impending fiscal disaster which were seen within the Ministry of Education as justifying the very quick implementation of the reform.

Carkovic's second objection was that such a thorough restructuring of the educational system would require not only the careful reformulation of curricula and teaching methods at all levels but also massive retraining of all the nation's teaching force and complete restructuring of the educational administrative apparatus. Implementation without such preparatory work was sure to lead to serious difficulty. This of course was a concern of the Radicals and Communists within the government.

His final complaint related to the availability of sites for the projected work-study programs. The problem was not simply that it was unclear how enough sites for on-the-job experience for all students would be found and matched to student interests and aptitudes. The problem resided in the fact that different regions of Chile were at different levels of technological development. Only the minority of students living in certain already favored areas of the nation could conceivably have access to on-site training in the most advanced technologies. Under these conditions, relying on local enterprises to provide technical training would mean that most students would not be trained in the more advanced technologies the nation needed for its development; they would be "middle level technicians" in name only. Moreover, this would create a new and uncontemplated type of social stratification based on geographic origin and would impede future mobility within the labor force.

On the following day, another editorial appeared in *El Mercurio*. This time it focussed on the proposals for massive in-service training of teachers. *El Mercurio* suggested that because of the government's "desire to -politically instrumentalize education, violating all types of pluralism," one could be sure that the "reeducation" provided would be political rather than technical, producing a "standardized and uniform teaching force, a grey bureaucracy," in which individuality would be non-useful, if not "counter-revolutionary" (16 March 1973).

On 18 March FEUC published another declaration. This time, it asserted that ENU was illegal since its implementation depended upon the Decree of Democratization which had been rejected by the *Contraloría*. Also, the proposal was unconstitutional because it proposed a unilateral view of the ideological problem of the nation and "assigns to education an official party orientation" (*El Mercurio*, 18 March 1973).

The next day, *La Nacion* attempted to reply to the escalating opposition attack in an editorial comment. However, it did not directly deal with any of the arguments; rather, it attacked the attackers.

> From the pages of the reactionary opposition newspapers we have seen the beginning of a virulent attack against the decision of the Popular Unity Government to apply the most modern educational objectives which will culminate in the Unified School, an aspiration of all the progressive teachers of Chile, and of the entire world. But not of course of the conservative, traditionalist and retarded elements who are at the service of bourgeois ideology and its imperialist and neocolonialist expressions.

The editorial was accompanied by a full-page feature story on a large Unesco educational project in Chile, called CHI-29, which had been headed by Mario Astorga since he left his post as minister of education. Again no specific reference was made to opposition arguments; the message was that Unesco supported the ENU proposition and that through this cooperative aid project it was providing the technical and administrative back-up and training required for the successful implementation of the educational reform (19 March 1973).

That same day, Jorge Tapia delivered a long speech to a joint meeting of ministry officials and SUTE and CUT representatives convoked to discuss the report. The speech provided the clearest and most detailed defense of the ENU proposal that had yet been developed, but it was reported in neither the government nor the opposition press (indeed, it was not published until August, 1973, in an issue of *Revista de Educación* No. 43-46, devoted to the government's reform proposals). Nonetheless, it provided a good indication of Tapia's position as it had developed by mid-March.

In response to the charge that government was trying to implement ENU too rapidly, the minister provided a carefully detailed explanation of the enrolment and financial crisis foreseen by the government, noting finally that:

> This government cannot now, and will not be able to, support the kind of university expansion which will result from the projections of secondary school development. . . . [Without policy changes] we are preparing the conditions for unemployment of the educated, that is we are preparing enormous contingents, thousands and thousands of Chileans, under such conditions, with such errors, that they will feel both frustrated and non-useful. And if we produce unemployment of the educated, we must also predict the rebellion of the educated, which would be more damaging than any other destructive force we could have. . . . This is why there are deadlines with respect to the National Unified School, to point out that this is urgent, that we have to do something rapidly, and to do it within these deadlines if we can. I want to be very clear: I welcome dialogue; I welcome critical observations, and support. But if the criticism or argumentation is exclusively political our attitude will also be exclusively political. (p. 24)

Tapia noted that the opposition was claiming that the constitutional requirement, in place since October 1970, for free and democratic discussion of any change in education required that Congress implement such a reform by law. To this he replied that, as a juridical scholar and as a member of the group which had written the Statute of Democratic Guarantees, he was convinced that while changes in the administrative structure of the ministry required a congressional law, an educational reform such as ENU could constitutionally be implemented by decree. This was his position "with neither doubt nor vacillation" (p. 25).

With respect to the argument that ENU represented an attempt to impose a single ideology in education, Tapia observed that the basic ideas in the ENU proposal had already been widely discussed in forums where all sectors were represented, that it was being discussed throughout the nation, and that the discussion would continue. He asserted that it was the attitude of the opposition which was anti-democratic and an offense against pluralism.

> We have to understand that this pluralism is one of the defining characteristics of the democratic way of life. Democratic thought and democratic life assume not only that different currents of thought will exist, but that these different currents can freely be expressed. This is what we habitually call freedom of opinion. And no one could seriously deny that in this country we have freedom of opinion, in every form it can take. But it assumes not only freedom of opinion, but the reciprocal willingness to listen to other opinions; to listen with real receptivity, based on the position that nobody is the exclusive, absolute and unique repository of the truth, and that it is therefore always possible to find in the opposing position part of the truth for which one is searching. . . . Even while we maintain with very clear emphasis the substantial value of the global conceptions each one of us has, it is still the case that no one is an autonomous and unique depository of truth. To the extent that we are intellectually and spiritually open, this brings us to the logical and human necessity to listen to our opponents, and to search together for a solution on which we can agree. (p. 21)

This plea for honest and open debate clearly reflected the traditional Radical opposition to ideological dogmatism and belief in the fundamental value and necessity of the principles of parliamentary democracy. Given the disputes within the Ministry of Education and government itself through which he had lived in the months since becoming minister, it could be read as an attack on the ideological extremists of both sides.

But he then turned the argument directly against the behavior of the intransigent opposition forces.

> How, then, can I accept the fact that in Liceo No. 4 in Valparaiso they threw the proposal in the wastebasket, saying they would not discuss it because it was illegal, because it was imposed, because it contradicted the Constitution? We sent the document there so that they could discuss it, and they refuse to discuss it. I do not understand this. Frankly, I am accustomed to democratic procedures, and after we have looked for such procedures I am left almost without alternative if in a democratic regime my opponent refuses to talk with me. (p. 23)

Even if this almost desperate plea for a return to the traditional Chilean style of democratic "convivencia" (living together) had been published immediately, it is highly unlikely that it would have had any effect upon the ever-more-polarized debate.

The next day, *El Mercurio* published yet another attack, this time in the form of a long analysis of the constitutionality of ENU written by Mario Calderon Vargas, previously a professor of law at the Catholic University and the lawyer for the Federation of Private School Parents and Guardians. After a detailed reiteration of various articles of the constitution, he concluded that the ENU proposal was a "flagrant violation." Noting the prohibition of any "official party orientation" in education, he observed:

> When a government, from the President of the Republic himself, not only does not deny its Marxist-Leninist nature, but reaffirms it on every possible occasion, when the two parties which today form Popular Unity also reiterate it, if they talk in an official document written by a socialist militant of "socialism," we are not going to believe that they are referring to a "humanistic" socialism, or to the utopian socialism of Owen. (20 March 1973)

Since the nation had just categorically rejected this political-philosophical position in the congressional elections, it was clear, he asserted, that the constitutional requirement for free and democratic discussion could not be met through debates in such government-controlled entities as the National Congress of Education or the National Council of Education. Only the full National Congress which had just been elected could rule in such matters.

On the following day, a brief reply to the opposition was published in *Puro Chile* (21 March 1973) in the form of an "exclusive interview" with the minister of education. It was simply reported that Tapia claimed:

> The National Unified School is not a "Marxist" invention. Rather, it is the school of the present and the future, supported by the highest educational authority in the world: Unesco. . . . There are sectors which are trying to block this initiative, using exclusively political criteria. . . . We accept the fact that some people will disagree, but it is inconceivable that some sectors will not even discuss the matter.

In contrast to this brief government reply, *El Mercurio* published a series of articles on the same day. First, there was an editorial criticizing the voluntary work aspect of ENU. It suggested that such work would be voluntary in name only, since any student who wished to enter university or get a good job would have to have a good record of "voluntary" labor. This meant that in reality it would be a source of unpaid forced labor for the socialized sector of the economy. This was only a "servile copy" of programs which had already been tried, and failed, in the Soviet Union and its satellites. Moreover, it claimed, supervisors in work sites would be chosen not for their technical skills but for their ideological correctness, which would expose inexperienced adolescents to the danger of accidents. "In this fashion, Marxism seeks the premature proletarianization of the new generations, moulding them into a pattern which is uniform and grey, but suitable for massive political and ideological control" (21 March 1973).

In the same edition, a declaration from Miguel Salazar, the president of FESES, was published. He began with a positive observation:

> In our opinion, the National Unified School is important for Chile, and it is a brilliant idea for Chilean education which should not be attacked on purely political grounds. Moreover, the National Unified School is not an invention of this government, but something that was contemplated in the educational reform plans of the Frei administration. (21 March 1973)

He then listed his criticisms. The plan was technically inadequate since little or no attention was given to problems of financing the reform, providing adequate facilities in the secondary schools for the new type of curriculum, or providing in-service training for the teachers. In spite of government claims that the proposal would be fully discussed by teachers before it was implemented, the proposed starting date of 1 July indicated clearly that the authorities had no intention of listening to the "majority voice." This factor, seen in conjunction with the evident intent in the Decree of Democratization to maintain tight central control, giving local councils only "consultative" power, indicated that "Chilean education will be totally controlled by Marxism. . . . They speak of integrating students into a socialist society. We think that students should be prepared without conscientization, so that later they can freely choose how, and from what point of view, to participate in a pluralistic society."

He noted that secondary students could not determine their strategy until after classes started on 26 March. However, "there is no doubt that the government will be faced with a rejection by between 60 and 70 per cent of the student body. . . . We will enter into dialogue with the Minister of Education. If he doesn't accede to the majority will, we will employ other means. I would not discard the possibility of a strike. We think that the fight for a free and pluralist Chilean education will be big and serious, but we will pursue it to the end."

On the same day, the paper reported condemnation of ENU by the Normal School of La Reina (a municipality in Santiago), Girls Liceo No. 5, and Sergio Aguilera, who had been superintendent of education during the last years of the Frei regime. Aguilera indicated that while he agreed with the idea of the National Unified School, he had no confidence in the form in which it was being applied. It was impossible to plan such a reform effectively in the time provided. Beyond this, any reform implemented by the Popular Unity government would place education "at the service of Marxist-Leninist ideology" (*El Mercurio*, 21 March 1973). The statements by Salazar and Aguilera reflected what became a common theme among moderate opposition sectors. While they agreed with the general idea of the National Unified School, its application in the form proposed in the ENU Report had to be opposed on both technical and ideological grounds.

On 23 March, the Federation of Private School Parents and Guardians (FEDAP) officially entered the debate through its representative on the National Council of Education, Isabel Dominguez. In an interview, she noted that there were many positive and negative aspects of the ENU proposal and even more questions yet to be clarified. For FEDAP, however, two points were fundamental. First, a change such as this had to be submitted to Congress. Second, the fundamental role of parents in the education of their children had to be recognized. "As parents we are not going to allow ourselves to be considered only as procreators, and later as productive entities. We will not delegate nor give up our right to educate our children" (*El Mercurio*, 23 March 1973).

The fact that the private school community also contained some supporters of the government was demonstrated by the publication on the same day of a declaration from the Left Front of Private School Students, a group which had split from the main-line private school student federation which was adamantly opposed to ENU and the governments. This group strongly defended ENU.

> ENU, far from bringing about a society of slaves, which is characteristic of capitalism, will lead to the integral liberation of man and give him the tools for developing his critical and creative capacity, which can only occur in the kind of society for which we are fighting. The intentions of the enemies of the people are clear in all of their campaign against ENU. They are trying to provoke a new bosses' strike, like that of last October, in order to stop the process of liberating our people. (*La Nacion* and *El Mercurio*, 23 March 1973)

THE CHRISTIAN DEMOCRATIC PARTY OFFICIALLY ENTERS THE DEBATE

Since the public debate had erupted, Christian Democracy, the largest single opposition force, had remained officially silent. There was debate within the party between those who rejected the ENU proposal completely and others who considered that the technical and structural change proposals were valuable and necessary extensions of their own reform and were therefore willing to negotiate to achieve a mutually acceptable educational change plan. Finally, on 23 March the party issued an official declaration:

> With reference to the report of the Ministry of Education regarding the National Unified School, the Christian Democratic Party declares:
>
> 1) The nation has been surprised by a proposal which would replace the existing educational system, thus jeopardizing the cultural values of the Chilean people.
>
> 2) Christian Democracy is aware of the need to perfect and improve the existing educational system according to the economic, social and cultural development needs of the current moment, since it was the initiator of a profound educational transformation which had as its objective integrating education with the aims and objectives of national development, in accord with a process of change which was a faithful reflection of majority thought.
>
> 3) The education reform initiated by our government, as a first step, contains the principles and fundamental bases that today one sees reflected, in a way, in the National Unified School scheme. Thus, our agreements, in the National Congress of Education (December, 1971), regarding the idea of a National Unified School characterized by the principles of pluralism, democracy and full participation.
>
> 4) However, the antecedents and information delivered by government authorities up to this moment regarding the National Unified School turn out to be, in their content and structure, lacking in consultation, contradictory, incomplete, sectarian, precipitate and unconstitutional.
>
> *Lacking in Consultation:* There has been a lack of real participation by the national community, thus contravening the agreements of the National Congress of Education.
>
> *Contradictory:* Given that they are trying to reconcile declarations of democracy and pluralism with affirmations which are completely ideological and clearly identifiable with the ends and methods of the minority government of Popular Unity.
>
> *Incomplete:* Given that the National Unified School Report that we are aware of is only a formulation of educational objectives and principles without further development.
>
> *Sectarian:* Given the fact that, in spite of the attempt to argue in terms of educational technique, they try to ignore the achievements and significance of the educational reform currently in operation, im-

plemented by the Christian Democratic Government, ignoring the fact that these were inspired by advances in modern education which were recognized by the highest international organizations.

Precipitate: Because they are trying to impose between now and the first of June a complete new educational structure without having available the necessary technical/pedagogical, administrative, juridical and budgetary support, all of which can lead to an anarchic situation with unforeseeable consequences.

Unconstitutional: Given that the report, in both its spirit and procedures, contravenes the dispositions of the constitutional guarantees.

Therefore, Christian Democracy declares: In conformity with what has been noted above, the Christian Democratic Party expresses its opposition to the National Unified School project of this government *in the terms in which it has been presented* (emphasis added). On the other hand, it is prepared to consider a project of law regarding the National Unified School which could contain as a previous condition a structure of democratization which would make possible the full and real participation of all the national community in the discussion and implementation of ENU through a national debate. The Party opposes, and will oppose without vacillation, any attempt to ideologically and politically utilize any kind of education change. Finally, Christian Democracy: 1) calls for the mobilization of all of its officials and members in order to analyze and discuss the National Unified School; 2) instructs its Parliamentary Members to immediately initiate the study and analysis of the legislative and juridical aspects of the National Unified School; 3) asks all Christian Democratic educational workers to join through their national association in the organizational work needed to make the Party's position known throughout the system. Finally, the Christian Democratic Party must note that the current situation involves everybody, and not just one political party. Therefore it will make available to the national community its technical, political and base level resources to aid in defining the orientation and future of Chilean education. (*El Mercurio*, 24 March 1973)

Although this official declaration was in many ways a strong attack on the ENU proposal, the language and tone were relatively moderate compared to the campaign being led by *El Mercurio*. But the fact that there were important sectors of the party which shared the more extreme *El Mercurio* viewpoint could be seen in an article written by "M" in the party's journal, *Politica y Espiritu*. The author began by observing:

The government of the so-called Popular Unity has initiated a new offensive with the very manifest goal of in fact terminating the educational pluralism which the Chilean people have won and which the Constitution guarantees. The pretext is the adoption of modern criteria and models of educational development. The vehicle is a set of measures which will lead to what its authors call the National Unified School. They try to create confusion by simultaneously advancing technical-pedagogical reforms with party conscientizing goals of a typically totalitarian type, to which they add the use of equivocal language and an attempt to leap over constitutional and legal requirements through the now well-known policy of "accomplished facts." (February-March 1973, p. 91-92)

The author added that the most positive aspects of the ENU Report represented a "natural unfolding" of the reforms begun by the Christian Democrats and then turned to the "now generally accepted concept of permanent education," noting how it was defined in the government's proposal: "of the masses, by the masses, and for the masses"

This is a good example of the confusion of plans and equivocation of language. The idea—not well expressed here—of the educative society appears acceptable to us, but this business "of the masses, by the masses and for the masses" in the mouths of Chilean socialists and communists—we know what they're talking about. For them, the masses will be the political directorships of their parties, and nothing more. Equally, the "socialist society" will be only one determined model of a socialist society: that which they have outlined and tried to impose—that of the so-called popular democracies.

THE DEBATE CONTINUES

As in many nations, the Sunday newspapers in Chile contain analyses of current political events. Sunday, 25 March produced several new developments in the debate over ENU. *La Nacion* published an interview with Ivan Nuñez regarding the National Unified School proposal which provided the first detailed analysis to appear in the government press of the enrolment and financial crisis which was the basis for the reform proposal and outlined carefully how it was based both on Unesco recommendations and on the historical experience of educational reform in Chile. He also replied specifically to several opposition arguments.

He first noted that "what appears to be a political attempt to proletarianize students is really nothing more than an adaptation of a worldwide educational tendency, adopted for strictly pedagogical reasons." He observed that the technical proposals had hardly been discussed by the opposition. "One notes that in this area we offer neither a target nor a weak flank." Indeed, the "polytechnical" proposals had already been implemented in several exclusive private schools, including those of the Salesian Order (the Catholic order of which Cardinal Silva Henriquez was a member). Given that situation, "they can hardly accuse them of Marxist conscientization." With respect to the charge that the government intended to mold students into a particular party line, he added the following:

> The Official Report does not have a party orientation. It does have a political definition, which is a very different thing. All the reports that have guided previous educational reforms have had a political orientation. All have been based on a particular conception of development . . . . It is legitimate that an Educational Reform of this type is preceded by a vision of the historical process within the nation, as has occurred with all previous reforms. . . . But this initial declaration does not mean that the students themselves are going to receive a party orientation. The same report notes the pluralist character of the reform, understood not as a mere dogmatic presentation of different doctrines, from which the students can passively and mechanically choose one or none. Rather, it is understood as the creation of conditions in which the students, in direct contact with reality, can critically form their own conception of the world, investigating it for themselves. This is true pluralism.

Beyond this, Nuñez claimed that the ENU proposition did not violate "freedom of education" since it contained specific guarantees of the continued existence of private schools and indicated various forms of aid they could receive to assist in the adoption of the new curriculum and structure. He finally rejected the charge that ENU was based on the Cuban educational system. The Cuban system was structurally very different from that of Chile and that proposed in the ENU Report. "Chile, faithful to its educational tradition, has attempted to go beyond what they have, without failing to recognize that the Cuban revolutionary process is more accelerated than our own."

La Nacion complemented the report of the Nuñez interview with an editorial entitled "Misrepresentations of the National Unified School," which summarized the superintendent's replies to opposition charges and concluded with the claim that "the reactionary right wants a battle and the forces of Popular Unity will respond to it because the interests of Chile and its youth demand it." It was becoming clear, however, that the forces of the government could not respond adequately to the opposition pressure. The "battle" was being fought not only in the pages of the press but also in countless meetings of teachers, students, and parents. Whenever possible, teams of government representatives were sent to these meetings to explain and defend the ENU proposal. They usually found that the opposition was well prepared with lists of questions and set speeches. It was generally evident that many of those who had actually read the ENU document itself had stopped after the first few pages which contained, in their opinion, alarming ideological propositions. Meanwhile, government supporters were either absent or unable to assist in the defense of ENU. Meetings of parents and guardians were suddenly overflowing. The typical experience of government officials is captured in this description:

> The first rows in the auditorium would always be filled with angry parents, some religious people, occasionally some military men whose children attended the school, in any event, members of the opposition. They would have the ENU Report with them. You could tell from their comments and questions that they had read it carefully. Most of our own supporters did not have the document, or had not read it, or didn't know what it was all about. The opposition had done their homework; our own supporters had not. The opposition always carried the meetings.

Several factors were at play. First, the government did not mobilize its own supporters. Again and again, parents, students, teachers, and lower-level government officials who supported Popular Unity have expressed to me their frustration at finding themselves in these meetings with no preparation, unable to defend the ENU Report. Indeed, reflecting the division within Popular Unity, many have stated that when they became fully aware of the nature of the proposal, often during the course of a meeting, they found that they could not in good conscience try to defend it publicly; their only alternative was to say nothing. Meanwhile, the opposition was ensuring that its supporters had copies of the report, analyses of it, and lists of questions to ask. At the same time, since the government teams ordinarily included one representative from each of the major Popular Unity parties, they gave differing interpretations of the ENU proposal. Summarizing his own experience as a member of such teams, Araya has noted: "All we accomplished was to create additional confusion. The Christian Democrats were better at explaining ENU than we were. It would have been better if we hadn't gone at all" (interview with Hugo Araya, 29 April 1983).

Moreover, the parents, usually middle or upper class but in many meetings including substantial contingents of working-class families, were evidently genuinely concerned about the effect of the government's plan on the fate of their own children. Two themes consistently arose. One was the problem of "socialist indoctrination," which was being discussed widely in the opposition media. The other was the question of linking education and work in a polytechnical scheme. The phrase consistently used in government documents and speeches was "educación y trabajo." In standard, traditional usage, "trabajo" referred to manual, lower-class work. The word for a non-manual, middle-class or professional occupation was "empleo." One sent one's children to school either to permit them to inherit one's own status as "empleado" or to give them the chance to rise from the status of "trabajador" to "empleado."

Popular Unity rhetoric consistently referred to all kinds of employment as "trabajo" and all levels of employees as "trabajadores" as a symbol of their desire to eliminate the invidious distinction between manual and non-manual work. However, the parents attending these meetings evidently were not persuaded by this semantic shift. Their expressed concern was that the intent of government policy was either to turn their children into "trabajadores" or to prevent them (in the case of working-class families) from becoming "empleados."

Lautaro Videla, the visitor general, who was one of the most active government spokesmen at these meetings, finally became so annoyed at this style of argument that, at a meeting of the Santiago Federation of Private School Parents and Guardians held in a private school in Santiago's most exclusive neighborhood on 24 March, he said to a packed auditorium: "Is everyone here a bum or a prostitute?" Shocked silence was followed by grumbling and shouting. He then said, "I thought that in a school like this, in a neighborhood like this, all the parents worked. Or if they didn't have a job they were housewives who worked at home. If you all work, how can you complain about the school teaching your children about work?" Of course, what Videla meant by "work" ("trabajo") and what the assembled parents understood the term to mean symbolized the incomprehension between the extreme left and the extreme right in the society.[6] On 25 March, *El Mercurio* reported this incident rather drily, noting that "the assembly was held in a tense atmosphere, and the moderator had to call for order so that the debate could proceed normally after the exposition of Lautaro Videla."

On that same Sunday, Tapia delivered a short speech on a national network to mark the commencement of the new school year. He began by outlining the basic characteristics of the National Unified School proposal and the reasons for proposing this reform, noting as well that on the following morning thousands of children would for the first time in their lives leave their homes to confront the new experience of schooling. Thinking of these young children and replying to the opposition forces in general and FESES' position in particular, he condemned those who were "sowing hatred and violence which is being incubated in parents, teachers and students." A national student strike would represent an enormous financial loss to the nation. "How can one then justify a national strike except under extremely grave circumstances, and without having exhausted all avenues of solution?'' With respect to the attacks against ENU he stated:

> Finally, I want to make the following categorical declarations: 1) The ENU proposal is still being discussed and there will be no final decision by the government until it judges that the discussion is complete; 2) No honest and capable individual can claim that ENU represents an attack against private education and freedom of teaching. Constitutional and legal norms will not be affected. Each individual or community will have the right to establish the kind of education they desire, or to complement official plans with the disciplines they consider necessary. (*La Nacion*, 26 March 1973)

Any possible calming effect of the declarations of Nuñez and Tapia on 25 March was eliminated by the publication by *El Mercurio*, on the same day, of an extensive comparison of the official ENU Report and the original ENU Commission Report. The analysis was headlined: ''Strange Mutilations and Changes in the Nuñez Report.'' It noted that the original report was labelled in its introduction as the ''definitive version.'' ''In good Spanish, 'definitive' means 'that which has been decided, concluded or resolved.' '' However, since there was a second version published in February, it had to be considered as ''even more definitive.'' *El Mercurio* concluded that it would be most appropriate to label the first version as the ''private report'' and the second as the ''public report.'' After a comparison of the texts of the two versions, the article concluded:

> This examination of the documents we have called ''the Private Report and the Public Report'' leads one to suspect that the authorities in the Ministry of Education do not want the public to be aware of their true intentions and their real thinking regarding the National Unified School. There is no other way to explain the suppression of entire sections and the significant changes in terminology. This means that we must analyze the Public Report regarding the National Unified School only in conjunction with all of the other documents produced by the Ministry and its personnel and other sources in order to reconstitute the thinking and deduce the position of Popular Unity with respect to the Chilean educational system.

In an editorial follow-up, *El Mercurio* stated that ''the first version clarifies the ends being pursued. These are nothing less than the Marxist-Leninist instrumentalization of education. . . . The tranquilizing comments from high officials within the Ministry of Education will not calm the alarm within the democratic school community. There have already been many occasions in which an officialist anaesthesia was followed by a bitter awakening among those who believed the promises of the government."

Over the same weekend, an article in the left-wing opinion and analysis magazine, *Chile Hoy* (no. I/41, 23-29 March 1973, pp. 16-17), appeared to confirm *El Mercurio*'s view of the "true intentions" underlying the ENU Report. In its analysis of the report and the debate surrounding it, an interview with Lautaro Videla was cited. Videla characterized the appearance of ENU as an "earthquake" which represented the "definitive entry of class warfare into education." The article asserted that the conception of ENU was sufficiently elastic that it could easily be applied either under the "communitarianism" of Christian Democracy or the humanistic socialism to which the ENU Report referred. However, it then quoted Videla as saying that "this is nothing more than a tactical step. . . . The National School will open up channels which will undoubtedly represent the extension of class warfare into education. There the force of the people will directly confront the old bureaucratic, individualistic and closed system of education." Videla rejected the Christian Democratic demand for pluralism and base-level decision making on the grounds that "this would mean atomizing the system." For ENU to serve their interests, the working class and the peasantry would have to use the tools provided by the Decree of Democratization and ENU to influence the direction of the system. "In this area the fight is also political and is a reflection of the class warfare that is opening up in other fields."

On 27 March, *El Mercurio* pushed its argument that the ENU Report did not represent the true intentions of the government a step further. In an article with the headline: "Marxist Inspiration of the 'Nuñez Report': Documents and Proof," an analysis was presented of several documents produced by the ministry previous to the ENU Report, including the "Contributions" to the National Congress of Education and the book published by the Socialist party in early 1971. After citing a number of examples of Marxist language and analysis in these earlier documents, the article concluded that:

> The Ministry of Education, through its public and private documents has pointed out that there is class warfare in the nation. It would therefore be ingenuous to think that when confronting the problem of educational reform they have adopted a neutral attitude, leaving aside political considerations. On the contrary, faced with a real crisis in the educational system they have sought for a solution which will favor the sector they say they represent in this class war. It is therefore insincere for government officials to complain because the opposition is trying to analyze the National Unified School Report from a political point of view.

In the same edition, *El Mercurio* replied editorially to Tapia's speech of the previous Sunday, referring to his arguments as a smokescreen. The minister's arguments, it said,

> cannot be reconciled with the authentic character of the proposal which has been underlined by the Superintendent of Education himself on diverse occasions. That functionary has been explicit regarding the final objectives being sought by Popular Unity with the political instrumentalization of schooling. Beyond that, other representatives of the Ministry of Education, members of the Socialist Party, have been claiming for some time that education is an ideal path for the construction of socialism.

THE CHURCH TAKES A POSITION

On 27 March, the Permanent Committee of the Bishops' Conference of Chile, under the chairmanship of Cardinal Raul Silva Henriquez, archbishop of Santiago, met in Santiago to consider the position of the Church. Several conservative bishops had been speaking out publicly against ENU, particularly Emilio Tagle Covarrubias, archbishop of Valparaiso, who had declared in a televised speech on 21 March that "The Church cannot accept the imposition of this type of policy in education" since the proposal showed a "lack of respect for the conscience of children, and does grave damage to the right of parents to provide the kind of education they desire for their descendants" (*El Mercurio*, 21 March 1973). At the same time, important sectors of the Church, influenced by the then-nascent theology of liberation, supported the Allende government and saw much of value in the ENU proposal. Allende himself was concerned about maintaining good relationships with the Church, and the Church had carefully preserved a position of political neutrality. Even the question of government subventions to fee-charging private schools had never been a serious issue for the Church since ecclesiastical authorities had themselves been reexamining the question of whether the Church should have schools which catered to the elite; and it hardly seemed reasonable that state funds should be used to subsidize the education of children whose parents were wealthy enough to pay for private schooling.

According to a source who was close to the inner circles of the Church at this time, the dominant position during the meeting on 27 March was that of the cardinal (for a thorough analysis of the role of the Church throughout the Allende years, see Smith, 1982, Part III), summarized as follows:

1) The government was legitimate. It had the right to exercise its authority.
2) The government clearly represented the popular sectors, and it was im-

portant that the Church be closely linked with those sectors.
3) The government had to respect the traditional values and feelings of the Chilean people; an important part of this was religion.
4) In education particularly, this meant that there could be no ideological imposition in the schools. The rights of parents to educate their children, or have them educated, in the values which they themselves held had to be respected.

As a result of their deliberations, the bishops issued the following declaration, which was made public by the cardinal in a press conference two days later:

1) A careful study of the National Unified School Report, Santiago, February 1973; the information we have regarding how it has been discussed up to now throughout the nation; and the understandable sensitivity of the Church regarding everything connected with education, prompts us to make the following declaration.
2) The report has, without doubt, positive aspects which we support without hesitation. We point out two. The first is the integration of all Chileans into an educational process which does not discriminate on economic, social or ideological grounds and which offers the same opportunities to everyone according to their abilities. The second is the integration of study and work, and the value given to physical work as one of the elements which contribute to the development of man and to the economic development and social progress of the community. We also see positive elements in the integration of people of all ages into the educational process, so long as the irreplaceable educational value of the home is respected.
3) Even though the Report declares itself to be very pluralistic, we see nowhere within it an emphasis on the human and Christian values which form part of the Chilean spiritual heritage, and to which a high percentage of Chilean students and parents adhere.
4) As Bishops we cannot cease to insist upon such "humanistic" values as: respect for man, and particularly the child; freedom of culture; the search for truth and the critical spirit and real conditions for its exercise; an equilibrium between the material values related to production and the spiritual values which contribute to the full development of man, including among these the real possibility of the Faith, and a life in conformity with Faith.
5) On the other hand, we see it taken for granted that the majority of the country accepts a proposition which declares itself to be "socialist, humanist, pluralist," and revolutionary, in circumstances where a considerable portion of the nation has shown itself to be in disagreement, either with the proposal itself or with the form in which it is to be put into practice.

6) With reference to the procedures through which the National Unified School is to be implemented in Chile, two facts call themselves to our attention. On the one hand there is a call for the extensive participation of the community in the debate regarding education; on the other hand this same debate will in practice be restricted to a minimum, and in some occasions excluded, and emphasis is placed on the fact that the ENU project will be implemented in any case, and within deadlines which are already rigidly fixed. The Report also presents practical difficulties—for private education among others—but its immediate implementation is being insisted upon, as though all the difficulties could be resolved on the spot. With regard to these two facts, the words "imposition" and "improvisation" come to mind even if one does not wish them to.

7) We must believe in the good intentions of the President of the Republic and the Minister of Education, with whom we have cordially spoken, and who we have asked for a *postponement of the implementation of the ENU plan* (emphasis in the original) in order to allow for a serious and constructive, truly democratic and pluralist, wide national debate, with the full and unlimited participation of parents and directors and teachers of public and private schools, students where their age warrants it, and all national organizations which are concerned about Chile's destiny.

8) Any plan for a radical reform of Chilean education will have to take into account, first of all, the parents, who have an irrefutable obligation to educate their children, and who must be given a real possibility of exercising that right and doing their duty. The United Nations Declaration of Human Rights, which has been signed by Chile, states: "Parents are the first and most important educators of their children. They have a preferential right in choosing the kind of education their children will receive."

9) This same plan must also have very clearly stated foundations and objectives, which correspond to other points of view of the entire national community, and not just one political group, however important it is or how good its intentions are. People pass on but documents remain. We must always bear in mind that others might use them or apply them with different criteria from those who wrote them, if the text itself is not perfectly clear and precise.

10) On the other hand, we view with pleasure the fact that a Project of Law is going to be presented, which has already been the subject of discussion between the Episcopate—after consultation with its respective organizations—and government representatives, establishing a National Council of Private Education, which will regulate in a form which appears to us to involve mutual respect and collaboration the relations between private education and the Chilean State.

11) We want to establish clearly that our intervention in the debate is

based exclusively on duties inherent in our roles as Bishops and apostles of Jesus Christ, and transcends any type of political party position. We respect politicians and parties, but we identify ourselves with none of them, and we do not want to be seen as supporters or adversaries in this terrain, but rather as exclusively concerned about the present and future of the Church and Chileans. (Oveido, 1974)

Shortly after the Bishops' Declaration was written and before it was made public, the cardinal telephoned Allende to inform him of the Church's official position. In his press conference on 29 March, the cardinal described his conversation with Allende as follows:

> The President of the Republic told me that he wanted an open, national dialogue, that this proposal was certainly not going to be imposed. I informed him—at this moment—that we had received information from the provinces and also from Santiago, that some individuals who believed themselves authorized to do it were stating the contrary. He told me that this was not the case, that it would not be the case, that it was against his principles and he would not accept it. Therefore, I have complete confidence and assurance that what we have asked for will become a reality, that is, the implementation of ENU will be postponed. (*El Mercurio*, 29 March 1973)

Allende then called Tapia and asked him to meet with the bishops immediately. Tapia recalls the attitude of the cardinal as being very "correct" and says that his questions, as well as those of the other bishops, were pointed and well-informed but not hostile. His impression was that the bishops were genuinely concerned regarding the surviving bits of revolutionary rhetoric in the final ENU document. He did not perceive them as having any sort of political objective in mind. The minister tried to "explain," "assure," and "give guarantees" regarding the government's intentions. Finally, one of the more outspoken conservative bishops, reflecting the opposition's problem of "who to believe," said, "Mr. Minister, I wish I could believe you."

What Tapia and the government wanted was a public declaration from the cardinal that the Church's doubts had been resolved and that they had the minister's assurance there was no need to worry. What they got was the cardinal's statement that the ENU proposal had both positive and negative aspects and that the Church had the assurance that the implementation of ENU would be postponed.

This relatively neutral stance could have been seen as a victory for the government, and it was lauded by the government press. *La Nacion* headlined its report of the Bishops' Declaration: "The Cardinal Proclaims the

Urgency of the National Unified School'' (30 March 1973) and followed with two long analyses which observed that the Salesian Order was already implementing ENU in its schools and that the basic ideas of ENU were found in the documents of the Medellin meeting of the bishops of the world and in various Chilean Church documents (29 March and 7 April 1973). It noted editorially that:

> The problems which worry the Church, and which are perfectly legitimate from its institutional point of view, can be discussed and clarified during a great national debate regarding such an important matter, which ought to exhibit the serenity and positive spirit of the Episcopal Document. (31 March 1973)

The opposition press reported the Church position without comment, or, in the case of *El Mercurio*, buried the report of the cardinal's press conference at the end of a report on an interview with the minister regarding another aspect of the ENU debate (30 March 1973). Despite the cardinal's insistence that the Church had no position regarding the political disputes of the moment and that it saw both positive and negative features in the ENU proposal, it was clear that the Church strongly objected to the plan. This was the first occasion since Allende had assumed office on which the bishops formally declared themselves to be opposed to a government policy initiative, and the impact was substantial. There was a widespread perception that the Church was even more strongly opposed to ENU than it was. In the polarized situation of late March, there was little middle ground left. In the view of most Chileans, one was either for the government or against it. If the Church could not completely support ENU, it was assumed that it was completely opposed.

In his press conference, Cardinal Silva Henriquez indicated clearly that he understood that he had the president's assurance that the implementation of ENU would be postponed pending a thorough national debate. He also described the kind of debate which the Church desired:

> It seems to me that always, and especially in these days, in the situation in which we are living, respectful dialogue that contributes something, is necessary. Therefore I would plead with all sectors of Chile that we try to understand each other, that we enter into dialogue with each other, that we reach conclusions with which we can all agree and which are useful for everyone. But this assumes, as I said, a kind of dialogue in which the opinions of the adversary are respected, in which no one is trying to take advantage of someone else and in which our truest values are recognized by everyone. (*El Mercurio*, 30 March 1973)

But the position of the government was not so clear. On the day before the bishops' meeting, expressing his exasperation at the nature and tone of the attacks on ENU and the refusal of much of the opposition to enter into serious discussion, Tapia had come close to calling opponents of ENU traitors. In an interview published in *El Siglo* (26 March 1973), he was quoted as saying: "if those sectors who oppose this measure with their mean and petty attitude succeed in dragging along with them large sectors of public opinion, they will be placing themselves in opposition to their own nation." Moreover, when Tapia was asked by a reporter from *El Mercurio* if the implementation of ENU would really be postponed, he appeared to contradict the cardinal's understanding.

> The debate regarding the Unified School is not new, and the teaching force understands very well that it has been going on for years. What is happening now is that we are asking for discussion, regarding a concrete proposal from the Ministry of Education, which cannot go on forever. If this had been carried out only among technicians it would have taken no more than 15 days, and I think that the established deadlines which have been fixed are more than sufficient, since this matter has already been dealt with fully and its aims and objectives were established by the National Congress of Education, which was held in 1971. I emphasize again that the deadlines provided are more than sufficient, but what is happening is that the opposition is giving this reform a political appearance, and is fighting against it just as they fight against everything that comes from Popular Unity, without even considering its benefits. We have already lost precious time trying to explain what the National Unified School *is not*.

ENU AS A COMMUNIST PLOT

Up to this time, opposition complaints, including even the most extreme attacks from *El Mercurio*, had identified ENU as a proposal based on Marxist-Leninist principles which was supported principally by the Socialist party, and any identification of ENU with the Communist party had been muted. Communist representatives within the ministry, following their party's cautious and pragmatic approach, had been less than enthusiastic about the ENU proposal. Nonetheless, at the end of March, an attempt was begun to characterize the educational reform proposal as part of the worldwide "communist conspiracy" which, through the Chilean Communist party, was attempting to capture the nation. On 30 March, *El Mercurio* published a series of abstracts regarding education from Communist party documents. The article began by citing passages from *Foun-*

dations of Scientific Communism, published by the Academy of Social
Sciences of the USSR:

> Based upon scientific principles, Lenin elaborated a plan for the con-
> struction of the socialist society. The integral parts of this plan are:
> creation of the material and technical bases for socialism, industrial-
> ization, collectivization of agriculture, and a *cultural revolution* (em-
> phasis added by *El Mercurio*).
>
> The objective of the cultural revolution is to affirm the advanced
> conception of the world [Marxism-Leninism], to free man from bour-
> geois influences and religious prejudices and all other antiquated cus-
> toms and conceptions, and to introduce new relationships and new
> customs into daily life.
>
> The socialist revolution nationalizes all avenues of ideological in-
> fluence: the press, radio, movies, theatre and publishing houses, and
> introduces *a new socialist system of teaching and education* (emphasis
> added by *El Mercurio*). . . . It transforms the schools and other teach-
> ing institutions, as well as all other instruments of ideological influence,
> into instruments of socialist construction and communist education.

El Mercurio then observed that "the Chilean Communist Party. . .follows
these doctrinal directives" and cited as proof a series of passages from a
book entitled *The Stage of Transition from Capitalism to Socialism* (published by "Quimantu," a government publisher), which it identified as a
Communist party document, although in reality it more nearly reflected
the thought of the Altamirano wing of the Socialist party. Key among these
passages was the following:

> Can education, in its various levels, play a positive role in the cultural
> revolution? It ought to, and can do so, if its content and orientation
> effectively reflect the Program of Popular Unity. Expansion of enrol-
> ment, raising the enrolment ratio, and establishing primary education
> free of cost are not enough. It is *necessary* to carry out a rigorous re-
> vision of the plans and programs of primary and secondary education,
> *in order that they reflect the requirements of the period of transition,
> in both the scientific-technical and humanistic-ideological fields.* (em-
> phasis added by *El Mercurio*)

Based upon these citations, the article reached the following conclusion:

> Thus, in order to truly understand the educational reform currently
> proposed by the Marxist-Leninist government, one must consider it as
> an aspect of the so-called cultural revolution. This process, which con-

stitutes a general and unavoidable law of the transition to socialism, implies the nationalization of all means of communication and the transformation of the school into an instrument of communist education. Beyond this, the cultural revolution prepares the path for the dictatorship of the proletariat—the first general law of the transition to socialism—and reinforces the directive position of the Communist Party.

An editorial commentary compared the ENU proposal to the writing of the French philosopher Louis Althusser, and concluded that "we thus see clearly outlined the central idea of the Ministry of Education regarding the use of education as an instrument within the strategy for seizure of power by the Marxist government of Popular Unity."

During this same final week in March, *Ercilla* (23-29 March 1973) published a striking editorial cartoon. It showed Marx and Lenin reading to a uniformed child from a book entitled "Marxist Unified School." This was depicted as a dream of Frei, labelled "nightmare of Catholics and democrats," and a dream of Allende labelled "sweet dreams of Marxists and totalitarians."

On the last day of the month, *El Mercurio* published a summary of all its previous attacks. It quoted liberally from documents published in Moscow to demonstrate the international communist origins of ENU. It quoted Videla's interview published in *Chile Hoy* to prove that the real and hidden intention of the government was to introduce "class warfare" into the classrooms of the nation. And it added a detailed textual analysis of the ENU Report to support the following conclusion:

> Given the nature of the current government, those who lead it and those who wrote the report, one understands that we are not dealing with an authentic democratic socialism but clearly with a Marxist-Leninist socialism, with a dictatorship of the proletariat under the direction of the Communist Party. . . . One must remember that for the communist pluralism stops when it produces ideas which are ideologically contrary to Marxist-Leninist socialism, as Soviet and Chilean theorists have repeated again and again. Discussion is only possible within socialism. To discuss the Marxist-Leninist ENU project from a democratic point of view is to be considered practically a traitor to the country.

On the same final day of March, *La Prensa* published, in an editorial commentary signed by "Plato," a vicious attack against the Radical party. Noting that Chilean parliamentary history contained many examples of "illustrious Radicals defending freedom of thought and education as the basic pillars of democracy and education," the author highlighted the "cruel irony" which saw a Radical minister of education, Tapia, following the lead of his immediate predecessors and implementing an educational reform proposal which "would cause the patriarchs of Radicalism to turn over in their graves." This clearly demonstrated, the commentary concluded, that the "Chilean Radical Party has become nothing more than a simple Department of the Communist Party, Chilean Section, a Department which is presented to the people as an independent party, only to give the Marxist government the appearance of pluralism" (31 March 1973).

At this point the Radical party was under enormous pressure. In spite of its long history as one of Chile's most important political forces, it had been steadily losing electoral support and had suffered several damaging internal splits. Within the Popular Unity coalition it was one of the weakest elements. Yet, it was still the dominant force in the field of education; though in this area of strength, it was being publicly identified as nothing more than a tool, first of the Socialists, and now, even more damaging, of the Communists.

Faced with this situation, the central figures of the party met for a private dinner in a central Santiago club, the Circulo Español. After a long discussion, which has been described by several participants as "frank but without recriminations," it was agreed that if there was to be any kind of educational reform, it would have to be something which could be supported by the Radical party, something which did not violate the position adopted by the party when it approved Hugo Araya's paper in November 1972. After this meeting, Araya produced an expanded version of his previous paper, taking into account the arguments which had developed since the previous November. This document, "Educational Change and the National Unified School" (Araya, 1973), is the most complete and developed version of Radical party thought regarding education in 1973. It was an example of the kind of "intelligent dialogue" for which the cardinal had appealed. However, in the turbulence of the accelerating political crisis, it had no impact whatsoever.

10

The Government in Full Retreat
April 1973

Over the weekend of 1 April, the position of the government was still not clear. In their Sunday editions, both *El Mercurio* and *La Prensa* featured long summaries of the evolving debate as they saw it. No new arguments were added, but the language became even more extreme. *El Mercurio* titled its report "National Unified School: Juvenile Captivity" and quoted extensively from the writings of Marx to demonstrate that "this project is directly descended from the Communist Manifesto."

Tapia spent the weekend visiting schools in the south of the country. During a press conference and speech in the city of Temuco, he made two observations which were immediately picked up by the opposition press. With reference to those who were attacking ENU, he said: "Whenever there is a project such as ENU which will benefit Chile, there is an immediate protest from those who would disunite, from those who destroy." He then turned to the implementation schedule: "There is no doubt that the National Unified School will begin this year, because there are many forms and levels in which it can begin." He qualified his assertion: "We are not slaves of deadlines. . . . The educational reform will be carried out, but deadlines are secondary and we cannot close off the debate because of them" (*El Mercurio*, 4 April 1973). The minister meant that even if the scheduled implementation date was postponed, the ENU proposal could be started on a small-scale basis. He also thought that such experimental application would demonstrate its technical flaws and could be used as a weapon against the Socialists (interview with Jorge Tapia, 19 April 1981). However, the impression left by his statement was that the government intended to proceed with the original schedule. This impression was reinforced by *El Mercurio*'s headline "Minister of Education says in Temuco: 'There is no doubt that the National Unified School will begin this year.' ''

This impression was particularly unfortunate because at approximately the same time the coordinating committee of the Ministry of Education, and the government itself, was deciding to accede to the bishops' request. Soon after the position of the Church became public, Allende met with the coordinating committee to discuss what the government's reaction should be. Not all members of the committee were present, and it is not clear whether some were not invited, or could not attend, or chose not to. The meeting took place on 2 April, immediately after Tapia's visit to the south. At the start of the meeting, Allende asked for Tapia's opinion. The minister did not respond immediately and suggested that the other members should first state their view. In the words of one of the participants: "It was a very strange meeting. All of the arguments had been made many times before. It was as though Allende were the judge, and each of us was presenting our best case to him." After listening to all of the arguments, Allende indicated his view that implementation should be postponed.

It is also not clear whether there was a formal meeting of the Coordinating Committee of Popular Unity. It appears likely that the president consulted as many members as possible by telephone, as was his habit when a crisis arose. However the decision was reached, several central figures in the ministry quickly became aware, through informal communications, that a decision had been taken at the highest level to postpone the implementation.

THE NATIONAL COUNCIL OF EDUCATION
AGREES TO POSTPONE IMPLEMENTATION

In the midst of all the public furor the National Council of Education had been meeting quietly to discuss the ENU Report. Following formal legal channels, the document had been written as a report to the council, and the members first discussed it on 13 March.

Members of this body included the highest level ministry officials, such as Tapia, Nuñez, Araya, Videla, Urrutia, Migone and Moreno; representatives of the deans of the major faculties of education in the nation and of public school and private school parents' organizations; a representative of private education; individuals from SUTE; and delegates from such community organizations as the National Agricultural Society and the Industrial Development Society. Although government members were always in the majority, there was substantial representation from non-government forces, and the National Council had a long tradition of thoughtful and mutually respectful deliberation. Throughout the ENU crisis this tradition was maintained. Participants in its debates have described the National Council as "having a very calm atmosphere" or as a "micro-climate of consensus and honest debate while outside they were shooting each other." Within the council individuals could shed their public roles and postures and work together to seek acceptable compromises. Throughout the debates, the report's main proponent, Nuñez, presided over the deliberations in a manner which was seen by other members as fair-minded and reasonable. Videla, who was publicly perceived as more intransigent, was seen by several other members of the National Council as one of its most skilled negotiators of compromises. Similarly, members representing agencies whose public position totally opposed ENU were able to work with government representatives toward a mutually acceptable resolution.

From the start of that first meeting in mid-March it was clear that if a formal vote were called, the government majority would carry the day. But forcing issues to a "government versus opposition" vote was not part of the style of operation of this body. Its traditional role had been to provide the incumbent government with a forum to test ideas and get a sense of the possible sources and strength of opposition to a proposal before it was publicly advanced. The Christian Democrats had earlier learned that when they ignored warning signals within the National Council, they often had to retreat publicly. The unusual feature of the situation in March 1973 was that the public argument regarding the government's reform proposal was occurring *at the same time.* In such circumstances the strength of the opposition forces within the National Council resided not in their numbers and not in signals of *potential* opposition, but in the fact that they clearly represented powerful political forces which were already active.

Within the council's debates the opposition representatives accepted the technical and structural aspects of the ENU Report with little question. Permanent education, linking education and work more closely, and better integration of the various types of schooling, both among themselves and within their local communities, were seen as generally accepted principles. Ernesto Livacic, the most influential opposition spokesman, referred to these ideas as "pedagogically impeccable." The fundamental objection of the Christian Democrats was, naturally, to the "subordination of education" to a particular ideology and regime. However, they indicated that they were prepared to continue discussing the proposal, for to reject it out of hand would close the door for a long time on any possibility of implementing needed changes in the educational system. The opposition had three other objectives: 1) that any educational reform proposal must be supported by a consensus derived from a broadly participative discussion; 2) that the results of the Frei reform should be seriously evaluated before the implementation of a new reform; and 3) that any reform proposal should be technically adequate and carefully planned.

The opposition's initial strategy was to delay a decision by the National Council until sufficient outside pressure could build up. At the first meeting, the Christian Democrats asked that implementation be delayed and that a broad national discussion be organized. When this suggestion was immediately rejected, they then began to ask for the technical supporting documents. The technical commissions working in the Gabriela Mistral building were, by the latter part of March, beginning to produce some support material, but almost every time one was produced, it found its way into the opposition press and was treated as evidence that the government intended to implement ENU immediately.

On Tuesday, 3 April, after the bishops' statement and after Allende had met with the coordinating committee, the National Council met to continue its discussion. Although Livacic was not fully aware of the government discussions, it seemed evident to him that Popular Unity would have to postpone implementation. He concluded that it would probably be easier to resolve the situation if he, rather than Tapia, suggested a postponement. Therefore, he proposed that the National Council take responsibility for organizing a "national debate" regarding educational policy, which necessarily implied postponement. If the debate were organized and controlled by the council, it might be possible to de-politicize the dispute sufficiently to develop a broadly acceptable educational reform proposal.

The first reactions from government representatives were negative. Tapia, however, concluded that it was an excellent resolution of the problem and declared that he supported the proposition. All of the government members immediately agreed. The council proceeded to produce a statement declaring that it was going to organize a new national debate and that the proposal would not be implemented until its completion. Thus, within five days of the public statement of the Church's position, the government formally agreed to postpone implementation of ENU and open the requested new debate.

However, the declaration of the National Council was not published in the government press until three days later (*La Nacion*, 6 April 1973). It was only the day after that that the decision of the National Council appeared in the opposition press, not as a news story but as a paid government advertisement (*El Mercurio*, 7 April 1973).

Tapia and other government participants in the National Council thought that this decision would "disinflate" the crisis. Tapia assumed that the opposition representatives within the Council really represented their sectors and that they would quickly communicate with their bases to take the pressure off the government. But this was not to be the case.

A number of factors seem to have been at play. Whatever representatives of Christian Democracy may have agreed to within the National Council, their party was becoming ever more sharply divided, with the sectors demanding absolute opposition to the government gaining strength. For example, in early April Eduardo Frei told a party meeting that there must be total and categorical "opposition to the Marxist attempt to implant totalitarianism in Chile. . . . I am being threatened by a spiritual death by Marxism and dictatorship. . . . I don't want even to live in a Marxist country" (*Ercilla*, 11-17 April 1973, p. 10). Beyond this, the opposition press— *El Mercurio* in particular—was subject to no effective political control. For those intent upon the downfall of the government, ENU represented too attractive an issue, gratuitously handed to them by the government, to let it die away. Moreover, there was a great deal of genuine concern regarding the government's intentions and an even more widespread mistrust of official government statements.

This could be seen in the speech delivered on a national radio and television network on 4 April by Patricio Aylwin, a powerful senator from the right wing of the Christian Democratic party. His purpose was to state the position of the party regarding ENU and to reply to several speeches delivered by Tapia, including his words in Temuco over the previous weekend. Aylwin noted that while Tapia and the government were calling for an open debate, Tapia had just said that to oppose ENU was to oppose the country. Aylwin replied:

> Where does this leave us? Does the government really want a free and democratic debate regarding educational reform, in which we can all participate with our own opinions in the work to which we have been invited, "to create together a new educational system for the nation"? Or is what they really want a farce, a mockery of debate, such as is practiced in the so-called "socialist" countries where the only thing one can do is agree, or risk being called "an enemy of the people or the nation"?

The senator also noted that although the government claimed that ENU would not be implemented until the debate had been completed, Tapia had said in Temuco: "The decision is taken. Do not doubt even for a second that the reform is going to go forward, and that 1973 is the year of the National Unified School." Aylwin continued:

> When is the government telling the truth? When it says that there will be no final decision until the debate has been completed, as it has promised the National Episcopate, or when it boasts that the decision has already been reached unilaterally to impose the reform by one means or another within 60 or 90 days?

Aylwin then emphasized that his party recognized the need for further change in the educational system. Their objection was not to ENU as such, but to "the form in which it has been presented by the government." Moreover, he insisted that any major change would have to be implemented by law rather than by decree. "This is our word: National Democratic School, at the service of all Chileans, yes. National Conscientizing School, at the service of an official party position, no" (*El Mercurio*, 6 March 1973).

In an editorial the morning before Aylwin gave his speech, *El Mercurio* had picked up this final theme. It noted that the technical aspects of the ENU proposal had been discussed by teachers for many years, had been introduced into various experiments, and had widespread support.

> Consequently, the debate is not for or against the National Unified School, which has received support from teachers of varying ideologies, but between the free school which Chile has had up to now and the conscientizing school proposed by the Marxist hierarchs enthroned in the Superintendency and the Ministry of Education. (4 April 1973)

A story appearing in the same edition illustrated the lengths to which *El Mercurio* would go in seeking examples to support its new theme that ENU was "communist." The "proof" offered was the fact that a few days previously Tapia had officially requested the renewal of the appointments of two East German advisors in agricultural education. One of the six reasons he cited was "the similarity between the educational system of the German Democratic Republic and that which the government is implementing in Chile." The following day an editorial entitled "Education for Communism" concluded that this demonstrated that the government was implementing the Eastern European educational model "behind the backs of the nation." This, claimed the paper, showed that the government "is in fact implementing the National Unified School, even after the President of the Republic and the Minister himself have promised to give a period of grace so that teachers, parents, guardians and the Church can present their objections" (*El Mercurio*, 5 April 1973).

On the afternoon of 5 April another Christian Democratic senator, Juan de Dios Carmona, introduced a completely new, and threatening, element into the debate. In a press conference he claimed that ENU would damage the integrity of the armed forces and the Carabineros (the national police force).

> When the Minister says that the project will definitely be applied this year, particularly to students in the first year of secondary school, he is indirectly submitting the Armed Forces and the Carabineros to a

transformation of their own specialized schools, since those schools will receive their students from ENU, dutifully conscientized in Marxist-Leninist socialism. This will begin, in the most subtle fashion, the gradual destruction of the essentially professional and non-political character of our armed forces. Even the most extreme leftists could not find a better way to attack them. (*La Prensa*, 5 April 1973)

This was clearly seen as a direct call for political intervention in the ongoing dispute by the armed forces. A few days earlier, *La Prensa* had published an editorial suggesting that members of the armed forces, *in their private capacity* as parents of children in school, had the right to involve themselves in the debate:

> Neither military discipline, nor any internal statute, nor any constitutional prohibition of political involvement, can deprive them of their right as parents to choose the education they want for their children and to protest if that right is violated or not recognized. (31 March 1973)

However, the author was careful to introduce this observation by noting that "the armed forces, as such, have nothing to say in the matter." Carmona appeared to be calling for an *institutional* intervention. Tapia responded immediately in a letter to the editor published the next day in *La Prensa*. He denied that he had said in Temuco that ENU would definitely be applied in 1973:

> What I have affirmed is that the government has introduced an educational reform proposal with the intention that it become a reality, but the deadlines and procedures for doing that are subject to revision, and that it will not be put into effect until the debate has finished. Contrary to what Senator Carmona says, we have responded favorably to the Cardinal's petition.

Tapia then replied to Carmona's claim that ENU would gradually destroy the professional integrity of the armed forces:

> The fantastic alarmism into which the senator has fallen exceeds all the limits of rationality, reveals an incredible disinformation, and can only be explained as a desperate attempt to oppose an educational reform which can only alarm reactionaries who are afraid of any social change that will lead to an authentic democracy. The schools of the Armed Forces have for many years followed a program which is very similar to the National Unified School; they will not receive conscien-

tized students, but rather men who are freer and more educated, prepared to better construct a new nation. (*La Prensa*, 6 April 1973)

Whatever he had *meant* to imply in his speech in Temuco, the words Tapia had actually used seemed to indicate a clear intention to begin at least a partial implementation. Tapia appears, both in his Temuco speech and in this letter, to have been carried away with his own rhetoric. Note again the proposition that ENU could only be opposed by reactionaries who feared all social change. This from a minister who was himself opposed to the proposal and who had privately indicated to opposition members in the National Council that it was not only in their own interest, but also in the interest of the Radicals and probably the Communists to delay implementation and have a new debate, since this would further isolate the Socialists who were the only strong supporters of the ENU proposal. He had indeed telephoned a prominent Christian Democrat and told him: "Look, you and the Communists have got to help us stop this thing."

Tapia was indeed willing to concede on the implementation schedule. Since the previous November he had remained convinced that it would be impossible and undesirable to do anything more than mount a few pilot or experimental projects during 1973. He considered this issue to be one of his most important "bargaining counters," but precisely for this reason he was not prepared to give in to opposition demands for postponement without wresting some sort of concession in return. He also had to convince the "internal opposition" of the need for postponement or await circumstances in which he could overpower them. Hence his *public* insistence throughout March, including the weekend just before the 2 April meeting with Allende, that the originally proposed implementation schedule should be maintained.

He had, however, seriously underestimated the strength of the opposition attack on ENU and the impact it would have on public opinion (as had most Popular Unity educational officials—even those who had predicted serious problems were generally surprised by the ferocity and degree of effectiveness of the attack). In such a highly charged atmosphere, the attempt to bargain in public had proven counterproductive. The government had finally been forced to agree to postponement without gaining any significant concessions. The minister's public defense of the original schedule served only to provide additional ammunition for the extreme opposition and to sow additional confusion regarding the government's attitude and intentions among more moderate opposition sectors, who were already steadily losing ground to the most adamant opponents of Popular Unity. In such a period of maximum confrontation the price of political miscalculation was very high.

THE DEBATE CONTINUES

In addition to these major events, throughout the first week of April the press on both sides continued the battle. *La Prensa* and *El Mercurio* carried story after story reporting individuals and groups who were rejecting ENU, claiming that it represented "mental colonization" of children or insisting that if the proposal were implemented they would formally complain to the Vatican. The government-supporting press finally became more active in defense of the proposal, focussing particularly on the attitude of the Church. On 6 April, *La Nacion* carried an article quoting at length from various Church documents published during the previous few years which supported the need for a reform of the type proposed by the government. This report also featured declarations from SUTE, CUT, and other organizations in support of ENU. All of the quotations were taken from a document prepared by the Technical Commission called "Foundations of the National Unified School," which supplied more than thirty pages of quotations from various authorities which could be used by government spokespersons defending the proposal. *Chile Hoy* (No. 42, 30 March - 5 April 1973) carried a careful analysis of the position of the Church as expressed in documents developed for the Second Vatican Council and the General Assembly of Latin American Bishops in Medellin (where liberation theology first became an important force) in order to demonstrate their similarity to the ENU Report (pp. 16-17). The same edition also featured a report on the opposition arguments titled: "National Unified School: New Pretext for Sedition."

During the same week, a Christian Democratic senator, Tomas Pablo, delivered a speech before the Senate, outlining the entire history of the development of the ENU proposal and the nature and basis of Christian Democratic objections to it. Emphasizing that his party recognized the need for further profound educational changes and that it was prepared to discuss and negotiate in order to reach a consensus regarding them, he concluded that the Christian Democratic objections could be summarized in two points:

a) The evident goal of ideological penetration which will in no way contribute to the liberation of people or the Chilean community.

b) The irresponsible adventurism of the project, which lacks the preparation and planning which are indispensable as a minimum guarantee of success in the fulfillment of its objectives. (The complete text of the speech was published in *El Mercurio*, 6 April 1973, and in the Sunday edition of *La Prensa*, 8 April 1973.)

At the end of this confusing week, Fresia Urrutia tried to clarify the government position. Along with other government representatives, she was invited to a meeting of directors and other representatives of private schools. The assembly announced the by-now standard objections to ENU: 1) it violated parents' freedom of educational choice; 2) it was ideologically unilateral; 3) it had not been subject to sufficient discussion; and 4) it had to be implemented by law rather than decree. However, they also stated:

> In spite of the above, there are aspects of the project which appear to us to be positive and which respond to an evident need for a reorganization of education. In this sense we hope that at the appropriate moment we will be given the opportunity to collaborate, contributing our own experience.

Responding to this relatively moderate opposition view, the director of primary education announced that: 1) there was no preemptory deadline for the implementation of ENU, and it would not be initiated on 1 July; 2) the proposal would be studied by the Education Committees of both houses of the National Congress; and 3) with respect to the problem of ideology, "the ideological aspect has not been totally defined, and the socialism which will be applied will be a type which the majority can support." Further questioning from the audience could not draw out an explanation of what that phrase meant (*El Mercurio*, 9 April 1973).

Over the same weekend, the provincial directors of secondary student federations throughout Chile had been meeting in Santiago to define a joint position with respect to ENU. At a press conference on Monday, 9 April, these student leaders announced that students supported the need for further democratization of education and the development of a more integrated educational system. But this would also have to be an educational system which was "free, pluralistic, democratic, and in which students could decide their own destinies." ENU, as presented, contradicted these principles since it proposed that education be oriented toward a determined political ideology. This was the moment, they insisted, "for the government to listen to the voice of the majority and decide to change direction . . . . We are open to dialogue, but if we don't accomplish anything by that means, or they don't want to listen, we can't discard the possibility of a strike."

With that threat publicly stated, the student leaders presented Tapia with a list of five questions, demanding a response within ten days: 1) Would ENU be implemented by law or by a simple decree? 2) Would the implementation begin in June? 3) Would there be widespread discussion? 4) Would the government respect the opinions revealed by that discussion? and 5) Why was the government already implementing ENU in some of the provinces?

Tapia immediately met with the directors of what was now being called the "Student Command." He told them that he would immediately answer their questions, but that he would also use the ten-day deadline to begin discussions with them regarding other kinds of issues they had raised, such as the lack of teachers or supplies, buildings in poor repair, and so on.

In response to the first question, he indicated that the government still expected to implement by decree, but that it would present the project to the National Congress for passage as a law if Popular Unity judged it to be "politically convenient." Regarding the implementation schedule and the national debate, the minister stated that the date of implementation would depend upon the nature and length of the debate. "If everything is not perfected ENU will not be applied in June. The Church asked that we provide more time and we are doing it." The debate would involve widespread participation, and the opinions expressed in it would be "taken into account." However, Tapia noted that the final decisions regarding the nature of the project and the implementation schedule would be taken by the National Council of Education.

It was quickly apparent to Tapia that the student leaders were not ready to enter into any sort of dialogue. He perceived them to be like any other group of young political party militants, captured by the rhetoric and slogans of the day and not disposed to talk seriously about what was happening. Their reaction focussed entirely upon the first portion of the ENU Report; they knew nothing at all about technical and structural proposals. The minister recognized that he was making no headway whatsoever with them.

Most damaging in this regard was the interchange regarding their fifth question. It became clear in the discussion that what the students were complaining about was the implementation of the First Integrated Year in some technical-professional schools as authorized by Circular 13. Tapia said that this did not represent an implementation of ENU, but was rather a special measure applied in only a few schools where unusual circumstances made it difficult for the regular plan of studies to operate. One of the student representatives told Tapia that in the school he attended, where the First Integrated Year was being implemented, the authorities had said they were putting ENU into practice. (It would not have been surprising for local authorities to take this position. Both Circular 13 and the 6 March circular signed by the directors of primary, secondary, and professional education had referred to this change as an advance implementation of ENU.) Nonetheless, Tapia told the students that what was involved here was an error on the part of the administration of this particular industrial school. To this, the students replied: "Look, Mr. Minister, we believe *you*, but you can't control the rest of the Ministry." Again, there was the problem of lack of internal consistency. Whose version of government policy was one to believe? At the end of the meeting Miguel Salazar, president of the "Student Command," informed the press that the minister had not provided "categorical replies" to the five questions, but "in fact maintained the same government position which youth have rejected."

On the following day, the first student strike against ENU occurred: a two-day walkout called in the province of Bio-Bio.

THE ARMED FORCES REJECT ENU

In spite of mounting pressure from within the various armed services and from the extreme sectors of the opposition throughout late 1972 and early 1973, the armed forces had continued to maintain their tradition of public neutrality on political issues. Even as individuals, members of the officer corps had usually carefully refrained from making public statements which could be construed as "political." Many officers had, however, participated actively as parents in school meetings called to discuss the ENU Report. The National Unified School proposal produced the first break with this tradition, the first occasion on which the military publicly declared its opposition to a policy of the Popular Unity government.

In early April the military had asked Allende to arrange a meeting with Tapia and other government representatives so that the officers, in their capacity as parents and grandparents, could enter into "frank dialogue" with government representatives regarding the proposal. The meeting was held on Wednesday, 11 April, in an auditorium in the Ministry of Defense. Approximately five hundred officers, of all ranks and from throughout the nation, were in attendance. The meeting was jointly presided over by Tapia; the Minister of Defense, Jose Toha; and the commanding officers of the army, navy and air force.[1]

Tapia began with a long speech in which he tried to explain, "very pedagogically," the technical aspects of the ENU proposal, why these were needed, and the details of the procedures for discussion and implementation. He tried to avoid inflammatory rhetoric and to present his understanding, and thus the understanding of the reformist wing of the government, of the underlying ideology and long-term goals of the proposal. Following this speech, a number of officers made observations or asked questions which appeared to Tapia to have been previously prepared and which did not take into account what he had just told them.

The most important response was a long presentation by Admiral Ismael Huerta. He gave Tapia a copy of a prepared document, which was immediately published in the opposition press. Huerta opened by insisting that "the present analysis is strictly individual," but it was interpreted as representing an institutional position of the military. In fact, *La Prensa* headlined its account of the meeting, which included the text of Huerta's document, "Curt Rejection of the National Unified School by the Armed Forces." Huerta noted that his analysis focussed solely upon "the possible consequences of the implementation of ENU, given the current tone of the project, upon the spirit and functioning of the armed forces." In his detailed analysis of the ENU Report, he appeared to be reflecting Senator Carmona's argument that the implementation of ENU would shortly present the armed forces with cadres of young men "conscientized" in a set of values completely contrary to the traditional military values and norms. This was a particularly sensitive issue for many military officers. Some spokesmen for MIR and the revolutionary wing of the Socialist party had already been calling upon "common soldiers" to refuse orders to attack "workers and peasants, their fellow-members of the proletariat" in case of an armed confrontation between the government and the military. Extreme leftists had also been discovered attempting to infiltrate the ranks and "politicize" enlisted men and conscripts, particularly in the navy.

Thus, for example, Huerta noted that the ENU Report was:

> an obvious attack upon the current educational system, of which we are all products. If these charges are true, then we ourselves are classist, egoist, authoritarian, unjust, exploiters, bureaucratic verticalists, who have no respect for work and are incapable of facing life. . . . In no part of the document is there mention of spiritual formation, which is a basic pillar of our own professional career. . . . There is no reference to education within the family. Nonetheless it is an accepted fact within humanist philosophy that the greatest educational influence occurs within the heart of the family. This is particularly true of the "military family" where we inculcate the most profound ideas regarding the norms of authority, discipline, hierarchy, justice, honesty, disinterest, abnegation, sobriety and good faith, and whose results can be seen. The children of both officers and troops always distinguish themselves. The Armed Forces mold young men from the very beginning in a framework of order, authority, discipline and hierarchy, which contrasts with the politicized and revolutionary ferment one finds in civilian schools.

The strongest part of Huerta's attack did not refer to the ENU Report itself, however, but to another document. He noted that Nuñez claimed in the introduction to the ENU Report that it reflected the popular will as expressed in the National Congress of Education. The admiral indicated that while he did not have a copy of the conclusions of that congress, he did have a document produced at the Center for In-Service Training entitled "Experimental Project for the National Unified School," which claimed in its introduction to be based upon the agreements reached in the National Congress of Education.

> In the five pages of this document there appear 16 times the concept of the revolutionary process, revolutionary action, etc., as well as terms such as: the Chilean road to socialism, bourgeois consciousness, cultural colonization, popular mobilization, conscientization, class conflict, confrontation by areas, citations from Marx, the road to revolution, and others.

This document appeared to contradict completely what Tapia had claimed at the beginning of the meeting about the nature of the ENU project and the government's intentions. Within the meeting, and in a press conference immediately thereafter, the minister insisted that the document was "apocryphal," that it had been prepared neither by the Center for In-Service Training nor by any other agency of the Ministry of Education, and that its emphasis on class warfare and inevitable confrontation did not reflect the government view.

Unfortunately, the document was quite real and, in a sense, authentic, even though Tapia did not know of its existence. It had been produced by a supporter of the revolutionary wing of the government for the preliminary ENU commission which had worked between May and August 1972. (Centro de Perfeccionamiento, 1972). It contained rhetoric and analysis which was even more revolutionary than that found in the first major ENU Commission report, which had caused the debate within the ministry in November and December 1972. It had never been formally accepted, but it had been printed on official Ministry of Education stationery, which carried the imprints of the ministry and the center, and it had been filed away at the Center for In-Service Training. Some weeks previously it had been removed from the Center's files (one informant uses the word "stolen," but that seems too strong as the document was not labeled confidential, nor was it carefully hidden away—I have found copies of it in the personal files of two different individuals) and passed to some very conservative members of the Church hierarchy, who eventually passed it on to Huerta.

As context, one should recall that about two weeks previously *El Mercurio* had published its detailed comparison of the final ENU Report and the earlier ENU Commission report, which it had labeled the "Public Report" and the "Private Report," concluding that "the authorities in the Ministry of Education do not want the public to be aware of their true intentions and their real thinking regarding the National Unified School." Here, then, was a situation in which the minister of education, involved in an extraordinarily delicate political confrontation with the officer corps of the nation's armed forces, was categorically denying the existence of an even more extremely revolutionary ENU document, which the officers held in their hands! It appeared to provide strong evidence to conservative sectors within the military and to conservative sectors of the Church who had seen the document first that there was indeed a "hidden ENU" behind the official statements, a proposal with a more sinister purpose, and that Popular Unity was thus playing a "double game."

Finally, after the interchange with Huerta and other officers, Tapia came to the exasperated conclusion that they were not listening to anything he said. The minister insisted that this sort of discussion had to stop since the audience seemed clearly unwilling to believe him. "The problem here is a question of confidence in the government. You are going to have to take a position, to define yourselves regarding your confidence in the government." Immediately the auditorium filled with murmurs and whispers, and clearly discernible shouts of, "Yes, Mr. Minister. That is the problem. We don't have confidence in the government." That was effectively the end of the meeting.

The next morning Tapia met with Allende. When he recounted the reaction to his challenge to the officers, the president asked what Toha's response had been. When Tapia replied that the minister of defense had said nothing, Allende looked very worried. This was the first clear signal that the armed forces had lost confidence in the government.

The officers corps was not, however, unanimous in its opposition to the government in general or to the educational proposals in particular. The commanding officers of each of the three services were committed constitutionalists. On 13 April, a meeting of approximately eight hundred officers was convened at the Military Academy in Santiago. General Carlos Prats, commander of the army and the former minister of the interior while the military were in the Popular Unity cabinet, strongly defended the government, particularly its educational policies and its policies regarding nationalization of industries. He was reported to have strongly criticized Huerta for the document he had produced regarding ENU, and to have said that if he had been minister of defense, he "would have ordered the arrest of those officials who spoke in so unprofessional and partisan a fashion during the April 11 meeting." Prats later denied this statement, but it was reported in *Ercilla*, which was known to have very good sources within the military and whose reports of military affairs generally proved to be accurate (*Ercilla*, 18-24 April 1973, p. 9 and 24 April - 1 May 1973, p. 9). Moreover, as Sigmund (1977, p. 208) has observed: "Subsequent events indicated that it [Prat's statement] reflected accurately the genuine divisions in the armed forces on the education and nationalization questions."

THE ATTACK CONTINUES ON OTHER FRONTS

On the same day that Tapia met with the armed forces, Wednesday, 11 April, the Plenary Assembly of the Bishops of Chile produced a public declaration and a letter to Tapia. The public declaration read as follows:

> 1. The Bishops of Chile reiterate the declaration of the Permanent Committee of the Episcopate regarding the National Unified School, and we support the efforts of the Cardinal, with the President of the Republic, to secure the postponement of the implementation of ENU.
> 2. We clearly declare that we are fundamentally opposed to the project because it does not respect fundamental human and Christian values, without prejudice to its pedagogical merits.
> 3. We invite student centers, teachers and parents to study the doctrine of the Church regarding education, in order to contribute positively to this debate, for which we are preparing a working document.
> 4. We thank the Minister of Education for his decision to postpone the implementation of the National Unified School, and we hope that the intermediate authorities will act in consonance with that decision, in order to avoid confusion.

In their letter to Tapia, the bishops added the following points:

> We want to make it very clear that our concern does not refer exclusively nor principally to private Catholic education, but to the entire educational process of the nation. . . . We cannot hide the fact that we have grave reservations regarding the ENU project, in spite of its positive aspects, because of its philosophical orientation, explicit and implicit, which we cannot share. (Text of both documents found in *Oveido*, 1974)[2]

On the following day, Tapia sent a letter to the cardinal formally confirming the decision of the government to postpone the implementation of ENU in order to permit a more extended debate. He added:

> I take advantage of this opportunity to express our willingness to receive the positive contributions the Bishops have requested from Christians, in order to establish an educational system suited to the current and future needs of the people. The government has never closed off dialogue, nor has it fled from the confrontation of ideas. . . . In this sense the National Unified School project can and should be discussed by all representative organizations of the national community, not only regarding its forms or methods of implementation, but regarding

its foundations. We are interested only in defending the central ideas which inform the National Unified School, which are the establishment of an educational system which is open and flexible, which combines theoretical work and study with practical work, which makes possible a permanent and creative education with equality of possibilities for all Chileans.

It worries us that the Bishops, according to their last public declaration, consider that the National Unified School "does not respect fundamental human and Christian values," for if this were the case there is no doubt that the project would have to undergo substantial modifications. However, the government believes that the National Unified School will permit the realization of such values. On this point in particular we are anxious to hear the proposals of the Catholic Church . . . . It cannot have escaped your attention that the government is supported by political forces with diverse ideological orientations—Marxists, rationalists, Christians—which is one more guarantee that we are not seeking to indoctrinate our youth. Disgracefully, a press campaign has exploded in the nation, using the most ignoble means to manipulate the conscience of the citizenry regarding that which is most dear to them: the destiny of their children. It is essential that we overcome this climate, which only favors those who are seeking by all means to nullify the rationality of democratic debate, stop the process of change, and submit the nation to obscurantism.

Tapia also emphasized that he had "personally proposed" to the National Council of Education that it develop a method of discussion which would guarantee a "serene and constructive" debate in which all could participate, that a subcommittee had been charged with this task, and that its report could be expected soon. (The letter was published in *El Mercurio* on 15 April 1973.)

On the same day that he sent this letter to the cardinal, Tapia also attended a special meeting of the education committee of the Senate. Here, too, he emphasized that ENU would not be implemented during 1973. Using the same arguments, he told the parliamentarians that the ENU Report had not been officially approved by the government and that it reflected the thinking of one sector only. The specific reasons for the postponement cited by Tapia were the "profound debate" resulting from the appearance of the proposal and the fact that the document had been written under such pressure for speed that programs of study necessary for its immediate implementation could not possibly be developed in time. (See *La Prensa*, 14 April 1973; *El Mercurio*, 15 April 1973; and *Ercilla*, 18-24 April 1973, p. 16. The *Ercilla* account noted that these were the "official" reasons for the ministerial decision, but that the real cause was the "rattle of the sabers" the minister had heard on the previous day.)

However, neither Tapia's letter to the cardinal nor his meeting with the senators significantly calmed the dispute. Immediately after the meeting, which started in the morning and extended into the afternoon, Jose Musalem, a Christian Democratic senator, stated:

> The truth is that in this affair the government is hiding its hand; its true face. First there was the report of December 15, which contained very clearly Marxist language. They hid it and produced another for public consumption, and even in this report one can see that the government intends to instrumentalize education in order to ideologize the children of Chile.

A National party senator, Victor Garcia, added:

> Behind a reform that could have some good aspects, there is a communist contraband, and the contraband is to turn all of our children into Marxists. (*El Mercurio*, 15 April 1973)

Also on 12 April, the National Council of the Christian Democratic party published an official declaration resulting from an emergency session, which noted that if the regime's actions regarding the National Unified School continued to threaten a violation of the Statute of Democratic Guarantees, the very legitimacy of the government would be called into question (*El Mercurio*, 13 April 1973). The National party also published an extensive report from its research division, which compared the text of the ENU Report to many of the quotations from classical Marxist works which *El Mercurio* had been using editorially and concluded that ENU represented "totalitarian imposition" and would bring "the disappearance of the family and the collective care of children" (*El Mercurio*, 12 April 1973). In that same edition *El Mercurio* published a large declaration, unsigned, but in the form usually reserved for announcing official government decrees, which referred to:

> The Unified School: Submission of Teachers to Communist Commissars. . . . Teachers cannot and will not accept their submission to the conscientizing manipulation of the Marxists. . . . They must stop by whatever means this communist-directed attempt to enslave them and poison the children of Chile. This was how it began in other countries which are now irremediably beneath the communist yoke.

On the following day, Friday the 13th of April, FESES brought thousands of students out for a march through central Santiago and a rally in front of the National Library. In his speech from the library steps, Miguel Salazar, president of FESES, claimed that while Tapia had agreed formally to the postponement and debate, he was still "mocking the students" by indirectly putting ENU into effect through the establishment of the First Integrated Year in technical-professional schools. Immediately after the rally, the FESES leadership met with Tapia who agreed: 1) to cancel Circular 13 which had authorized the First Integrated Year; 2) to send official memoranda to all schools that very day, or on Saturday at the latest, announcing this decision; and 3) to have published in the nation's press as soon as possible an official declaration of that decision (*La Prensa*, 14 April 1973).

Tapia assumed that this additional concession would finally calm the opposition and permit the new national debate on educational policy to proceed in an orderly fashion. He was so confident of this that over the weekend he left to attend the annual meeting of the Andean Pact ministers of education in Caracas, where he presented the technical portions of ENU as Chile's new educational structure, a presentation which was supported and approved by the assembled ministers. His assumption about the effect of his action was incorrect.

On the day that Tapia left for Caracas, 15 April, Carlos Moreno, director of professional education, published the declaration Tapia had promised to the students. However, Moreno *did not withdraw Circular 13*. Rather, he defended it, insisting that it was not an advance implementation of ENU but simply an attempt to provide a transitory solution to problems faced by certain technical-professional schools which were facing unusually high first year enrolments (*El Mercurio*, 15 April 1973). This action caused a great deal of consternation among the Radicals and Communists within the Ministry of Education. When Tapia heard about it, he was furious. It was seen as yet another example of subordinate officials within the government acting independently of official policy and instructions, adding to the image of a government whose word could not be believed.

In the edition in which it published Moreno's declaration, *El Mercurio* offered yet another "proof" that the government intended to implement ENU in spite of its agreement to a national debate. The subject of attack this time was a National System of Workers' Education (SINET), which had been presented at a national seminar late in March. SINET had been under discussion within the government for some time, and various aspects of it had been debated and approved by the National Council of Education. Technically, it represented an attempt to better link all of the existing separate programs for workers' education within various sections of the Ministry of Education and in other ministries into a single national system, through which a worker could easily progress from any starting point, including basic literacy, up to high-level technical training. The SINET proposal embedded the detailed structural mechanisms required to meet this goal in the same kind of ideological analysis which characterized the ENU proposal. It stated, for example:

> It will be of no use to workers to learn perfectly how to operate a machine, or even how to manage a productive process, if the relationships of production are still capitalist. . . . Any Chilean worker who enrols in SINET, whatever his educational level or area of technical specialization, will enter a system in which he will learn profoundly and permenently the ideology of the proletariat, as well as technical skills from a scientific perspective.

From such examples, *El Mercurio* concluded that SINET was another example of the "predominant objective found in all of the educational initiatives of this government, Marxist conscientization" and concluded that it was a "complement of the National Unified School."

In a follow-up editorial, the paper linked SINET with the Circular 13 issue and the promulgation of the Decree of Democratization to demonstrate that:

> lately the strategy of the Ministry of Education has been elusive, as they pretend that the ENU initiative has been filed away in the face of generalized repudiation.

These examples were:

> proof that Marxism may have been forced into a strategic retreat, but has in no way abandoned the idea of implanting ENU. . . . The battle against the National Unified School will continue until the proposal has been authentically rather than fictitiously buried. (*El Mercurio*, 15 April 1973)

THE COMMUNISTS REFUSE TO SUPPORT ENU

One major theme of the attack against ENU throughout April was that it was in reality a "communist" initiative, in spite of the fact that within the coordinating committee the Communist party representatives had never strongly supported the proposal. On 19 April the party declared publicly that it did not support the ENU Report even though it considered the technical and structural aspects to represent important and necessary changes. The declaration took the form of a statement by Luis Guastavino, a member of the Chamber of Deputies, to a meeting of the communist members of SUTE. He observed that the "monstrous campaign orchestrated by the reactionaries and *El Mercurio*" against ENU had as its underlying purpose nothing less than bringing down the government before Allende could complete his term of office.

Guastavino then strongly criticized the ENU Report on the grounds that it had been written and presented in such a way as to invite such a response from the opposition:

> We criticize the fact that they have not taken into account the experiences through which we have already lived, when important initiatives of this government have come to a bad end because of the manner in which they were presented to public opinion.

As a pedagogical concept ENU was "irreproachable," and only the most reactionary elements could oppose its central ideas. However, "we cannot identify ourselves with the particular proposal which has been developed, and we have significant objections to it. The documents we write ought to instruct rather than confuse."

The Communist party, he stated, was sympathetic to the doubts and concerns expressed by the bishops of Chile regarding the ENU Report and also agreed with Tapia's response to the cardinal. In this context, the party was prepared to enter actively into the "serene and democratic debate" which was required in order to produce "needed improvements" (*Puro Chile*, 19 April 1973).

This declaration appeared just as Tapia was returning from Caracas. He was neither surprised nor upset by the position taken by the communists.[3] Indeed, the fact that the statement criticized the "ministry" but not the "minister" provided him with some additional ammunition in his own battle with the Socialists in the ministry (interview with Jorge Tapia, 9 December 1981). However, the position taken by the communists enraged those Socialists within the ministry responsible for the ENU proposal. They believed that the Communist party had already given its support to the project and regarded this declaration as an act of self-serving "treason" to the cause of the government. The always tense relationships between the Socialists and Communists now ruptured completely.

Allende had to intervene yet again. He called another meeting of the representatives of the different parties in the ministry. The tension was so great that as people assembled, the communists stayed in a separate room until Allende arrived. Again he lectured them all on the need to stop the "partisan bickering" which was threatening to destroy the government.[4]

Allende's plea had little effect. Internal disputes brought most work within the ministry to a standstill. Hernan Vera, a Chilean educator who had been seconded by the Organization of American States to work with the technical commissions, became so disgusted with the situation that he left his position. When he presented his final report to Tapia, he told him: "You don't need a technical advisor. You need a political advisor who can help you get these people to work together" (interview with Hernan Vera, 6 May 1981). Tapia sent a letter of resignation to the president, hoping that if it were refused, it would give him some power and control over the warring factions (interview with Jorge Tapia, 9 December 1981). Allende refused to accept his resignation, but the gesture did not have the desired effect, and the crippling arguments continued.

BY LAW OR BY DECREE? THE FINAL GOVERNMENT RETREAT

During this last part of April, with the Ministry of Education in complete disarray, the opposition attack escalated. Every day there were more students in the streets, and their activities were becoming more and more violent. Every day *El Mercurio* published additional attacks upon the ENU proposal. It appeared that adamant opposition forces, their nostrils catching the "smell of blood" from a crippled government, were moving in for the kill. The Federation of Students of the Catholic University (FEUC), which had opened the attack upon ENU in early March, joined the battle once again with a series of public declarations (see *El Mercurio*, 24 and 25 April 1973), and published a widely read book titled: "ENU: Control of Consciousness" (FEUC, 1973), which brought together all of its previous declarations and added several new critical analyses. There was almost no response from the government media beyond an occasional attack upon the character of the opponents, which could only help to alienate and weaken the decreasing moderate opposition sectors. For example:

> The intransigent position of the traditional right—now aided by Christian Democracy—should not surprise anyone in the country who understands their retrograde and classist ideology, the egoism of this privileged group, their intellectual myopia, and their close-minded defense of their caste interests. (*La Nacion*, 25 April 1973)

Having forced the government to postpone the implementation of ENU pending the outcome of the new national debate, the opposition stressed two issues: 1) apparent attempts by Popular Unity to implement ENU indirectly, particularly through SINET, Circular 13, and the already promulgated Decree of Democratization; and 2) insistence that any educational reform proposal must be implemented by a law passed by Congress rather than by ministerial decree. The second issue assumed particular importance during the latter part of April.

The problem of how to implement an educational reform proposal was a difficult issue for the opposition. Within the National Council of Education, the question was never seriously considered because the Christian Democrats who were members of that body were fully aware that the educational reforms of their own regime had been implemented by decree (interview with Ernesto Livacic, 24 September 1982). Even *El Mercurio* had recognized late in March that "the text of the Constitution is not explicit regarding this matter" (29 March 1973). Nonetheless, the opposition claimed that because the National Council of Education was ultimately controlled by the government, the only way to ensure the fulfillment of the demand of the Statute of Democratic Guarantees for a free and democratic discussion of proposed educational changes was to submit them to the two houses of Congress. Even many moderate Christian Democrats, still anxious to achieve a compromise with the government, were insistent upon this point because they feared that without control by Congress, where the government was in a minority, Popular Unity could ultimately use the provisions of the Decree of Democratization to do whatever it wanted.

For the government the issue was the very maintenance of its authority. Tapia, who had been quite happy to be able to postpone implementation of ENU, was particularly insistent on this point; this issue was not one of his "bargaining counters." As a legal scholar, he was quite sure that both the constitution and precedent gave the government the authority to establish an educational reform by decree. The Statute of Democratic Guarantees had been quite consciously edited to maintain this formal authority. The central question was "the power of the executive to execute," a power which had been under attack by the opposition on all fronts for months (interview with Jorge Tapia, 19 April 1982). On this issue the revolutionary Socialists agreed with Tapia because they were sure that any educational reform bill passed by congress would be totally unsatisfactory from their point of view (interview with Ivan Nuñez, 21 September 1982). Araya, however, favored the congressional route. He was concerned about the tangled, confusing, and sometimes contradictory body of educational legislation that had developed over the years, which permitted the "hotheads" in the ministry to take advantage of obscure and forgotten clauses to do whatever they wanted, independent of official policy. He saw the development of a new general law as a way to eliminate this possibility (interview with Hugo Araya, 22 September 1982).

Thus, the predominant position within the ministry, the result of an unusual commonality of interest between the minister and the revolutionary Socialists, was to insist upon implementation by decree. However, as pressure upon the government became more and more fierce and as it became increasingly clear that the call for a new ENU debate was not having the predicted calming effect, it became evident that something more had to be done. Late in the month, somewhere between 20 and 25 April, first the coordinating committee of the ministry, and then the coordinating committee of Popular Unity, met to discuss the issue. In both groups it was agreed that the government should accede to opposition demands by agreeing to work towards the passage of a *general law* which would establish *basic policy and guidelines* for an educational reform so long as the ministry could retain the prerogative to establish specific details by decree.

With this decision, the government retreated completely from the educational reform proposal it had made public less than two months before and bowed to all of the principal objections from the moderate opposition sectors. The only way it could have met the demands of the extreme opposition was to have agreed to say nothing at all about education and, indeed, to have agreed to stop governing the nation!

While the government was deciding this, violence in the streets escalated to unprecedented levels. On 26 April, a FESES rally in front of the Ministry of Education was attacked by a large group of government-supporting students who had just left a rally in the Caupolican Theater (the largest public auditorium in Santiago). Serious clashes developed, a number of windows were broken in the presidential palace (which was less than half a block away from the Ministry of Education), and the police had to use tear gas and water cannons to break up the riot.

The next morning over breakfast, Tapia, along with several of his key officials, met with Renan Fuentealba, president of the Christian Democratic party, and several of his key officials. Tapia and Fuentealba had known and respected each other for a long time. They recognized that an agreement had to be struck in order to get the students off the streets and deescalate the violence. During a long discussion, they agreed 1) There would be no implementation, direct or indirect, of ENU until a general educational law was passed by Congress. The only thing that would happen in 1973 would be a full debate in which all sectors of the nation could participate. 2) Circular 13 would be suspended. The Christian Democrats also thought that agreement had been reached on suspension of the Decree of Democratization, but Tapia had not agreed to that proposition.

After the meeting, the Christian Democratic participants went to their party headquarters to draft a memorandum for the minister summarizing their understanding of the accords. As they were writing this document, the headquarters was attacked by a CUT-sponsored counterdemonstration responding to the previous day's attack on the presidential palace. During the violence, gunfire was exchanged and one of the demonstrators was killed by a shot alleged to have come from the party building. In the ensuing mutual recrimination between government and opposition, no further accommodation appeared possible.

The following day, 28 April, Gerardo Espinoza, minister of the interior, announced to a closed session of Congress that the government had decided ENU would be implemented only by law after full discussion in the congress (*El Mercurio*, 28 April 1973). In the even more heightened climate of confrontation and violence, the potential impact of this final government concession was lost. The government had retreated completely and publicly, but no one seemed to have noticed it or believed it.

11

Educational Compromise During the Final Destruction of the Popular Unity Regime

Throughout the May-August period the public attack against the government's educational policy continued unabated. The major concessions by Popular Unity had not calmed the situation, and mistrust of the government's ultimate intentions with regard to education remained widespread. Three themes dominated the opposition arguments during these final months: 1) a continuing assertion that ENU, and with it all Popular Unity educational proposals, were "communist" attempts to impose a totalitarian ideology in Chile; 2) an attack against a program of teachers' workshops, which was identified as yet another attempt by the government to implement the ENU proposal indirectly; and 3) a set of objections to the new national debate regarding education proposed by the National Council.

ENU AS A COMMUNIST INITIATIVE

This theme was carried forward vigorously by *El Mercurio* throughout May. The paper carried a long series of detailed critical analyses of education in the Soviet Union and its satellites. These articles were based upon, and quoted liberally from, official reports and documents published in the Soviet Union. These were available to specialists in Soviet education but were not the sort of material ordinarily used by even a major newspaper such as *El Mercurio*. There is speculation that it came from the CIA as part of its support for *El Mercurio*, but it could have been provided by Chilean scholars who specialized in Soviet affairs. Whatever the source of the background information, it was used with considerable effect to advance the argument that: 1) ENU was a faithful copy of Soviet educational programs; 2) such programs had failed in the Soviet Union and in Eastern

European nations; and 3) these failures had been recognized even by Soviet authorities. The headlines of the various articles in themselves clearly outline the nature of the argument developed by *El Mercurio*.

> 5 May: Failure of Polytechnical Education in the Soviet Educational Model;
> 6 May: Exploitation of Students in Soviet Agriculture;
> 7 May: Educational Calamity in the Soviet Union;
> 8 May: Deficiencies in Soviet Polytechnical Education Stripped Naked;
> 10 May: Deficient Preparation of Students in the USSR Because of Polytechnical Education;
> 11 May: Soviet Self-Criticism of the Failure of Polytechnization;
> 12 May: The Educational Black Market in the USSR;
> 21 May: Reform of Soviet Education After the Failure of Polytechnization.

El Mercurio summarized the articles by observing editorially that (14 May 1973):

> The proven failure of the Soviet experience with polytechnical education has not stopped those who, years later, want to implement it here. Such an educational system could have some advantages, but these are dissipated by the oppressive form in which the official proposal is presented. The controversial Circular 13 of the Ministry of Education, which appears to still be in effect in spite of official claims that it has been withdrawn, and the National System of Workers' Education (SINET), sponsored by CUT, which complements ENU, are indicators of the tenacious official insistence on implementing the National Unified School. . . . If one adds to these the educational councils created by the Decree of Democratization of education, one must be convinced of the Marxist threat hovering over Chilean education.

This attack on the polytechnical aspect of ENU was complemented in early May by another complaint regarding the Marxist nature of the textbooks used in the national literacy campaign. In an editorial published on 3 May, *El Mercurio* noted that when the Communist party announced its opposition to the ENU Report, it suggested that a campaign to eradicate illiteracy in the nation could at least be mounted without objection. But, claimed the paper, even in this area the communist influence was evident. As proof of this assertion, portions of a booklet entitled "Suggestions for Literacy Training," which had been attacked by the newspaper some months earlier, were cited. Part of the booklet's introduction read:

We have particularly taken into account the great Cuban experience and the very important experience of the first years of Soviet Power. Both nations effectively eradicated illiteracy. Mobilizing the entire nation, particularly working youth, they were able to provide literacy to those who had not been able to achieve it under capitalism.

The editorial then noted that all of the "key words" and "themes for reflection" (following Freirian methodology) included in the booklet were clearly derived from the Basic Program of Popular Unity or other official government sources. It asserted that "there is not even the slightest hint of pluralism in the text. Everything is reduced to proselytizing for the cause of Popular Unity." From all of this, the following conclusion was derived:

This Marxist literacy manual clearly shows once again the intention of the government to utilize education politically at all levels. The National Unified School and the educational councils created by the Decree of Democratization were based upon a desire for spiritual, educational and political control. Here one sees it even in the teaching of the first letters. . . . Thus the repeated claims of neutrality by the Ministry of Education evaporate. This Ministry is considered by communism as a vital instrument for penetrating the widest possible sectors of the nation.

Six days later Tapia replied in a letter to the editor (*El Mercurio*, 9 May 1973). He stated that in early April he had requested a report from the literacy commission regarding its programs and texts. After receiving the report, he had issued a decree which declared that the textbook cited by *El Mercurio*, as well as another designed for use among Chile's small indigenous population, clearly violated the constitutional guarantees regarding democratic and pluralist education and were to be immediately withdrawn from official use. Once again, a minister of education was put in the position of having to disavow the actions of his subordinates publicly.

THE TEACHERS' WORKSHOPS ISSUE

This issue first surfaced in early June (*El Mercurio*, 8 June 1973) and continued as a major source of opposition complaint through early August. It was yet another example of an independent initiative by one group within Popular Unity creating problems for the minister of education, while calling into question his credibility and thus the credibility of the government itself.

In this case, the problems originated in the small MAPU group within the ministry. Following MAPU's position that fundamental social change could only be the product of a process which started at the base level and worked its way up through the system, Rodrigo Vera, the dominant Mapucista in the Center for In-Service Training, had been quietly developing a program based upon teachers' own experiences and understandings of their students and the environments from which they came. Starting with a small-scale pilot project involving secondary level philosophy teachers in 1971, he slowly expanded the program, experimenting and evaluating all the while, until it was ready for widespread implementation in July 1973. On 20 July, small groups of teachers in each school were to meet to begin a diagnosis of the social reality from which their students came and collectively to develop programs which could more closely link their school with its community. It was assumed, based upon the MAPU position, that the reality in which each school was immersed was different and that the appropriate educational solutions, involving both the school and its community, would also necessarily vary. This was to be the start of a process through which local groups of teachers throughout the nation would, in cooperation with their own communities, adapt national curricula to local needs and change their teaching methods in order to better link schools to their immediate environments.

La Prensa mounted a concerted attack on this proposal, claiming that it was yet another example of a "hidden" implementation of ENU (see the editions of 1, 2, 5, 8, 12, 13, and 15 July. It is interesting to note that after mid-June, *El Mercurio* had almost nothing to say on this issue.) The argument here was rather strained, asserting that these workshops were similar to the local councils proposed by the Decree of Democratization. Because that decree was a necessary complement to the implementation of ENU, the workshops themselves were an attempt to implement ENU indirectly. The fact that such an argument could be both asserted and widely accepted indicates the degree of sensitivity created by the controversy during the previous months. Even innocent proposals for change were assumed to have hidden intentions. To some extent the government had invited this sort of attack by defining ENU as the keystone of a *totally integrated* national educational system which included all types of formal and non-formal education from the pre-school years to old age. Under such a concept, *any* change or innovation in any aspect of education could be defined as related to ENU.

This particular proposal also alarmed the dominant sectors within the Ministry of Education—the Radicals, the two wings of the Socialist party, and the Communists. The workshop idea, if fully implemented, might have created a genuine grass-roots change process. Local solutions might have been developed for local problems, outside of the official control of the government. Since all major parties in Popular Unity were committed to a centralizing, control-oriented conception of the role of the state, none could fully accept the idea of a process not controlled and directed by the government.

Consequently, as soon as the workshop proposal was attacked by the opposition and thus became widely known within the government itself, it became an orphan—disowned by every political group except MAPU.[1] As the opposition campaign gained momentum, Vera came under strong pressure from the government to abort the workshop plan. He ignored the pressure. Late in July the sub-secretary of education went out to the Center in a great fury to insist that Vera abandon the program. Vera, however, was already out in the field helping with the implementation of the workshops and could not be reached from Santiago. Again it appeared that the government was unable to control its own officials.

CONTROL AND ORGANIZATION OF THE NATIONAL DEBATE

In late May the National Council of Education published a document entitled "National Debate Regarding Education" (Consejo Nacional de Educación, 1973; this was first published as a mimeographed council publication, then as an official announcement in the nation's press, and finally as a small booklet for distribution throughout the nation). The document was designed to guide and orient the discussion which the National Council had called for when it announced the postponement of ENU's implementation. Its language and tone were entirely different from the ENU Report and the various government documents which had preceded it. There was not a hint of the "revolutionary" analysis which had been the center of controversy during March and April. The document started with a brief description of the enrolment/financial crisis which would soon confront the educational system if changes were not introduced. Faced with this situation, the authorities advanced educational proposals to serve the following basic purposes (p. 2):

1. The National System has to make educational services available to all persons from birth to old age because, especially in these times of rapid change, human beings of whatever age have needs which can be met through education. Put simply, this is what should be understood by Permanent Education.
2. The National System should promote both education within the family and the formal levels of pre-school, primary, secondary and higher education, as well as the wide and varied set of educational activities carried out in work centers, neighborhoods, and in social and cultural organizations.

3. The National System should offer to the community an education which enables it to create and participate in the process of social, economic and cultural change, and which favors the full personal development of those being educated. Among other things, this makes it necessary:

   a) to ensure continuity of studies to the highest level compatible with the capacities and interests of each student and with the possibilities of the nation;

   b) to deal with individual differences among students as well as with differing national, regional and local needs;

   c) to integrate theory and practice, education and life, study and work.

4. There must be real democratization of the system. This means:

   a) promoting the entrance into, survival within and progress through the National System for all of the population; and

   b) participation by students, teachers, parents and guardians, that is, the school community, and the citizenry in general, in the planning, execution and evaluation of educational activity.

5. It appears reasonable to establish priorities and advance gradually in the reform process, taking advantage of that which is valid in the existing system and of the pedagogical and social experience accumulated in the country.

The remainder of the document was taken up with a series of questions to which specific answers were sought from the groups participating in the debate. One set addressed to all participants was followed by separate questions directed at particular types of participating organizations: parent and guardian associations; teachers' organizations; secondary level students; community organizations; and labor unions. Generally speaking, each group was asked to do four things: to describe in both general and specific terms what it perceived to be the most important educational problems of the nation; to identify what it understood to be the causes of each problem; to suggest solutions which could be implemented both at the national level and at the level of their own community; and to indicate how their groups could contribute to the solution.

All groups who wished to participate were asked to send their replies, including identification of the group and its size, by certified letter no later than 31 July. Finally, it was indicated that "the National Council of Education will establish procedures for objectively evaluating the responses and will in due course issue a new official publication, which will make the results widely known" (p. 5).

Two classes of objections surfaced immediately. First, the most adamant opposition sectors insisted that the debate would violate the constitution because its sponsoring body, the National Council of Education, was constitutionally prohibited from undertaking such an exercise. This was so because the National Council was numerically dominated by government representatives and supporters; consequently, it did not fulfill the mandate of the Statute of Democratic Guarantees that all educational changes be subject to free and democratic discussion. This was linked with a second set of concerns, which had widespread support among those who were convinced that the government's words and actions could not be trusted. For them, the statement in the document that the National Council would "establish procedures" for evaluating the responses was considered far too vague. Who, it was asked, would control the participation to ensure that only the opinions of legitimately established groups would be taken into account? Who would actually evaluate the responses? What guarantees were there that the summaries produced would accurately reflect the information received?

Throughout July the argument on these issues continued. The most extreme opposition sectors suggested that no one should participate in the proposed debate because it was so evidently unconstitutional. The Christian Democratic party, the private school parents' federation (FEDAP), and other major organizations indicated that they would recommend that their members participate only if satisfactory arrangements were developed for evaluating the responses.

On 5 July, as part of another cabinet shuffle, a new minister of education was appointed, Edgardo Enriquez Froeden. Enriquez was an older man (sixty in 1973) who had important links both to the government and to the armed forces. He had been rector of the University of Concepción from early in 1969 to January 1973. Two of his children were leaders of MIR. For thirty-one years he had served as a medical doctor for the armed forces, attaining the rank of captain in the navy. In his first public statement, he said that any educational reform proposals would be implemented by a law and that his immediate priority was to ensure that the forthcoming national debate was carried out in a satisfactory manner (*El Mercurio*, 8 July 1973).

While most of the major political parties, the Church, and a wide array of other organizations were issuing statements and documents designed to guide their members and sympathizers regarding the national debate,[2] the new minister initiated a series of meetings with the education committee of the Senate and other "experts" to resolve the problems surrounding the debate. By now the 31 July deadline specified in the original National Council document had been abandoned. In early August the National Council announced that it had agreed to opposition demands and would appoint by decree a technical evaluation commission to preside over the debate and analyze its results (Consejo Nacional de Educación, August 1973).

Shortly thereafter it was announced that the Christian Democrats and FEDAP were satisfied with the arrangements and had agreed to participate fully (see *La Prensa*, 4 and 14 August 1973; and *La Nacion*, 17 August 1973).

However, by mid-August the final nationwide political crisis was fully underway. It was impossible even to begin the formal consultation process. Because of a national transportation stoppage, there was no available mechanism either to get the discussion guide booklet out to groups throughout the nation or to get their responses back to Santiago.

THE DEEPENING POLITICAL CRISIS

From May 1973 onward there was within the Chilean political system what Tapia has called "a growing sense of the inevitable, a final collapse of the Unidad Popular's basic project" (Tapia, 1978a, p. 58). The government had been forced to retreat on its last major policy initiative, ENU. It was almost totally paralyzed. If any initiative were to be seized to prevent the destruction of the regime and with it the political institutional system which had proved incapable of resolving the increasing crisis of legitimacy created by the election of Allende, it would have to come from the opposition. But the ENU debate had not only identified the two major institutions presumed to be neutral, the Church and the military, as opposed to the government, it had also strengthened the hard-line elements within the major opposition party, the Christian Democrats.

In mid-May the national assembly of the Christian Democratic party met. Two motions were put before it. One was presented by Renan Fuentealba, outgoing president of the party. It emphasized the commitment of the party to "humanist socialism" and recommended a policy of "revolutionary opposition" to the government. It reflected the view of those Christian Democrats still prepared to try to seek a compromise.

Fuentealba's motion lost. In its place, a motion proposed by Patricio Aylwin was approved. Echoing the debates over ENU, it accused the government of attempting to establish a "communist tyranny" in Chile and instructed the party to use every legitimate means to ensure that the regime respected the constitution and the laws of the nation. Shortly thereafter, Aylwin was elected party president, along with a hard-line slate of officers. As Valenzuela notes (1978, p. 92):

In a skillfully orchestrated set of political manoeuvres, former-president Frei succeeded in convincing the convention to adopt the thesis that Chile faced the prospect of a Marxist dictatorship, and that the party's response could only be one of continued and invigorated opposition.

This position won by a narrow 55 per cent to 45 per cent margin over the thesis maintaining that Chile's problem was not too much authority, but too much anarchy. According to the progressive wing of the party, the nation's chaos could only be overcome through a policy of rapprochement and accommodation. The election of Patricio Aylwin to the presidency of the organization signalled the determination of a narrow majority to refuse to take any initiatives at finding a political solution unless the president was genuinely willing to capitulate to its demands.

But these were demands that Allende could not possibly meet. The extreme elements within his own coalition were increasingly militant and radicalized and absolutely unprepared to accept a compromise. One example of their attitude was a media attack against members of the judiciary who had frustrated a government proposal, as "old shits" (viejos de mierda) (Sigmund, 1977, p. 210). Beyond this, moreover, acceptance of the Aylwin-wing demands would have meant the collapse of the very coalition from which the president drew what legitimacy still remained to him. As Tapia has observed (1978a, p. 58):

> It is very hard to avoid concluding that, whatever course Allende might have taken to evade direct confrontation, the original "model" for peaceful revolution would have had to undergo a profound transformation. As in the beginning, one question echoed insistently: consolidation or revolutionary advance? For either alternative, the immediate cost was the collapse of the coalition, the program and the viability of the project. That price was seen as too high by all involved, and led to continuing what had seemed the only internally acceptable form of political leadership: maintaining, in the name of ideological pluralism, the political stalemate and paralysis of all organized, political, leadership.

In short, if Allende had accepted the demands of the now dominant opposition forces, he might as well have relinquished the leadership role for which he had fought during most of his political career.

What little middle ground was left was further eroded during the first week in June. The ongoing dispute between the presidency and the congress regarding the definition of the areas of the economy had been submitted to the Constitutional Tribunal, one of the legal institutions for resolving differences in interpretation of the constitution. During this week the tribunal ruled that it was not competent to judge the constitutional dispute. With this decision, "the very conflict was finally left without a single referee" (Valenzuela, 1978, p. 93). Another institutional mechanism for conflict resolution had failed. What was left was a naked confrontation; what was left was armed conflict.

The first signal of this new situation occurred on 29 June, when one garrison of the army attempted a coup. The attempt was quickly put down by the military under the decisive leadership of General Prats. The constitutionalist elements within the armed forces still predominated, but the attempted coup was a clear indication of the unrest within the ranks. It led to a series of increasingly desperate attempts by moderate sectors to strike some sort of compromise which would avoid the seemingly inevitable downfall of the government.

> If Allende had been ambivalent before, his actions after the attempted coup clearly indicated that he was prepared to come to some kind of agreement with the Christian Democrats in a last effort to structure a compromise that would defuse the political opposition. The Christian Democrats were still the largest party in the country, and their leaders commanded great respect among vast sectors of the opposition. Even though many people were no longer interested in preserving the traditional system, a compromise between the president and the principal opposition party would have made any coup attempt, or for that matter any attempt to spark armed confrontation by the masses, extremely costly. . . . But compromise among the centrist forces still faced the perennial constraints of the last two and one-half years; both government and opposition faced the virulent opposition of the extreme Right and the extreme Left. Furthermore, the leadership of the Christian Democrats had shifted to the conservative side. The level of trust was at an all-time low. . . . Debatable issues had all but disappeared. (Valenzuela, 1978, p. 94)

During July and early August there were several attempts to arrange a compromise between the government and opposition. Each attempt failed, as moderate sectors were blocked by their extremist colleagues. August saw a repeat of the October 1972 strike which brought the entire nation to a standstill. The remaining constitutionalist forces within the military collapsed under the pressure, removing the last important obstacle to a coup.[3]

A COMPROMISE OVER EDUCATION IS NEGOTIATED

In the midst of this chaos during the last weeks of the regime, attempts to resolve the educational policy crisis continued. Finally, after the efforts of the new minister of education had produced the agreement by Christian Democracy and FEDAP to participate fully in the proposed national debate on education, a more fundamental compromise was quietly worked out between the Christian Democrats and the government. The result was a Project of Law which was drafted by the Christian Democrats and placed on the congressional agenda a few days before 11 September.[4] (Partido Democrata Cristiano, September 1973).

This final document did not deal with the *content* of an eventual educational reform. Considerations of content were to await the results of the national debate and the work of the technical commissions. Rather, it emphasized two more basic issues: 1) guaranteeing the existence of private education not controlled by the government; and 2) establishing mechanisms and guarantees for the consideration and approval of whatever specific educational change proposals might be produced by the public deliberations.

The first twelve articles of the proposed law dealt with private education. Most of these articles referred to private schools which "cooperated with" the national education system and which were required to follow officially approved programs of study and administrative norms. There was little dispute over these sections, which essentially ratified what already existed as a consequence of a variety of laws and decrees. The purpose was to guarantee the continued existence of such private education under the existing rules. Much more controversial was a clause which authorized a new category of "independent" private schools, which would not be obliged to use official programs. Government representatives had great difficulty accepting the concept of schools which would be totally free of control by the state. This, however, was an essential agenda item for the Christian Democrats, who saw the possibility of establishing such schools as a necessary guarantee for those parents who were afraid that official curricula might become too "communist" and who did not wish to have their children "indoctrinated" in an ideology to which they were bitterly opposed. The compromise solution authorized the establishment of such "independent" schools, which could organize their teaching programs and their administrative and financial affairs in any manner they wished. But this authorization was qualified by the statement that such schools could receive no benefit whatsoever from the state and that their certificates and diplomas would not be officially recognized and would have no legal or regulatory status.

The next set of articles reaffirmed and strengthened the role of the National Council of Education, specifying that no change in education could be implemented without discussion in and approval by the council. Membership on the council was restructured to broaden its base within the community and to provide a relatively even balance between government and non-government representatives, with the added provision that members had to be "democratically elected" by the organizations they represented. There was little dispute over these articles in spite of the fact that they strengthened the power of the opposition to block government initiatives in the area of education.

The final article (Article 17) provided a much stronger check upon government efforts to change education. Under the constitutional system then in place a decree law could be annulled by the *Contraloría*. However, a negative ruling by the *Contraloría* could be overridden by a decree of insistence, a decree signed by the president and all of his cabinet ministers. Article 17 placed educational change proposals in a special category, to which a decree of insistence would not apply. As the Christian Democratic negotiators understood the constitution, this provision effectively meant that any educational reform proposal would have to be approved by both houses of Congress. By agreeing to these provisions, Popular Unity was guaranteeing there would be no significant change in education without the approval of its opponents.

How, then, was it possible, after all that had happened before, to arrive at this final educational policy compromise? Both sides saw it as a key element in a desperate last-minute attempt to avoid the military intervention whose probability was becoming more and more apparent. The Christian Democratic negotiators saw themselves "in the middle," trying to arrive at a proposal which would be minimally acceptable to Popular Unity representatives but which would also provide necessary guarantees to those who were openly advocating military intervention. One of the government negotiators who had been a vocal advocate of the revolutionary socialist position explained their activity as "one last attempt to avoid a coup. We had to try to do something." Both sides wanted to demonstrate publicly that a compromise could be reached even in the area that had been the subject of such rancorous and damaging debate over the past few months and which affected almost every family in the nation. They hoped that this could be the start of a process of arriving at compromises in other areas which would allow Popular Unity to continue governing until the next presidential elections and save the political institutional structure of the nation. But the compromise came too late.

Also too late was a broader attempt to resolve the institutional crisis. This attempt originated with Allende and his close advisors. As Valenzuela notes:

> The device decided on was a plebiscite, to be held during the second week of September, calling for the election of a constitutional assembly to resolve the crisis. The Communist Party was intent on the move, and secretary general Luis Corvalan supported it vigorously. To Corvalan's irritation, Allende insisted on trying to bring the balking Socialists around to his position, though he was determined to proceed without their support if necessary. Through the good offices of the

Cardinal, the Christian Democrats were approached directly to obtain their reaction to the plebiscite proposal. General Pinochet and other army generals Allende deemed loyal were informed of his plan on 7 September. Over the weekend the minister of the interior and others worked frantically to come up with the wording for the President's speech, announcing the plebiscite, and they still had legal problems to resolve the night of 10 September. (1978, p. 105)

One source has described the scene in the Christian Democratic party headquarters on the night of 10-11 September. There was constant telephone communication between the Christian Democrats, Allende (and presumably some of his aides), and Cardinal Silva as they tried to work out final details of the plebiscite announcement which it was hoped could be made public the next day. Late in the evening, the telephone rang. The person who answered it listened for a moment, and "his face turned white." The coup was under way. Within hours Allende was dead, and the dream of Popular Unity turned into a nightmare.

12

Conclusion

The question to be addressed in this final chapter is the relative importance of the ENU controversy among the myriad factors at play during the final months of the Allende government. Within the vast literature which has developed during the past twelve years attempting to explain the fate of the Popular Unity government in Chile, there are lengthy debates over the importance of a number of factors: the actions of the government itself and its principal internal opponents; the economic situation of the nation, as a consequence of Popular Unity policy and/or the economic "sabotage" by the Chilean right wing and/or the economic "blockade" mounted by the United States; the direct foreign attempts to destabilize the regime; the breakdown, under increasing political polarization, of the centrist mechanisms of negotiation which had maintained the stability of the political system for so many decades, and so forth.

One of the Christian Democrats most centrally involved in the negotiations leading to the final educational compromise between his party and the Popular Unity government maintains that the ENU proposal was the single most important cause of the government's downfall. "If the law we produced had been in place earlier, there would have been no ENU controversy, and therefore there would have been no coup. We were six months too late." But studying the Allende years can also easily lead one to the conclusion that no single factor predominated; that the entire project was doomed from the start; that the main lesson to be learned is that for a minority coalition government (itself internally divided) to attempt to implement revolutionary change in a highly polarized parliamentary democracy is to invite disaster. Lautaro Videla, one of the most active hard-line advocates of the ENU proposal, has concluded that "ENU was born dead. And Popular Unity was born dead" (interview, 19 May 1981).

In attempting to understand the fate of the Allende regime and the role of the ENU controversy within it, three sets of actors need to be considered: 1) the members of the government itself and their active supporters; 2) the opposition forces within Chile; and 3) the opposition forces outside of Chile—principally the United States government. It should be evident that I do not place much weight upon the influence of the activities of the United States government. Its well-documented *attempts* at influencing events in Chile (particularly the CIA support of *El Mercurio*) clearly made the task of the government harder and the task of the internal opposition easier. But I have encountered no convincing evidence that this influence was decisive. (Indeed, the history of this epoch in Chilean history can be read as an example, reinforced by many other examples during the past decade, of the limits of the effective use of power by a large nation against a small nation several thousand miles away.)[1] The view taken here is that the most significant elements of the drama were played out in Chile, by Chileans.

Within this context one can easily focus only upon the actions of the government. This can lead to a "Greek tragedy" explanation (as reflected in the quotation from Radomiro Tomic in the introduction): hubris leading inevitably to disaster. But this view discounts the actions and intentions of the Chilean opposition forces, who were searching for ways to defend their own interests. It is equally easy to concentrate only on the actions of the opposition, which discounts the extent to which the actions of the government and its supporters contributed to their own calamity.

What I have tried to demonstrate in the preceding chapters is the dialectical tension between these two sets of actors and their actions. Neither can be understood without the other. In the early chapters the emphasis is primarily upon the actions of the government. In later chapters the intentional activities of the opposition become increasingly important. This reflects my perception of how events unfolded. During the early part of the Popular Unity epoch, the opposition had not developed a coherent and effective strategy. Particularly in the first year, the government was surprisingly successful, and such problems as it had were largely consequences of its own mistakes, which, however, had a cumulative effect. As the months passed, a coherent opposition strategy began to emerge, which became an increasingly important factor in the government's difficulties. Indeed, the central importance of the ENU proposal was precisely that, at a politically very delicate moment, it handed to the extreme opposition forces the tool they had been looking for to crystallize, and mobilize support for, their campaign to delegitimize the government.

One can never, of course, "prove" through historical analysis that the removal or alteration of any single factor, such as ENU, in a complex political situation such as that experienced in Chile during the Allende years could have altered the ultimate outcome. As suggested in the introduction, what has been offered here is one interpretation of these events. Others reading this account of the complex process through which the educational policy of the Popular Unity government was developed and the debates which resulted from its public presentation may come to different conclusions.

My position is that if there were any way to save the Allende regime after the congressional elections of March 1973, it would only have been through heroic compromises by both the government and opposition. These would have been very difficult to achieve under the best of circumstances, but such compromises were not totally impossible as the last-minute negotiations over the educational law and the plebiscite proposal indicate. It was in this context that the ENU proposal, in the form and at the time it was presented to the public, had a devastating political impact upon the Popular Unity government. The ENU dispute reinforced the perception that this was a government that could not govern and could not be trusted to abide by the constitutional and legal norms even in a matter so sensitive as the education of children. It frightened and alienated many of the remaining middle sectors whose support, or at least neutrality, was essential to the survival of the regime under the existing parliamentary system. It brought the two remaining major neutral institutions, the Church and the armed forces, into open opposition. Within the internally divided military, still officially neutral, whose highest-ranking officers were committed constitutionalists, the ENU dispute legitimized the open expression of political dissent and lack of confidence in the government.

In a sense, the most remarkable aspect of the results of the election of March 1973 was their similarity to the outcome of the 1969 congressional election. In spite of four years of extraordinary turmoil and intense competition for voter loyalty, the patterns of support for the major political parties had shifted very little. Referring back to the analysis of the overall political situation in 1970 at the end of Chapter 2, it would appear that there had been relatively little change in the patterning of commitment to the existing socioeconomic order (the dimension along which the political "left" and "right" are typically located). What these results masked, however, was a shift on the other dimension: commitment to the existing consitutional order.

The revolutionary wing within the government coalition, which advocated rapid and if necessary violent elimination of the existing constitutional order, had lost ground in the Lo Curro meeting of Popular Unity in June 1972 and was further weakened by the resolution of the October Strike. However, its position was strengthened by the unexpectedly favorable electoral results in March 1973. However, those same results convinced the most adamant opponents of the government that they could not decisively defeat it electorally and that military intervention was their only alternative.

A small minority had believed this from the very beginning, but they had not been able to bring a "critical mass" of Chileans to their point of view.

The position of the opposition forces who still maintained at least a qualified commitment to the traditional governmental institutions had been steadily eroded by a number of factors such as: 1) the failure to resolve the dispute over the definition of the three areas of the economy and the associated use by the government of quasi- or extra-legal means to take over private enterprises and farms; 2) the apparent inability of the government to maintain a minimum of order and stability in basic and pervasive institutions such as the schools; 3) the continuing confusion over which government spokesmen one could or should believe on basic policy issues and the perceived inability of senior government officials to direct and control the actions of their subordinates; 4) the apparent inability of the government to manage the economy so as to control now rampant inflation and ensure at least minimal supplies of foodstuffs and other basic consumer items; 5) the evident progressive deterioration of the informal mechanisms of negotiation which had permitted the political system to absorb and settle divergent demands from increasingly polarized social groups (a deterioration which had begun well before Popular Unity came into power). It was no longer self-evident that "honest brokers" could be found to negotiate the compromises upon which the traditional system had depended. Nonetheless, in March 1973 there still appeared to be among these sectors a substantial residue of loyalty to the Chilean democratic institutions in which they had long taken great pride.

If they maintained allegiance, not necessarily to the government in question but to the ongoing institutional order, a coup would be, if not impossible, then very costly. If they were convinced that the government was prepared to destroy the traditional institutional structure in pursuit of socioeconomic policy goals they did not necessarily support, then a military coup would be seen as the lesser of two evils. If they came to believe that the government represented a serious threat to their most deeply held personal or familial values, they would be prepared to sacrifice the constitutional order to get rid of the regime.

The debate over the ENU proposal was a critical factor in tipping the balance among these middle sectors away from support for the constitutional order and toward acceptance of a coup. The hard-line Socialists within the Ministry of Education who supported ENU had no conception of the political impact it might have. As one of them noted in trying to explain this miscalculation: "We had a very restricted Leninist view, with a narrow understanding of power. During discussion of the ENU project within the Party throughout the period, December, January, or even after the crisis exploded in March, the concern was always with specific groups, like the Church or the military, whose actual or potential power was clear.

It never occurred to us, and we never perceived the anti-ENU reaction as coming from 'the middle sectors.' It would have helped if we had read Gramsci.'' Those within the government who strongly opposed the ENU proposal had recognized the potential for political disaster that it represented and had consequently fought to abort it or at least modify it. But even these individuals were surprised by the strength and tenacity of the opposition attack and the extent to which the media and opposition party campaign against the proposition struck a deeply resonating chord among large sectors of the body politic.

This was certainly not the first occasion since the advent of the Popular Unity government in which the opposition media, particularly *El Mercurio*, and the opposition parties had mounted a sustained attack against a government policy. Indeed, such attacks were a constant of political life in Chile from September 1970 onward. The question to be addressed is why the campaign against the ENU proposal had such a pronounced effect. A simple answer relates to the pervasiveness of schools as social institutions. Most Popular Unity policies directly affected only a small proportion of the population. Disputes over limits of the social property sector of the economy and illegal or quasi-legal takeovers of enterprises or farms had an immediate impact upon few Chileans. Even the "Papelera" controversy, to which *El Mercurio* (and apparently the CIA) devoted so much attention was of direct concern to only a small minority of the population. Complex arguments over the constitutionality of various government measures were hardly likely to capture the avid attention even of the well-educated sector of the population. While the results of public opinion polls indicated that the middle sectors felt themselves to be the group most seriously affected economically by the government's policies, the inflation and shortages affected families differentially. But every family had children, grandchildren, nieces or nephews, or cousins in school. This explanation of the effect of the ENU proposal was advanced by many of the individuals interviewed for this study, but is not wholly satisfactory. The massive educational reform implemented during the Frei regime had created relatively little political controversy; indeed, it seems to have been one of the more popular of that government's initiatives. Chileans were not inclined to automatically oppose educational change.

The explanation lies rather in the way in which the ENU proposal, as presented, keyed into the value structure of Chileans. Silvert and Jutkowitz (1976) and Silvert and Reissman (1976) report the results of the best available empirical examination of the values and attitudes of Chileans from all social strata. One of their interests was the extent to which Chileans were prepared to accept change in each of five basic institutional spheres: the family, religion, the political system, the economy, and education. The results of this very extensive study were that "the most obvious conclusion

. . .useful to social scientists and policymakers alike, is that the Chileans interviewed are most prone to change in education and the economy, least prone to change in familial and religious matters, and very undecided and presumably conflicted over political change" (Silvert and Jutkowitz, 1976, p. 17).

This explains why there was little disagreement, either within the government or between the government and the opposition, regarding the technical or structural aspects of the ENU proposal. As the Frei reforms had shown, Chileans were quite prepared to accept changes in this area. But the hard-line socialist rhetoric in which the proposal was wrapped allowed it to be portrayed by the opposition as an attack against the *family* (socializing children into a value pattern which would alienate them from the beliefs of the parents) and their *religion* (particularly when the Church declared itself in opposition to the proposal). Instead of capitalizing upon the willingness of Chileans to accept changes in education, the proposal, because of its ideological content, threatened them in precisely those areas where they were least likely to accept change. It also hardened their "conflicted" attitudes toward changes in the political structure.

The principal political vehicle of the Chilean middle class was the Christian Democratic party. Popular Unity constantly had difficulty understanding the position of this party and its constituents. As Sergio Bitar has observed: "The eminently sociological and structuralist analysis of Christian Democracy by Popular Unity emphasized its multi-class base and concluded that it would be possible to attract many of its members given the character of many of the measures which would aid laborers and white-collar workers. The policy toward this party was affected by an underestimation of the ideological elements which held its membership together" (Bitar, 1978, p. 15; see also Bitar, 1977). It was precisely these ideological elements—including the party's attachment to Christianity (the Church) and private education as a guarantor of educational freedom for the family— which were seen to be threatened by the ENU proposal. This both improved the cohesiveness of the party at the ideological level and strengthened the hard-line elements within the party.

The ENU proposal was certainly not the only factor at play in those critical last months of the Popular Unity regime; but it was one of the most important elements. The nature of its impact was dramatized for me in late August 1973 during a family birthday celebration to which I had been invited. Most of the men present were middle-aged armed forces officers of fairly senior rank. Naturally, the main (practically the only) subject of conversation during a very long evening was the nation's political situation, and the arguments were heated. The educational reform proposal was a theme to which the discussion kept returning, each time with greater vigor. As we were downing our last round of pisco before heading home, one of the officers turned to me and said in a loud voice, apparently trying to summarize for me the entire discussion: "Look, these Marxists can wreck the economy, and we can recover. We've done it before. They can change the political institutions, and we can change them back if we want. But they had better keep their damned hands off my kids!" In the cooler words of Anibal Palma (interview, 25 May 1983), the language in which the ENU proposal was presented was "a monument to the damage that can be caused by ideological intransigence."

Appendix 1

ORGANIZATIONS AND ACRONYMS

ASTECO	Technical School Teachers Union (pre-1970)
CUT	National Workers Federation
FECH	Federation of Students of the University of Chile
FEDAP	Federation of Private School Parents and Guardians
FEDECH	Federation of Teachers Unions (pre-1970)
FEUC	Federation of Students of the Catholic University
FESES	Federation of Secondary School Students of Santiago
INACAP	National Technical Training Program
ODEPLAN	National Planning Office
SINET	National System of Workers' Education (proposed)
SONAP	*Liceo* Teachers Union (pre-1970)
SUTE	Single National Teachers Union (post-1970)
UPCH	Primary Teachers Union (pre-1970)

Appendix 2

FREQUENTLY CITED NAMES

Name	Position*	Party
Altamirano, Carlos	Secretary-General of the Socialist Party, Jan. 1971 - Sept. 1973	Socialist
Araya, Hugo	Technical Secretary, Superintendency of Education	Radical
Arenas, Sergio	Head of Planning and Budget Office, Ministry of Education	Radical
Astorga, Mario	Minister of Education, Nov. 1970 - Jan. 1972	Radical
Aylwin, Patricio	President of Christian Democratic Party, May 1973 - Sept. 1973	Christian Democrat
Balocchi, Roberto	Staff member, Planning and Budget Office, Ministry of Education	Socialist
Dominguez, Andres	Policy analyst and speechwriter, Ministry of Education	MAPU
Enriquez Froeden, Edgardo	Minister of Education, July 1973 - Sept. 1973	Radical
Espinoza, Jorge	Director of Secondary Education, Nov. 1970 - Jan. 1972	Communist
Fuentealba, Renan	President of Christian Democratic Party, May 1972 - May 1973	Christian Democrat
Gonzalez, Gilberto	Staff member, Planning and Budget Office, Ministry of Education	Communist
Leyton, Mario	Director, Center for In-Service Teacher Training	Christian Democrat
Livacic, Ernesto	Member of National Council of Education (Subsecretary of Education during Frei government)	Christian Democrat

Name	Position*	Party
Migone, Aida	Director of Secondary Education, Jan. 1972 - Sept. 1973	Communist
Moreno, Carlos	Director of Technical-Professional Education	Socialist
Nuñez, Ivan	Superintendent of Education	Socialist
Palma, Anibal	Minister of Education, June 1972 - Nov. 1972	Radical
Rios Valdivia, Antonio	Minister of Education, Jan. 1972 - June 1972	Radical
Salazar, Miguel	President of FESES, Nov. 1972 - Sept. 1973	Christian Democrat
Suarez, Waldo	Subsecretary of Education	Socialist
Tapia, Jorge	Minister of Education, Nov. 1972 - July 1973; (Minister of Justice, Nov. 1970 - Nov. 1972)	Radical
Urrutia, Fresia	Director of Primary and Normal Education	Radical
Videla, Lautaro	Visitor-General of Education	Socialist
Yunge, Guillermo	President of FESES, Nov. 1971 - Nov. 1972	Christian Democrat

*If dates are not specified, the individual held the position throughout the Allende period.

Notes

NOTES TO THE INTRODUCTION

1. It was particularly common for North American observers to refer to Popular Unity as a "Marxist" regime. Western European observers tended to focus more on the "socialist" nature of the government and its proclaimed intent to use peaceful and legal means to achieve revolutionary change. Allende regularly insisted that while he himself, and many Popular Unity supporters, accepted one variant or another of Marxist theory, his *government* was *not* Marxist.

2. I first heard this quotation in a news report on a portable radio in a darkened hotel room in Santiago (a terrorist bombing had cut off the city's electrical supply) late in August 1973. I immediately copied it down, for it seemed to me to capture perfectly the situation of the nation in that late winter.

3. Recently, a few works have appeared that analyze education under the Popular Unity government (for example, Fischer, 1977; Bermudez, 1975; Castro, 1977; Nuñez, 1979; Vivallo, 1978). However, in all of these works except that of Vivallo, education under the Allende regime is treated as one portion of a more general historical analysis which also covers pre- and post-Allende regimes, and the analytical emphasis is on the differences in educational policy stances among several regimes as a function of their general ideological positions. None of the cited works provides a sufficiently thorough analysis of the causes and consequences of the ENU proposition, although all (especially Fischer, 1977, and Vivallo, 1978) contain important material which has been used in the development of this book.

4. Notable exceptions to this tendency are brief articles by Schiefelbein (1975) and McGinn, Schiefelbein and Warwick (1979) regarding education decision-making in Chile and El Salvador during the 1960's.

5. Unfortunately, neither of these clipping files maintained a record of the page number on which a particular newspaper article was found. Consequently, for consistency's sake, all references in this book to newspaper reports include the date but not the page number.

6. The appendices which follow the final chapter contain a list of the frequently mentioned individuals, with their official position and party affiliation, and a glossary of frequently encountered organizational acronyms.

NOTES TO CHAPTER TWO

1. Under the Chilean Constitution, a president cannot succeed himself, although he may run again after a one-term interval. Thus, Alessandri could not be a candidate in 1964 and Frei could not run in 1970, in spite of the fact, ironically, that each was probably the most generally popular political leader available at the end of his term of office.

2. This account relies heavily on the very useful book: *El Partido Socialista de Chile*, by Julio Cesar Jobet (1971), as well as on interviews with various participants in the Chillan Congress, particularly Ivan Nuñez and Lautaro Videla.

NOTES TO CHAPTER THREE

1. For an excellent discussion of the planning and implementation strategies adopted by the Frei government's educational policy-makers, see Schiefelbein (1975) and Schiefelbein, McGinn and Warwick (1980).

2. In addition to Nuñez' monograph on the history of Chilean Teacher Unions (1982b), interviews with Lautaro Videla were particularly helpful in clarifying developments in the teachers' union movement in the immediate pre-Allende years.

3. Apart from his official bureaucratic role, Videla was also very influential in the policy formulation process within the ministry. He got along well with and was respected by key figures from the various factions within the Popular Unity coalition as well as from the Christian Democrats. According to several informants, he also used his trips on behalf of the Ministry of Education to serve the same "troubleshooting" and information gathering roles on behalf of the leadership of the Socialist Party—an interesting combination of responsibilities!

NOTES TO CHAPTER FOUR

1. There were also calls for more attention to physical education and a pledge to stimulate further university reform efforts. The university reform process in Chile is outside the scope of this work.

2. The attempts by the U.S. government to block Allende's election by the Congress, or failing that, to stimulate a military coup, have been well documented and need not be repeated here. What is most significant for the present analysis is that those attempts failed. Even when they produced their most extreme consequence, the assassination of the army's commander-in-chief, Rene Schneider by right-wing extremists, "the result was to intensify the determination of the Congress, the armed forces, and the country to follow through with the constitutional process" (Sigmund, 1977, p. 123).

NOTES TO CHAPTER FIVE

1. The document also contained eight pages of recommendations regarding university enrolment targets and plans of study which are not of concern here.

2. "Ningún cabro quedará sin matricula." *Chilean slang uses the words cabro* or *cabrito* (goat or baby goat) to refer to a child in exactly the same way English uses the word "kid."

3. In a study in which I was involved at this time, we had to locate a sample of students who moved from primary to secondary school between 1970 and 1971. Compared to the traditional record-keeping systems still used in the rest of the nation, the computerized records were very complete and accurate.

4. I was at this time associated with the educational planning office within the Superintendency of Education. The discussion of internal government procedure until June, 1971, when I left Chile, is based on my observations as a foreign participant observer, except where some other source is specifically mentioned.

5. It is to the credit of these new officials

that many of them frankly recognized the need for expertise and their lack of it. During this period and for many months thereafter, I was frequently called upon to provide "crash courses" in research and planning techniques and to work with others in arranging longer term training opportunities. These efforts could not, however, solve the immediate problem in the first months of the regime.

6. A well publicized but typical example was the case where a school with five hundred poor children enrolled received fifty pairs of shoes to distribute. A wave of jokes swept Santiago concerning the criteria which would be used to determine which children got a left shoe, a right shoe, both shoes, or no shoes at all.

7. It should be noted that under Chilean civil service regulations, all nominees had to have met minimum qualifications with respect to seniority and type and level of education.

8. For early statements of the Communist party position, see lead editorials in the party newspaper, *El Siglo*, 23 and 27 March 1971. These were commentaries on Allende's first major speech on education, which simply repeated his main points with approval.

9. *El Mercurio*, which was and is Chile's "paper of record," was controlled by the Edwards family, one of the most influential families in the traditional Chilean oligarchy. The paper's publisher in 1970, Augustin Edwards, fled the country on the day of the presidential election. He was actively involved in the plotting in the United States to try to prevent Allende from assuming the presidency (see Sigmund, 1977, pp. 111, 115).

10. It should be noted that the level and extent of state subventions to private schools had been a contentious issue for

years. The very complicated system in existence in 1971 was the product of political compromises struck by several previous governments as they had wrestled with the problem. Thus, what was new here was not the issue itself but the fact that it was being dealt with by a government which had, before the election, publicly proclaimed its intent to eliminate private schools.

11. However, a widely believed rumor had Allende telling high Church officials that while the government did not have the resources or the desire to take over private schools right away, "eventually we will have to do it." I heard this story several times in early 1971 and have had it quoted to me several times since by individuals closely associated with the private school movement.

12. See, for example, *Ercilla*, 26 May 1971; *La Segunda*, 6 September 1971, which complained of a test question which asked students to analyze and critique a passage from the writings of Ernesto Guevara and compare it to Christian morality; *La Tribuna*, 25 October 1971, referring to a communist teacher who asked her students to read the biography of Guevara rathe0 than to study Chilean national heroes; or *El Mercurio*, 11 December 1971, praising a group of students from a Santiago secondary school who had refused to take a test whose sole purpose, they claimed, was "political concientization."

13. The issue raised here by Pablo has since become a very common criticism of the Freirean methodology, suggesting that it is not truly liberating, but is rather a subtle, and therefore especially insidious, way of imposing the educator's worldview upon the subject.

NOTES TO CHAPTER SIX

1. SONAP added to the terminological confusion by approving a resolution at its national convention which referred to the "Unified School for Development." Although the description was general it appeared to be about the same thing as the "National Unified School" in the Six-Year Plan (SONAP, 1971, pp. 9-10).

2. Vivallo (1978, pp. 166-78) provides a very detailed discussion of this document.

3. Most of the information contained in the preceding three paragraphs is taken from an interview with Ivan Nuñez, 15 November 1980.

4. Ministerio de Educación Pública, October 1971. All citations used here are taken from the version published in *Revista de Educación*, no. 36-38 (1972, pp. 71-98).

5. The document which was distributed in

October included a fifth theme: *Bases for a Proposed Law for Democratization of Chilean Education.* There was no discussion of this topic in the text, and the topic was eliminated from the version published in the *Revista de Educación* after the National Congress was held. Also missing in the final published version was a brief introductory outline of the contents, followed by the slogan: "ONWARD TO SOCIALISM: LET US BUILD THE NEW CHILEAN EDUCATION."

6. See Chapter 4 for a discussion of the role of the *Contraloría.*

7. FESES had just completed an election for its leadership, which had been won by the opposition.

8. A note on the relationship between the major parties and their student federations will be useful here. All of the main parties had youth or student wings. I have discussed the relationships between the party and its youth wing with members of all of the major parties. Rarely were the youth wings given direct commands by their party's central committee. The typical pattern was described this way by one informant: "Look, these 16 or 17 year old kids would be invited to a dinner or a meeting with the highest officials of the party. General issues would be discussed, and possible actions that students might take to assist the party would be referred to. But you could not tell these proud young men what they were supposed to do." Indeed, I have been told of a number of occasions in which youth leaders of various parties argued openly and vigorously against the policy decisions of their elders. Moreover, the student movements often undertook street

actions, demonstrations, or takeovers of buildings at times and places which were awkward or embarrassing to the main party. During conversation with Chilean political figures about their party youth groups, the tone most commonly encountered is one of fond exasperation, with frequent references to the "uncontrollable effervescence of youth" and stories of their own days as student political leaders. There is no question but that all of the parties that had the capability were actively aiding their students in school and association election campaigns, although they could not easily control the students' behavior.

9. Through the latter part of October and into November, secondary student federations in the rest of Chile held their elections. Although Popular Unity won a few notable victories, for example, in the provinces of Concepción and Cautín, generally the opposition, particularly the Christian Democrats, received the most votes.

10. Edwards was the publisher of *El Mercurio.*

11. The assassination of Hernan Mery, a land reform worker, was a cause célèbre among the Chilean left at this time.

12. In the next week SUTE held its first national conference. Discussion centered on the same themes as in the National Congress of Education, and the same positions were taken by government and opposition forces. Indeed, the overlap was so great that the Christian Democratic contingent walked out of one of the working commissions, complaining that they were dealing with exactly the same agenda as in the just concluded National Congress (*La Prensa,* 20 December 1971).

NOTES TO CHAPTER SEVEN

1. This is Jorge Tapia *Valdez,* who later became minister of education, and who figures prominently in later chapters. He should not be confused with another well-known Chilean of this epoch, Jorge Tapia *Videla.* Tapia *Videla* appears nowhere in this manuscript. Therefore, all references to "Tapia" or "Jorge Tapia" can be understood to refer to Jorge Tapia *Valdez.*

2. Tapia had been a central figure in the negotiations for the Statute of Democratic

Guarantees. Since the inauguration of the government, when he became minister of justice, he had been engaged in secret negotiations with the Christian Democratic senator Tomas Pablo. This was the first occasion on which these negotiations became publicly known (interview with Jorge Tapia, 23 May 1983).

3. The government claimed that these economic difficulties were the result of an external economic blockade, orchestrated by the United States, and internal sabo-

tage, involving hoarding and black market manipulation by the economically most powerful groups. These factors were clearly present and *aggravated* the economic situation. However, it would have been extraordinarily difficult for a government pursuing the combination of policies adopted by Popular Unity to have avoided the damaging combination of severe shortages and very high rates of inflation. Valenzuela (1978, pp. 61-70) provides a particularly cogent and brief account of the effects of the regime's economic policies. A long-time Socialist related to me an indicative incident. In mid-1972 he was asked to accompany the dean of a Russian school of industrial engineering on a tour of industries which had been socialized, in order to evaluate the worker self-management procedures. At every factory they visited, they arrived to find that there was no one working. "They were always in political meetings." After several days of this, the Russian said, "Comrades, you can't let this happen! If you're going to make a revolution, you have to *work*."

4. It is interesting to note that in August, while the deliberations within the ministry were still underway, *El Mercurio* published two long and detailed articles outlining what it claimed were the educational policy directions of the government. These were based to a very large extent upon Araya's paper. It is also interesting to observe that these two articles are descriptive and quite calm in tone, containing none of the inflammatory rhetoric which one had seen in the reportage of the National Congress of Education and which would soon reappear (*El Mercurio*, 7 and 13 August 1972).

5. Although FESES was the largest and most active of the student federations, it represented only the students of public *liceos* in Santiago. Students from other branches of secondary education, from private education, and from the various universities all had their own separate federations.

6. The selection process worked as follows. After a vacancy was formally announced, anyone who had the appropriate qualifications and time in service could apply and send credentials to the Ministry of Education. The background documentation required regarding each year of an applicant's career was very extensive. A ministerial committee then examined all of these applications, applying to them a set of criteria set out in regulations and selected a short list of three candidates. The credentials of these three were then considered even more closely, and a decision was finally made by the minister of education. One of the many bureaucratic absurdities of the Chilean system was that every school directorship in a nation several thousand miles long had to be decided in Santiago, ultimately by the minister himself. This elaborate process was designed to ensure that selections were made on technical rather than political grounds, although as we have seen the government had already circumvented the regulations in the naming of several hundred primary school directors, and it was certainly not the first government to have manipulated or ignored the regulations.

7. This was something rare in Chilean history—students in the streets demonstrating in *support of* a minister of education.

8. Student leaders in these incidents have indicated that they were under very strong pressure from their political parties to refuse to compromise with the government, to prolong the situations as much as possible.

9. Palma would have left his post in any case. He was sure that he could not, under the circumstances, continue as minister of education, and his party had asked him to be a senatorial candidate in Santiago for the March elections. It is indicative of Palma's relationship with Allende that after that campaign he was appointed general secretary of the government, responsible for the presidency's relationships with the media. Palma was the only non-Socialist to hold this position, which was one of the few major posts which fell within Allende's personal authority rather than within the interparty quota system.

NOTES TO CHAPTER EIGHT

1. Information contained in this chapter is derived from interviews with many of the participants in the struggles within the Ministry of Education, including Jorge Tapia, Ivan Nuñez, Hugo Araya, Aida Migone, Andres Dominguez, Lautaro

Videla, plus many other officials. Specific sources are noted only when a direct quotation is used.

2. Throughout this text, the Spanish acronym for the National Unified School, ENU, is used, since this is how the proposal is generally known to students of this period of Chilean history.

3. This report circulated in the ministry in mimeographed form. Some copies are dated 15 December others are dated simply December 1972, and still others have no date. In all cases, the content is the same.

4. The concept of permanent education and the distinction between the two areas of education were introduced into the document by Nuñez. In October 1972, the first world meeting to examine and evaluate a draft of the Faure Commission report was held in Santiago, at the initiative of Felipe Herrera, a Chilean who was a member of the Unesco commission which had produced the report. Nuñez was the only official of the Ministry of Education to participate in this meeting. He immediately inserted the principal themes of the Unesco report into the ENU document.

5. This perception was based not only on his reading of the document itself but also upon discussions within the government in which the minister participated. As one example, a proposal was advanced to mount a publicity campaign for the educational reform proposal under the slogan, "ENU—UNE" (ENU unites). This idea was rejected by a hard-line militant who was very close to Allende on the grounds that the purpose of ENU was not to unite but to "rupture" (interview with Jorge Tapia, 23 May 1983).

6. Throughout 1971 and 1972, international aid funds were available to establish such a "data base" system, and a plan had been developed within the ministry for the use of the funds. The proposal foundered on the problem of equal representation of the several coalition parties. The available money would not have permitted the provision of necessary technical training to representatives of each party, and agreement could not be reached on who would be included and who excluded.

7. This was in contrast to the experience of the Christian Democrats, who had announced and begun implementation of their own reform very quickly, which allowed them to implement it fully by 1970.

8. Indeed, many Christian Democrats also believed that this general policy direction was both necessary and a logical extension of their own reform efforts. For a Christian Democratic criticism of the government's failure to act quickly to implement further needed educational changes, see Livacic (1973).

9. Although the coordinating committee was the center for the disputes within the ministry regarding ENU, the debate was occurring throughout its divisions and offices. Positions taken by individual members of the committee often reflected not only their perceptions of the stances of the individual members of other parties within this central committee, but also their understanding of the general stance within the ministry and the government taken by the party those other actors represented. Thus, for example, the Socialists in the coordinating committee saw the Radical members of the committee not only as individuals with their own peculiar positions but also as representatives of the more general "Radical party position" within the ministry, as they understood it from other interactions, which ranged from formal meetings to coffee-break gossip, and vice-versa. When reference is made here to the position of the "Radical party" or the "Socialist party," it must be understood that that position was interpreted differently by different members of the same party and by individual members of other parties.

10. Interestingly, Tapia also considered that the ENU proposal could help government candidates in the March elections. However, his analysis of the political situation brought him to the belief that it would be a positive influence only if the ideological rhetoric so important to Nuñez and Videla was significantly softened. Otherwise, it would have a negative impact on the Popular Unity fortunes.

11. It is an interesting commentary upon the lack of communication between the central educational policy planners in the ministry, and their respective parties that while the opposition press had obtained and publicized a copy of the ENU Commission report which was being revised in January, the annual meeting of the Socialist party members of SUTE held in early January proceeded without being fully aware of either the first report or the fact that it was under revision. The

conclusions reached by this group of active Socialist teachers emphasized the need to carry out the "unanimous agreements" of the National Congress of Education, spoke of the National Unified School in very general terms, and lauded the First Integrated Year proposal as a very major and *permanent* change in secondary education, rather than as the two-year transition arrangement which the ENU Commission had proposed (*La Nacion*, 14 January 1973). The opposition and its press were better informed regarding the details of the proposed educational policy than were the teacher members of the government party which was, for the most part, strongly supporting it!

NOTES TO CHAPTER NINE

1. The Popular Socialist Union, a small party which had split from the Socialists in 1967, ran a separate list of candidates but played no significant role in the results.

2. Anibal Palma, who by this time was in charge of Popular Unity's liaison with the media, has made the same observation. Each side read its own newspapers, watched its own television station, and listened to its own radio stations (except that *El Mercurio* was widely read), paying little or no attention to what the other side was saying (interview with Anibal Palma, 12 December 1982).

3. With respect to CIA aid for *El Mercurio*, estimated to be at least $1.5 million (which probably prevented the bankruptcy of the newspaper since it was being financially squeezed by the government), Sigmund has observed (1978, p. 285): "This may have made a psychological difference to the opposition, but given the politicization of the Chilean populace, it is difficult to believe that the absence of some organs of communication would have led the opposition to give up the battle. Many groups in Chile, and not all of them wealthy, felt—were—directly threatened by Allende's policies and ideology, and they did not need CIA propaganda to inform them of that fact."

4. Given the overall political situation, it is likely that any kind of significant educational reform proposal by the government would have been fiercely resisted by the opposition. As one government participant in the debates said: "We could have given them the Faure Report, labelled as ENU, and they still would have complained." However, the particular language used in the opening section of the ENU Report made it a very easy target for attack. As another Popular Unity actor noted: "It was like handing a loaded rifle to your enemy."

5. Many Chileans have recounted stories of bitter arguments among friends and family members with respect to the ENU proposal. A typical observation is the following: "Old friends, even members of my own family, started swearing viciously at me, or even refusing to speak to me, because I was seen as somehow vaguely associated with ENU."

6. It should be noted that this issue did not surface only among parents from the extreme right. It was a more general phenomenon, encountered in parent meetings in middle-class and working-class neighborhoods as well. It was assumed not only within Popular Unity but by significant sectors of Christian Democracy that the pejorative connotation of the word "trabajo" had disappeared from Chilean culture except among the extreme right. The widespread reaction of parents on this issue suggests that when it came to the destiny of their own children, the traditional value stance was still powerful.

NOTES TO CHAPTER TEN

1. The description of this meeting is based upon press reports, particularly *La Segunda*, 11 April 1973 and *La Prensa*, 12 April 1973; interviews with Jorge Tapia, 9 December 1981 and 19 April 1982; and interviews with other sources.

2. It is interesting to note that on this day when Tapia was meeting with the military officers and the bishops were meeting to discuss the government's educational reform proposal, the Decree of Democratization of Education, which had been slightly but not significantly modified by the government and then approved by

the *Contraloría*, was officially promulgated (*Diario Official*, 11 April 1973). In the heat of the debate over ENU, the official establishment of this decree, which had itself been the subject of such intense argument just months before, went practically unnoticed. The only press report that can be found is a brief note in *La Nacion* two days later.

3. Tapia notes that Luis Corvalan, secretary general of the Communist party, assured him when they were together in the prison camp on Dawson Island after the coup that the party's central committee had never been informed regarding the details of the ENU proposal (interview with Jorge Tapia, 9 December 1981). This is not surprising. I have noted above that *none* of the central committees of the parties comprising Popular Unity had been fully informed regarding the proposal, nor had they given it their approval.

4. The precise date of this meeting is not clear. From the testimony of various participants it appears to have taken place between 20 and 25 April.

NOTES TO CHAPTER ELEVEN

1. The Christian Democratic objections were very similar to those of the governing parties. They were very suspicious of any apparent attempt to create centers of power outside of the legislature which they controlled.

2. See, for example, Partido Democrata Cristiano, July 1973; Consejo Nacional de Educación Particular, July 1973; Frente de Trabajadores Radicales en Educación, July 1973; Conferencia Episcopal de Chile, June 1973; Santalices, et al., 1973; and Federación de Institutos de Educación, 1973.

3. I was in Chile during August 1973. The entire nation was paralyzed. One afternoon late in the month I was hitchhiking from the downtown area of Santiago to a meeting in an outlying district (since there was almost no gasoline to be found and the public transit system was not operating, those few who had functioning vehicles routinely picked up anyone who needed a ride). I got into a car and discovered that the driver was a powerful moderate Christian Democratic senator. In the course of our brief conversation, he said that he could see no solution to the crisis, that it was an absolutely hopeless situation, but that he still had faith that somehow, someone could find a way to resolve the situation.

4. The exact date on which the law proposal was placed on the agenda for eventual discussion and decision by the two houses of the Congress is not clear. Since it was never discussed either by committees or by the full Senate or Chamber of Deputies, there is no trace of it in the available formal records of congressional debates. The document I have is a copy from the files of a member of the Christian Democratic party who participated in writing it. Sources consulted both from the party and from the Ministry of Education agree on the authenticity of this version and on the fact that it was placed on the congressional agenda shortly before 11 September.

NOTES TO CHAPTER TWELVE

1. However, even if one accepts the view that the downfall of the Popular Unity government was inevitable because the United States government simply would not have permitted a Marxist president to complete his six-year term, one could argue that the lack of political skill in handling the ENU proposal contributed to and accelerated the inevitable.

References

Allende, Salvador. "Palabras del Presidente de la República Compañero Salvador Allende, Pronunciados en el Estadio Chile al Iniciar el Año Escolar 1971." Santiago: Dirección de Informaciones y Radiodifusion de la Presidencia de la Republica, 25 May 1971. Mimeograph.

Araya, Hugo. "Politica Educacional del Gobierno de la U.P.: Medidas Inmediatas." Santiago: Superintendencia de Educación, October 1970. Mimeograph.

"Medidas de democratización inmediatas del año 1972 derivadas de las conclusiones del Primer Congreso Nacional de Educación." Santiago: Superintendencia de Educación, 1972a. Mimeograph.

"Democracia y educación." Santiago: Superintendencia de Educación, 1972b. Mimeograph.

El Cambio educacional y la Escuela Nacional Unificada. Santiago: Impresos CHI-29, April 1973.

Ariagada, Genero. "La izquierda: un nuevo militarismo." In M.A. Perez Yoma, ed. *Subversión y contrasubversión*. Santiago: Centro de Investigaciones Socioeconomicos, 1978, pp. 139-78.

Astorga, Mario, and Araya, Hugo. *Formulación de una nueva educación en el gobierno de la Unidad Popular*. Santiago: Ministerio de Educación Pública, Ediciones Cultura y Publicaciones, 1971.

Cariola, Patricio, and Garcia Huidobro, Juan Eduardo. "Nuevas politicas de la educación particular y el programa de la Unidad Popular." *Cuadernos de Educación* (October 1970): pp. 456-62.

Castro, Pedro, *La educación en Chile de Frei a Pinochet*. Salamanca, Spain: Ediciones "Sigueme," 1977.

Centro de Perfeccionamiento. "Proyecto experimental de Escuela Nacional Unificada: tomado del Programa de Trabajo, 1972, del Centro de Perfeccionamiento, Experimentacion e Investigaciones Pedagogicas. Ministerio de Educación." Lo Barnechea, Chile: 1972. Mimeograph.

Comision Racionalizadora de Matricula. "Informe de la Comision Racionalizadora de Matricula sobre el proceso de matricula 1971." Santiago: Superintendencia de Educación, 15 May 1971. Mimeograph.

Comité Permanente de la Educación Particular. "La educación particular ante el documento 'Educación.' " Santiago: July 1972. Mimeograph.

Conferencia Episcopal de Chile. *El Momento Actual de la Educación en Chile: Documento de Trabajo*. Santiago: Documentos Revista Mundo, June 1973.

Conferencia Nacional de Trabajadores de la Educación del Partido Socialista. "Documentos de la Conferencia Nacional de Trabajadores de la Educación del Partido Socialista, Enero de 1968." In *Aportes socialistas para la construcción de la nueva educación chilena.* Santiago: Editorial Universitaria, 1971, pp. 42-54.

Consejo Nacional de Educación, "Puntos de acuerdo y conceptos alternativos del Primer Congreso Nacional de Educación para definir las lineas de politica educacional en el Gobierno de la Unidad Popular." Santiago: July 1972. Mimeograph.

"Debate nacional sobre educación." Santiago: Mimeograph. Also printed as a supplement to *Revista de Educación,* May/June 1973.

"Boletin No. 3: explicación sobre el debate." Santiago: August 1973. Mimeograph.

Consejo Nacional de Educación Particular. "El Consejo Nacional de la Educación Particular a sus bases y a la opinion publica en general." Santiago: 26 July 1973. Mimeograph.

Coombs, Philip A. *The World Educational Crisis: a Systems Analysis.* New York: Oxford University press, 1968.

Duran, Claudio. "Psycho War of the Media in Chile under Allende," *Media Probe* 2, no. 4, 1976.

Duran, Claudio, and Urzoa, Patricio. "On the Ideological Role of *El Mercurio* in Chilean Society." In *The Political Role of the Media. LARU Studies* 2, no. 3 (1973): pp. 45-64.

Faure, Edgar, et al. *Learning to be. The World of Education Today and Tomorrow.* Paris: Unesco, 1972.

Federación de Institutos de Educación. "La enseñanza particular y el informe ENU." In *Revista de Pedagogía.* No. 176 (July 1973): pp. 97-100.

FEUC. *ENU: el control de las conciencias.* Santiago: Federación de Estudiantes de la Universidad Catolica, Departmento de Estudios, 1973.

Fischer, Kathleen B. *Political Ideology and Educational Reform in Chile.* UCLA, 1977. Unpublished Ph.D. Dissertation.

Frente de Trabajadores Radicales en Educación. *Postulaciones del Partido Radical en relación al Debate Nacional sobre Educación.* Santiago: Partido Radical, July 1973.

Gil, Federico G. *The Political System of Chile.* Boston: Houghton Mifflin Company, 1966.

Jobet, Julio C. *El Partido Socialista de Chile.* Santiago: Editorial Unversitaria, 1971.

Landsberger, Henry A. and Linz, Juan J. "Chile 1973/Spain 1936: Similarities and Differences in the Breakdown of Democracy." In Federico G. Gil, et al. eds. *Chile at the Turning Point. Lessons of the Socialist Years, 1970-1973.* Philadelphia: Institute for the Study of Human Issues, 1979, pp. 399-438.

LaTorre, Carmen Luz. "Recursos asignados al sector educación y su distribucion en el periodo 1965-80." Santiago: Programa Interdisciplinario de Investigaciones en Educación, 1981.

Linz, Juan J. et al. *The Breakdown of Democratic Regimes.* Baltimore: The Johns Hopkins University Press, 1978.

Livacic, G. Ernesto. "Tres años de la experiencia Allende en materia de educación." In *Politica y Espiritu* (April 1973): 50-54.

Maira, Luis. "The Strategy and Tactics of the Chilean Counterrevolution in the Area of Political Institutions." In Federico G. Gil, et al eds. *Chile at the Turning*

Point. Lessons of the Socialist Years, 1970-1973. Philadelphia: Institute for the Study of Human Issues, 1979, pp. 240-73.

MAPU. "Cuestiones centrales sobre los cuales este Congreso debe pronunciarse a juicio del MAPU." 1971. Mimeograph.

McGinn, Noel.; Schiefelbein.; Ernesto, and Warwick, Donald. "Educational Planning as Political Process: Two Case Studies from Latin America." *Comparative Education Review* 23, no. 2 (June 1979): 218-39.

Ministerio de Educación Pública. *Algunos Antecedentes para el planeamiento integral de la educación chilena.* Santiago: Comision de la Planeamiento de la Educación, 1964.

"Analisis critico de la realidad educacional de Chile en la perspectiva de la nueva sociedad y calendario escolar." March 1971. Mimeograph.

"Bases generales para la formulacion del Plan Operativo 1972 y marco de referencia para la formulacion del "Plan sexenal del sector educacional.' " July 1971. Mimeograph.

"Temario de los Congresos Provinciales y Nacionales de Educación." August 1971. Mimeograph.

"Congreso Nacional de Educación: Segundo Aporte del Ministerio de Educación a sus debates." In *Revista de Educación.* No. 36-38, 1972, pp. 71-98.

"Anteprojecto de Decreto General de Democratización." July 1972. Mimeograph.

"Informe sobre Escuela Nacional Unificada." December 1972. Mimeograph.

"Informe sobre Escuela Nacional Unificada." Published as a supplement to the *Revista de Educación.* February 1973.

"Decreto General de Democratización." Decreto No. 224, 6 March 1973. Published in the *Diario Oficial.* 12 April 1973.

"Instruye sobre etapa inicial del trabajo educacional del presente año." Direcciones de Educación Primaria y Normal, Educación Secundaria y Educación Profesional. Circular No. 15-12-14, 6 March 1973. Mimeograph.

Muller, Herbert J. *The Uses of the Past. Profiles of Former Societies.* New York: Oxford University Press, 1957.

Nuñez, Ivan. "Discurso para celebrar el comienzo do los seminarios de perfeccionamiento para los profesores de nival medio." 25 February 1971. Mimeograph.

Tradición, reforma y alternativas educacionales en Chile, 1929-1973. Santiago: Centro de Estudios Economicos y Sociales, 1979.

"Desarrollo de la educación chilena hasta 1973." Santiago: Programa Interdisciplinario de Investigaciones en Educación, 1982a.

"Los organizaciones del magisterio chileno y el estado de compromiso. 1936-1973." Santiago: Programa Interdisciplinario de Investigaciones en Educación, 1982b.

Oveido, C. Carlos. ed. *Documentos del episcopado. Chile. 1970-1973.* Santiago: Ediciones Mundo, 1974.

Palma, Anibal. "Discurso del Sr. Ministro de Educación Sr. Anibal Palma en la Asamblea Inaugural del Quinto Congreso de las Asociaciones de Padres y Apoderados de la Comuna de Los Condes." Santiago: Ministerio de Educación Pública. 29 June 1972a. File copy taken from tape recording.

"Declaracion del Ministro de Educación Anibal Palma Fourcade por Cadena de Radio." Santiago: Ministerio de Educación Pública. 24 September 1972b. File copy taken from tape recording.

Partido Democrata Cristiano. "Enfoques al temario de Congreso Nacional de Educación." In *Presencia* (edición especial), n.d.

"Pauta de orientación para dar respuesta al documento 'Debate Nacional Sobre Educación' del Consejo Nacional de Educación." Santiago: Partido Democrata Cristiano, Departmento Tecnico, Comision de Educación, July 1973. Mimeograph.

"Projecto de ley que reglamenta garantias constitucionales." Santiago: Partido Democrata Cristiano, Departamento Tecnico, Comision de Educación, September 1973. Mimeograph.

Paulston, Rolland. *Conflicting Theories of Social and Educational Change: A Typological Review*. Pittsburgh: University of Pittsburgh, Center for International Studies, 1976.

Program Basico. *Programa Basico de Gobierno de la Unidad Popular*. Santiago: Impresa Horizonte, 1970.

Retamal, M. Orlando. "Algunas ideas sobre la educación en el transito del capitalismo al socialismo." In *Aportes Socialistas para la construccion de la nueva educación chilena*. Santiago: Editorial Universitario, 1971, pp. 91-95.

Santalices, C. Romulo. *La ENU. Control de las consciencias o educación liberadora?* Talca, Chile: Fundacion Manuel Larrain, May-June 1973.

Schiefelbein, Ernosto. "The Politics of National Planning: The Chilean Case." *Educational Planning* 1, no. 3, January 1975.

Schiefelbein, Ernesto, and Farrell, Joseph P. *Eight Years of Their Lives: Through Schooling to the Labour Market in Chile*. Ottawa, Canada: International Development Research Centre, 1982.

Sigmund, Paul E. *The Overthrow of Allende and the Politics of Chile, 1964-1976*. Pittsburgh: University of Pittsburgh Press, 1977.

Silvert, Kalman. "Election, Parties and the Law." Santiago: American Universities Field Staff Letter, 10 March 1957.

Silvert, Kalman, and Jutkowitz, Joel M. *Education, Values and the Possibilities for Social Change in Chile*. ISHI Occasional Papers in Social Change. Philadelphia: Institute for the Study of Human Issues, 1976.

Silvert, Kalman, and Reissman, Leonard. *Education, Class and Nation: The Experiences of Chile and Venezuela*. New York: Elsevier, 1976.

Smirnow, Gabriel. *The Revolution Disarmed: Chile. 1970-1973*. New York: Monthly Review Press, 1981.

Smith, Brian H. *The Church and Politics in Chile: Challenges to Modern Catholicism*. Princeton, New Jersey: Princeton University Press, 1982.

SONAP. "Resoluciones de la VII Convención Nacional sobre situación educacional." 1971. Mimeograph.

Suarez, Waldo; Nuñez, Ivan; and Videla, Lautaro. *Aportes a la formulación de una politica educacional*. Santiago: Ministerio de Educación Pública, Ediciones Cultura y Publicaciones, 1971.

Tapia, Jorge. "The Difficult Road to Socialism: the Chilean Case from a Historical Perspective." In Federico G. Gil, et al eds. *Chile at the Turning Point. Lessons of the Socialist Years, 1970-1973*. Philadelphia: Institute for the Study of Human Issues, 1979a, pp. 19-75.

"The Viability and Failure of the Chilean Road to Socialism." In Federico G. Gil, et al eds. *Chile at the Turning Point. Lessons of the Socialist Years, 1970-1973*. Philadelphia: Institute for the Study of Human Issues, 1979b, pp. 297-315.

Valenzuela, Arturo. *The Breakdown of Democratic Regimes: Chile*. Baltimore: The Johns Hopkins University Press, 1978.

Vera, Hernan. "Algunas notas para la comprensión de las reformas educacionales propuestas por el gobierno en el informe sobre la ENU." May 1973. Unpublished report.

Vivallo, Rudecindo J. *Education in Chile Under the Allende Government*. Temple University, 1978. Unpublished Ph.D. Dissertation.

Zemelman, Hugo. "The Political Problems of Transition from the Assumption of Political Power to Revolutionary Power." In Federico G. Gil, et al eds. *Chile at the Turning Point. Lessons of the Socialist Years, 1970-1973*. Philadelphia: Institute for the Study of Human Issues, 1979, pp. 274-93.

Index